A Lens on Deaf Identities

Perspectives on Deafness

Series Editors
Marc Marschark
Patricia Elizabeth Spencer

A Lens on Deaf Identities

Irene W. Leigh

OXFORD
UNIVERSITY PRESS

2009

OXFORD
UNIVERSITY PRESS

Oxford University Press, Inc., publishes works that further
Oxford University's objective of excellence
in research, scholarship, and education.

Oxford New York
Auckland Cape Town Dar es Salaam Hong Kong Karachi
Kuala Lumpur Madrid Melbourne Mexico City Nairobi
New Delhi Shanghai Taipei Toronto

With offices in
Argentina Austria Brazil Chile Czech Republic France Greece
Guatemala Hungary Italy Japan Poland Portugal Singapore
South Korea Switzerland Thailand Turkey Ukraine Vietnam

Published by Oxford University Press, Inc.
198 Madison Avenue, New York, New York 10016
www.oup.com

Oxford is a registered trademark of Oxford University Press.

Library of Congress Cataloging-in-Publication Data
Leigh, Irene.
A lens on deaf identities / Irene W. Leigh.
p. ; cm.—(Perspectives on deafness)
Includes bibliographical references and index.
ISBN 978-0-19-532066-4
1. Deafness. 2. Identity (Psychology) I. Title. II. Series.
[DNLM: 1. Deafness—psychology. 2. Self Concept. 3. Social Identification.
WV 270 L528L 2009]
HV2395.L35 2009
362.4'2—dc22   2008034961

9 8 7 6 5 4

Printed in the United States of America
on acid-free paper

FOREWORD

To naïve observers, deaf people are a little like the Borg in the *Star Trek* films. Deaf people think alike, behave alike, and have the same life experience. You meet one deaf person, you've met them all. This antiquated, one-size-fits-all approach persists, even in this day and age.

In *A Lens on Deaf Identities*, Irene W. Leigh gives us exciting insight into one of the most diverse groups of people alive today. Deaf people share a common trait: hearing loss severe enough that their lives, and indeed their world views, are primarily visually and spatially oriented.

Dr. Leigh opens by writing about identity and labeling—two of the basic instincts that humans use in trying to classify other humans. By addressing these issues early on, Dr. Leigh prepares her readers to retreat from the phenomenology of the deaf experience and to focus on the diverse nature of deaf and hard-of-hearing people and the deaf community.

The multidisciplinary approach of *A Lens on Deaf Identities* does not cover everything you might want or expect. However, it will certainly prompt you to explore further. Dr. Leigh raises more questions than answers. This will certainly engender vigorous academic discourse.

Dr. Leigh goes where few scholars are willing to venture. She has combined scholarly research with an autobiography. In so doing, she has produced a work that gives her readers rare insight into the diversity of deaf people. Through Dr. Leigh's cogent and powerful scholarship, she breaks down preconceived societal notions about deaf people.

Dr. Leigh promotes no agenda, nor does she offer solutions. Rather, she presents her audience with a broad tapestry. On its face, this is a psychology text, but Dr. Leigh covers a broad range of disciplines so seamlessly that the reader hardly notices her segues. I commend this book to anyone who wants to learn more about deaf people and the deaf community through the eyes of a distinguished deaf scholar.

I think it is important to explain my own relationship with Dr. Leigh. I met her for the first time in 1969, when I was a student at the Lexington School for the Deaf, and she was the school's new director of guidance services. My first contact with her was very affirming. She emanated positive energy and great optimism for her work. I knew that she was deaf like me, but that she was somewhat different.

I may not have understood fully then, but I do now. I had deaf parents and a younger deaf brother. My entire family used American Sign Language (ASL) as its primary means of communication. In contrast, Ms. Leigh was raised using oral/aural methods of communication. At that time, Lexington espoused oral/aural methods; thus, Ms. Leigh and I communicated orally. Despite this difference, she was easily approachable. She made other students and me feel that we were very much welcome in her presence.

Today, it is a reflection of our diverse, pluralistic society that we see so many different cultural facets experienced by different deaf people. Some of us grew up with family members who are deaf; others grew up being the only deaf member of the family. All of us have experienced events and situations that can be experienced only by those of us who are deaf. There is always a commonality; yet there are differences that set us apart as well. Dr. Leigh will help you understand these similarities and differences.

Since joining the Gallaudet University faculty in 1992, Dr. Leigh has been an exemplary scholar. She taught in our APA-approved program in clinical psychology. She is now chair of the department of psychology. She conducts empirical and applied research, and publishes widely. She serves her department, her school, and the university in a staggering number of roles, and gives each role more than 100 percent. I am not exaggerating when I say that every time I turn around, Dr. Leigh seems to be working on a new book. She is oft-cited in the literature. She has become a mentor to many new scholars, guiding them through the intricacies of writing dissertations, submitting research for publication, and writing and publishing that elusive first book.

Dr. Leigh is one of the most highly respected professors at Gallaudet University today. She was named our Distinguished Faculty Member in 2003. She has inspired countless people through her high standards and her unceasing pursuit of excellence. Some of her colleagues in the department of psychology have adopted a new verb—to be "Ireneized"—as an endearing term of affection. Quite simply, no one can spend time with her and not feel her energy and her influence.

Forty years after our first meeting, I continue to ask Dr. Leigh for advice and words of wisdom. It is an honor to be colleagues with her.

Stephen F. Weiner, Ed.D.
Provost
Gallaudet University

Preface

What are the questions that prompt this journey, and why is it important to undertake it?
    Robert Kegan (1982, p. 2)

A number of years ago, I was told by an oral deaf woman that I was not deaf. She claimed she was the one who was deaf, not me. She never went to a school for the deaf, she disavowed the deaf community, and she had never used a hearing aid. Yet she claimed that because I can use a hearing aid, even though I also must rely on speechreading, I am not deaf. I protested! I am deaf to the heart and core of my being, but in her eyes, I did not fit her conceptualization of "deaf."

A deaf acquaintance recently questioned whether I am truly deaf despite the fact that I socialized with deaf peers while growing up, have never been separate from the Deaf* community wherever I have lived, and have the ability to understand and communicate with different constituents of this community. Again, I protested. But clearly, our conceptualizations of my deaf identity did not match.

When I was a child attending what would be described today as a large oral-based mainstream program for deaf and hard-of-hearing children within a city public school that served the hearing children of its neighborhood, I recall no fights over hearing-deaf issues or how to communicate. We were all deaf and unified by that common bond. There were signing deaf children of deaf parents at my school. We knew peers attending the state school for the deaf, but never did I sense that there was such a thing as "us" versus "them."

Because I can talk, deaf children from a culturally Deaf family who saw me speaking while ordering food at restaurants thought I was hearing, even though I typically used American Sign Language (ASL) or Contact Sign (ASL mixed with English sign order) with them. Their

* "Deaf" refers to deaf people as a cultural group while "deaf" denotes the audiological condition of severe to profound hearing loss.

parents had to disabuse them of this perception. Is it typical to disqualify deaf persons who can talk from being Deaf? Does this mean that even if I am seen signing, when I am seen speaking, I am therefore "hearing?"

When I speak to supermarket cashiers, they hear the voice of a deaf person. Surprisingly often they will respond to me as a Deaf person and acknowledge that I need visual communication by attempting to sign a simple concept such as "Thank you." This is very affirming for me and for Deaf individuals who prefer to use ASL, but not for those deaf individuals who prefer spoken language. These individuals will often develop standard answers to demonstrate they are not sign language users and perhaps to show their resentment at being automatically categorized as something they are not.

Again and again, I see deaf persons giving themselves or being given different identity labels. These labels include Deaf, deaf, oral deaf, Oral Hearing Loss, hearing impaired, acquired hearing loss, hard of hearing, deaf with a "hearing mind," Black Deaf, Deaf and Hispanic, People of the Eye, and so on. At times, to identify themselves more descriptively, deaf persons will use phrases such as "I have a hearing loss," "I'm deaf and I have a cochlear implant," or "I'm a lipreader." Whatever label you name, I have seen it used.

The use of these labels and descriptions contradicts the very notion of a single "deaf experience," considering that individual experiences and the emotional feelings, whether positive or negative, attached to these experiences give rise to individual and particular perceptions of one's deaf or hard-of-hearing identity. The complexity of "deaf" identity is further compounded by the fact that different versions of the deaf or hard-of-hearing self emerge in different situations, and external perceptions of that self will vary according to the observed and the observer.

As an individual who cannot imagine giving up my deaf self, confronting the diverse perceptions of "deaf" through my own experiences and observations inspired the following questions: How are identities formed? How do identities influence one's path through life? How does the concept of "difference" influence identity formation? What is deaf identity? Is it a multiplicity of identities, each of which is inextricably tied to time and space, language and communication? What about hard-of-hearing identity? How has the popularization of Deaf culture influenced identity formation? Can deaf people be deaf in different ways? What are the implications of specific constructions of "deaf" or of specific labels on the lives of deaf persons? How have these evolved over time? When a naïve hearing person comes across the path of a deaf or hard-of-hearing individual, what are the standard responses to that person and why? What can we learn from history? Does it matter? If so, how does it matter? What does the future hold for deaf identities?

To start this journey and answer my own questions, I explore identity and identity-related theories grounded in the field of psychology, as I am a psychologist by training. I also briefly venture into other realms, such as sociology, history, philosophy, anthropology, medicine, science, technology, education, history, government and politics, sociolinguistics, Deaf Studies, and Disability Studies in my quest for illumination. However, because the professional is always informed by the personal, I occasionally interject myself and my experiences into the thread of this book. In this way, you, the reader, can get a sense of how my experiences have shaped my identity "worldview" while you react with your own perspectives and decide whether I have captured the essence of what various deaf identities are all about.

To explore the topic, I start with an explanation of the identity construct in Chapter 1 and present some perspectives on the evolution of identities and how people categorize themselves. This provides the background for issues related to how deaf and hard-of-hearing persons label themselves and the meanings of these labels. I then examine Deaf culture as a linchpin for the exploration of deaf identities, yet in uneasy relationship with disability identity, before addressing why deaf identities matter at all. While d/Deaf identities do differ from hard-of-hearing identities, in the interest of expediency I have opted to use "deaf identities" to cover both groups except when I specifically refer to the individual groups.

Chapter 2 focuses on perspectives from theory and research related specifically to deaf identities. Chapter 3 addresses the dangers of assuming that a specific deaf identity category fully explains the person. In Chapter 4, I explore the roles of family and school in creating or modifying deaf identities. Chapter 5 presents a brief historical overview of deaf identities and how these have influenced present-day perspectives; in Chapter 6, I expand on how hearing society perceptions have created situations that have either enhanced or suppressed the potential of deaf and hard-of-hearing persons to achieve in life. I examine not only oppression and related constructs but also the resiliency of people responding to less than ideal conditions.

While deaf and hard-of-hearing people have always been diverse in terms of background variables, including family cultural affiliation and socioeconomic status among others, the extent of this diversity has become increasingly pronounced in recent decades (as it has for people who hear). Chapter 7 addresses this phenomenon related to ethnicity, sexual orientation, and additional disabilities. In Chapter 8 I explore the overt and subtle influences of technology and the use of genetic findings on how deaf identities are evolving. And finally, in Chapter 9 I have endeavored to achieve some resolution in answering the questions I posed at the beginning of this project. I will not claim to have answered all of the questions. This is an extremely complex area rife with multiple nuances, and I may certainly have missed some nuances or interpretations that may broaden our understanding of deaf identity meanings. I may also have created misinterpretations of what others have tried to express. If so, I look forward to future scholarly efforts that will facilitate ongoing exploration of this area of study.

This book is the culmination of my life experiences, the review of the literature required to buttress the statements I have made, and the essential editorial and review input that is part of any book process. First, I owe Marc Marschark and Patricia Spencer a huge expression of gratitude for their encouragement when I approached them with my proposal for this book. I want to thank Alesia Howard and Cara Miller, two graduate research assistants who roamed the library and the Internet in search of identity-related literature. They made it that much easier for me to bring this book to fruition. I am indebted to Serena L. Krombach for the first eye and critique as I worked on the proposal, to Leslie Anglin for the final editing of this book, and to Sarah Harrington and Mark O'Malley for guiding me through the publication process. John Christiansen's eagle-eyed review helped to ensure that I was on target in terms of book content. Kathleen Arnos, Susan Burch, and Virginia Gutman provided feedback related to their areas of specialization. The help of Robert Pollard, as well as the anonymous reviewers who guided me in the shaping and revising of this book, is also gratefully acknowledged.

Going back to the "beginning," I thank first of all my late hearing parents, Paul and Hilde Wolff, for creating in me an unwavering positive sense of self as a deaf person. The deaf and hearing peers I grew up with facilitated the process of solidifying my d/Deaf identity. I owe much to Elberta Pruitt, former principal of the Alexander Graham Bell School in Chicago, Illinois, for her persistent efforts to open access to challenging postelementary school education opportunities for me in the face of institutionalized societal expectations that I as a deaf student could not succeed.

As I went through life, relying mostly on speaking and eventually as a young adult becoming comfortable with the use of ASL, performing as a professional working with deaf people, and experiencing parenthood, I encountered more and more the complexities of identity. My hearing daughter has said that she felt herself to be the minority inside her family, and the majority outside. My deaf son, growing up immersed in mainstream hearing society, went to Gallaudet University in his junior year to explore his d/Deaf identity. As part of life's journey, after my children were in college I joined a new family grounded in Deaf culture and ended up working with diverse students and colleagues at Gallaudet University. This project owes much to the significant roles all these individuals have played throughout my life. Many of them have reflected back to me their perceptions of who I am as a person who feels deaf at the core of my identity. It is quite apparent that my self-perceptions and the perceptions of those others in my environment do not always match. How these have influenced my determination to be who I am became the driving force for this book.

Contents

A Lens on Deaf Identities

1

Identity and the Power of Labels

I, however, cannot accurately describe myself without using the word deaf.
Bonnie Tucker (1995, p. xix)

Interest in identity and the self goes back to ancient times (Hoffman, 1996; Mischel & Morf, 2003). Philosophers, theologians, anthropologists, historians, sociologists, psychoanalysts, and psychologists among others have explored the topic from numerous angles as part of their desire to understand the human condition. For centuries the stable social context typical of many historically homogenous societies lent itself to relatively clear demarcations of self and cultural identity. Yet this vaunted stability has entered an increased state of flux, spurred in large part by the rapidly emerging diversity in societies.

The emergence of this diversity is due in part to the effects of a globalization process that reflects "a cluster of related changes that are increasing the interconnectedness of the world" (Croucher, 2004, p. 13). Immigration and technology have been the prime driving forces in transforming the degree and intensity of intercultural contacts in various ways, mostly by bringing contrasting groups of people into closer proximity to one another and thereby creating opportunities to explore different identities (Arnett, 2002; Camilleri & Malewska-Peyre, 1997; Croucher, 2004; Hermans & Dimaggio, 2007). The recent explosion of self- and identity-related literature (e.g., Côté & Levine, 2002; Harter, 1999; Holland, Lachicotte, Skinner, & Cain, 1998; Leary & Tangney, 2003) reflects the influence of cultural collision and the desire to examine implications for identity.

The identity messages created by exposure to families of origin, neighborhood, country, world, ethnic/religious groups, and other diverse groups incorporating gender, abilities, sexual orientation, socioeconomic class, special interests, and so on require that a multiplicity of information about self and others be integrated into a coherent sense of self. This information can include private/internal, public/revealing, cultural, and inherited components, as well as perceptions of "destiny" (or fate) (Mottez, 1990). Within societies that offer different options, identity explorations are often fueled by the desire to escape

3

from the uncertainty of where one belongs (Bauman, 1996; Hermans & Dimaggio, 2007).

WHAT IS IDENTITY?

Identity is a complex and developing cognitive and social construction encompassing an array of characteristics or identity components that connect the person to specific social groups (e.g., Baumeister, 1997; Erikson, 1968, 1980; Grotevant, 1992; Harter, 1999; Leary & Tangney, 2003; Moskowitz, 2005). This construction is based on one's understandings of the biological (i.e., race, disability, gender, age), psychological (i.e., drives, intellect, competencies, self-understandings), social (i.e., cultural, social roles, the resolution of conflict and crisis), and religious-spiritual aspects of our beings (Tatum, 1997). It is also a dynamic and ongoing compilation of the meanings of past experiences, present experiences, and our images of what is possible for us in the future (Tatum, 1997).

The literature on identity is replete with debates about the nature of identity. These debates can be categorized into two basic perspectives: primordialism or essentialism, and constructivist or nonessentialism (Croucher, 2004; Woodward, 1997, 2002). Within the essentialist perspective, identity is conceived of as essential, relatively fixed, predetermined, or "natural," based on specific "authentic" characteristics that clearly define an overarching identity construct and create a related sense of belongingness, shared historical truth, and stability. A child of culturally Deaf parents, for instance, is more likely to acknowledge belonging to and identifying with Deaf culture as a dominant identity with a set of essential Deaf-related fixed characteristic values imparted by the parents that reflect specific ways of "being" and connecting with others.

In contrast, the nonessentialist perspective is based on a social constructivist framework. Specifically, identities are not inherently in the self or created by the individual's surroundings. Rather, the self as an ongoing process constructs itself and is constructed by the social environment in the guise of political, economic, and sociocultural forces that contribute to shared meaning systems or cultural contexts that evolve over time (e.g., Baumeister, 1997; Cushman, 1995; Lyddon, 1995). The interplay between one's psychological characteristics and the family, culture, and context will ultimately define that person (Bronfenbrenner, 2005; Szapocznik & Kurtines, 1993). Within increasingly complex and pluralistic cultural milieus, individual construction of malleable and multiple identities becomes more the norm than the exception.

Using the nonessentialist perspective, a culturally Deaf adult can manifest different identities surrounding that core Deaf identity, depending on environmental contexts. For this adult, one specific Deaf cultural identity may emerge at the local Deaf festival, while a different kind of Deaf cultural identity may manifest itself in a situation involving a specific Deaf ethnic group. In another example, if a socially isolated deaf person has never been exposed to another deaf person until finally meeting a group of deaf and hard-of-hearing people in adulthood, self-perceptions of deafness in isolation can gradually metamorphose into self-perceptions of a specific kind of "deaf" or "hard-of-hearing" person as exemplified by the group members. This involves internal identity changes in response to a more complex social framework incorporating deaf and hearing members, thus repudiating the notion of a fixed deaf identity. These identity changes then become pivotal for selecting behaviors, changing self-representations, and in turn influencing one's cultural world.

IDENTITY EVOLUTION

The evolution of self and identity is a multidimensional, reflexive process involving psychological motivation, cultural knowledge, and the ability to perform appropriate roles (Fitzgerald, 1993). The end result is not a static, but rather a dynamic construction of identity, mediated by the individual's social position as well as cultural, linguistic, and social experiences. Throughout the process of individual development, as one transitions from situation to situation and learns new information about the self, such as group identification, abilities, self-perceptions versus perceptions created by others, etc., this evolving information interacts with the cognitive framework of the personal self and one's psychological motivation to reshape meaning and self-perceptions (Kegan, 1982).

While the prevailing notion is that adolescence is the linchpin for identity resolution (Erikson, 1968, 1980), identity evolution is actually a lifelong process (Grotevant, 1992; Harter, 1999). The toddler becomes aware she is a girl, a daughter, possibly a granddaughter, and as she interacts in the neighborhood and at school, she becomes aware of herself as a friend and a pupil. Throughout subsequent stages of development, she may identify herself as a camper, lacrosse player, member of a religious and ethnic group, college student, Peace Corps volunteer, wife, partner, mother, working woman, and so on. And if she is deaf, running throughout all these identities will be that layer of deaf, having a hearing loss, being hearing impaired, hard of hearing, "I have a cochlear implant," or whatever identifier she selects to frame her different-hearing uniqueness at different points in time, knowing that it colors many of the identities she assumes.

The evolution of self and identity has been approached from three different theoretical approaches: evolutionary psychology, symbolic interactionism, and ecology (Forgas & Williams, 2003). The first approach relies on a Darwinian-based perspective, which posits that the sense of self evolves as a programmed response to the inherent need to manage interactions with other members of the human species in ever-increasing, sophisticated ways (Buss, 2004). This evolutionary pressure facilitates the development of skills in inferring the internal states of others and thereby accumulating the social information needed for maintaining one's sense of self and ensuring that others respond to that person in optimal ways.

The symbolic interactionist approach relies on the premise that the core self emerges out of the interaction between one's cognitive, symbolic, interpersonal, and collective systems. This evolving self is a social construct dependent on the process of constructing symbolic representations of self as subject, agent, or observer (the I-self) and then self as object, categorical, or observed (the Me-self) based on interpersonal experiences that in turn influence self-perceptions and identity. These experiences are converted into symbolic representations through, for example, language, visual images, and emotional reactions. Different aspects of the core self emerge depending on whom we interact with and where we are. This theoretical approach is based on seminal work done by theorists working in the late 1800s, including William James and George Herbert Mead (see Forgas & Williams, 2003; Harter, 1999 for a review).

The third theoretical perspective focuses on the ecological domain related to intergroup, collective, and cultural aspects of the self. Different environments will give different messages to the individual that can influence self-perceptions and identity. In particular, subtle contextual cues via social feedback in various environments can ultimately influence whether individuals identify with or separate themselves from relevant reference or social groups (Biernat, Eidelman, & Fuegen, 2003; Brewer & Pickett, 2003). However, there is a role for internal motivation in influencing whether individuals proceed to internalize or reject this feedback.

Erik Erikson (1968, 1980), a developmental psychologist, played a premier role in popularizing the psychosocial nature of identity and interposing this construct within the life cycle. While Erikson's work was rooted in psychoanalysis, he was among the earliest to combine the biological, cultural, and individuality/self-responsibility perspectives. While acknowledging that identities develop as the child grows, Erikson identified adolescence as a critical transition point for identity, noting that if identity issues are not resolved at that time, the risk for identity diffusion and problematic psychological functioning during subsequent stages of life increases. His psychosocial theories of identity evolution made the interconnections between personal and social worlds, between psychology and sociology, more explicit than heretofore had been the case (Côté & Levine, 2002; Evans, 1967).

Successive authors (e.g., Côté & Levine, 2002; Côté & Schwartz, 2002; Foddy & Kashima, 2002; Holland, Lachicotte, Skinner, & Cain, 1998;

Thoits & Virshup, 1997) have reinforced the psychology–sociology interconnection through exploring the influence of social structures on how the self evolves and is shaped while at the same time becoming self-regulating in terms of incorporating specific identities. This process requires psychological confidence in handling relationships, making life/identity choices, taking responsibility, and overcoming societal obstacles. The degree to which flexibility in identity choices exists will clearly be subject to the availability of choices in the relevant macrosocial context as well as to individual responses to that social context. Specifically, exposure to diverse ways of being deaf is subject to the availability of deaf social groups and the differing social messages on the value of the deaf identities associated with these groups. This creates opportunities for psychological processing to determine which of these identities fits with one's self-perception.

Self-esteem has a place in identity evolution. Recent research validates the idea that enhanced self-esteem may be a consequence of achieving a positively distinct social identity, not necessarily that the need to increase self-esteem motivates social identification in the first place (Brewer & Pickett, 2003). Group identification, even with stigmatized or disadvantaged groups, may come about not because of the need to buttress self-esteem but more as a consequence of the search for self-definition in ambiguous situations, with the identification process ultimately bolstering self-esteem. Supporting this premise is a meta-analysis of self-esteem studies with deaf samples including deaf children, adolescents, and adults (Bat-Chava, 1993). Bat-Chava's findings strongly suggest that self-esteem is associated with having a community of people who share one's group membership, both in childhood and in adulthood. This serves to protect deaf individuals from attitudes that often devaluate them.

It appears that the universal need for belonging facilitates identifying with social groups and thereby avoids social exclusion (Baumeister & Leary, 1995; Baumeister, Twenge, & Ciarocco, 2003). However, the need for belonging does not sufficiently explain how individuals select groups to connect with. Brewer and Pickett (2003) use the concept of "distinctiveness" as a factor that facilitates the selection of social groups to identify with, separate from the positive evaluation of these groups. The need to be included, "similar to," and belong has to be balanced with the need for differentiation and individuality so that one no longer feels too different and isolated, but rather feels connected and not lost in the group. There can be different levels of inclusiveness within specific social categories, depending on whether criteria for belonging to a category or group are more specific or more general. For example, a broadly inclusive group might be a national group, such as the Asian American group, which incorporates multiple Asian American heritages, such as Chinese, Thai, Korean, Pakistani, and so on. More specific identification with the category of Japanese persons who are Christian will decrease the level of inclusiveness, while those within this specific group will achieve a sense of greater similarity. Hearing loss or hearing difference represents a broadly inclusive category, with different levels of inclusiveness being represented by, for example, people who have a hearing loss, and then more specifically by people who have a cochlear implant.

Even though social and personal identities often have enmeshed relationships within one's core identity, it helps to understand that social identities are concerned with group belongingness and involve "we" and "us," while personal identities involve "I" and "me" and address the question, "Who am I?" Observing or being involved with social groups will influence personal identity. The more collective identity predominates, the less dominant personal identity will be, and vice versa. At times, gravitation toward a collective group may contradict one's personal self-schema (Onorato & Turner, 2004). For example, joining a popular group in which one does not believe may be based on the desire to escape "outsider" status.

How society and individuals construct identities is inextricably tied with social policy and personal ideology (Forgas & Williams, 2003; de St. Aubin, Wandrei, Skerven, & Coppolillo, 2006). Social policies reflect visions about the nature of specific groups of people. The personal ideology of individuals reflects their political and religious/moral values and convictions, and also their self-identities. Those perceptions in turn will influence that particular society's goals in the guise of public policy, family approaches to childrearing, educational planning, and the structure for people's lives. In this book, the role of social forces will be examined as these interact with individual perceptions about being d/Deaf.

SELF-CATEGORIZATION: RECOGNITION OF SIMILARITIES AND DIFFERENCES

In the process of developing one's identity, individuals self-categorize based on what they know about social groups, the saliency of these groups for their lives, associated emotional meanings related to group membership, and how they see themselves connecting with each group (Tajfel, 1981; Turner & Onorato, 1999; Woodward, 1997, 2002). As they self-categorize, they tend to label themselves and others in terms of relevant social categories or symbolic systems of representation (Brewer & Pickett, 2003; Simon, 1999; Turner & Onorato, 1999). These become classificatory structures that incorporate fundamental distinctions between "us and them." Extending this logic, one is either male or female; either within one cultural or religious group or another; either a parent or not a parent; either hearing, hard of hearing, or deaf.

Labels are a form of stereotyping based on one's perceived identification or similarity between the self and members of a specific category or group as contrasted with perceived differences between the self and outside group members. The labels themselves are based on an amalgam of interactions between one's motives, expectations, knowledge, and reality related to the meaning of the label. The meaning of the labels will typically vary in level of inclusiveness, content, and type depending on the social context of the groups. Much depends on personal perspective and the valence of the label being utilized. How we weigh the relative importance of each label is part of the dynamic process of identity evolution.

Often, categorizations or labeling may be subject to cognitive simplification or distortion because the process involves making sense of complex schema and organizing or simplifying information to eliminate fuzziness and emphasize differences (Oakes, 1996). This can inadvertently lead to the creation of meaning and identity in the guise of facile labels, empty of nuances and not reflective of one's state. For example, it is easy to assume that a person labeled as hard of hearing is part of a group forever on the margin, unable to fully assimilate into hearing or Deaf groups. Despite the tendency to stereotype, the hard-of-hearing label is not that clear-cut due to the presence of different ways of being hard of hearing, as we will see in this book. The focus on differentiating categories can limit or deny the possibility of similarities between categories as well as potentially create rationales for exclusion.

THE EFFECT OF DEAF LABELS

While the hearing–not hearing dimension is only one of many possible identities that a person can harbor, it is a complex dimension that has profound implications for personal adjustment and connections with others (Higgins & Nash, 1996; Leigh & Lewis, 1999). This dimension incorporates multiple identity labels, such as hearing impaired, hard of hearing, oral deaf, late deafened, and Deaf. Each label indicates varied choices about self-representations, communication and language choices, individual functioning, and socialization with hearing and/or deaf persons. Those who select their labels and those who label others may perceive the criteria for each label differently. Consequently, to provide generally acceptable definitions of deaf-related labels can become a futile task.

For example, the generally accepted definition of "hard of hearing" is "less deaf" (Wilson, 2001). But what does that really mean in terms of objective criteria?* Because of the variations of decibel level at each frequency as indicated on audiograms of hearing levels, the

---

* See Appendix for decibel criteria for hard of hearing.

hard-of-hearing category can include those who hear nothing without hearing aids, and others who can hear vowels without hearing aids. But increasingly, profoundly deaf people who rely on spoken language are being labeled hard of hearing, decibel criteria notwithstanding (e.g., Punch, Creed, & Hyde, 2006). To complicate matters further, hard-of-hearing individuals may use or discard audiological definitions and sociological definitions depending on meaning and context. One may say she is hard of hearing in the audiological booth and Deaf at a Deaf social function, thereby failing the criteria of spoken language user. Another may say he is hearing with bad ears despite being audiologically hard of hearing.

To cite another example, "hearing impaired" is a term frequently used to gently indicate one's hearing loss (Kannapell, 1994; National Association of the Deaf, 2005). This label is not popular with Deaf people for whom the term "impairment" is a subtle reflection that their hearing difference makes them appear dysfunctional, less capable than they are. They reject the hearing-centered focus on impairment and deficit because they view themselves as intact and communicatively competent (Corker, 1994; Kannapell, 1994; Lane, Hoffmeister, & Bahan, 1996; Padden & Humphries, 2005). Others do not have an issue with the negative semantics; they view hearing impairment as a fact, an explanation for communication needs, so hearing impairment has a different meaning for them.

Padden and Humphries (1988) emphasize the need to look at the individual's "center" as the determining factor in identifying the meaning of relevant labels. They also acknowledge an interesting phenomenon: specific labels can establish either commonality or marginality, depending on who is doing the categorizing and what their centers are. When individuals with different centers ascribe different labels to a particular individual, the possibility for a collision of meanings for the affected individual exists. This is exactly the paradoxical situation Cheryl Heppner (1992) found herself in. She reported being condemned to a sort of zombie land where the hearing people who recognized she was deaf and the Deaf people who called her "hearing" (see discussion in Chapter 3) or hard of hearing all held her at arm's length, making it difficult for her to internalize a clear deaf identity.

The potentially divisive nature of labels has led individuals to recognize problems related to labeling people as hard of hearing, Deaf, hearing impaired, oral, or sign language user, because of this need for "other versus us" when there essentially is a common bond (Aiello & Aiello, 2001). There are times when the commonality of experiences overrides these labels, particularly when it comes to equality in accessibility, civil rights, technology, and employment, for example. But human nature being what it is, the tendency to categorize in order to differentiate groups is not going to go away.

Adding to the inherent complexity of labels and meaning, labels can also change over time (Bat-Chava, 2000; Breivik, 2005; Haualand & Hansen, 2007; Leigh, 1999a; Padden, 1996). Based on a study involving 34 oral deaf adults, Leigh (1999a) noted that 19 provided audiological definitions for their chosen label, while 15 used functional definitions. Half of the sample reported re-examining and changing labels, mostly because of changes in perceived meanings of these labels based on new experiences and new information. For example, Martha Sheridan (2001) went from being a child in a hearing school who "had trouble hearing," felt different, and didn't understand what being deaf meant or even that she was in fact "deaf" to readily identifying herself as Deaf in adulthood. And Kristin Buehl reports using and discarding labels as her self-perceptions changed.

> If I had a dollar for every label I insisted on using to describe myself, I would be rich now! I went through several phases where I would request for people to refer to me only as hearing-impaired, deaf, hard of hearing (with a cochlear implant), someone who happens to have a hearing loss, or, at one time when I was a kid, someone with broken ears. My opinions constantly change due to my ever-changing, individualized preferences depending on the situations in which I find myself. Who knows what label I'll come up with next, but I guarantee you that it'll be something new and reflective of how I feel at that time, not how other people or organizations want to label/view me. (K. Buehl, personal communication, May 25, 2006)

DISABILITY AND DEAF: CATALYST FOR IDENTITY

On the face of things, a difference in hearing *is* a disability, considering that the word "deaf" represents a functional deficiency in the ear. As the concept of disability is based on diagnostic classification to denote a specific pathology or dysfunction (DePoy & Gilson, 2004), "deaf" or any nomenclature referring to types of hearing loss qualifies as a disability. Hearing loss tends to be portrayed as an affliction that cuts individuals off from human contact because of lack of access to sound and spoken language (Baker, 1999; Bauman, 1997; Baynton, 1997; Sparrow, 2005). This portrayal often translates into the binary opposite of "normalcy" instead of a variation of the human condition, itself construed as normal. As such, how one internalizes identity vis-á-vis the hearing dimension has profound implications.

A review of disability studies has led Scott-Hill (2004) to distinguish four main models of identity. First is the deficit model, which focuses on the impairment. Because functional limitations are assumed, the related identity is perceived to be negative and in need of correction or normalization. The dominance model is based on inequalities of power caused by society's dominance of persons with disabilities that facilitates their unity and in this process empowers them to resist this domination. However, the notion of persons with disabilities being connected primarily through resistance to negative, oppressive frameworks is limiting in terms of identity construction. Third is the cultural difference model, which assumes a cultural relationship among persons with specific disabilities (i.e., deaf) separate from others. From a social-relationist perspective, the separatist characteristic is manifested by groups for whom the goal is that of minority rights and social autonomy. Within-group differences are not tolerated in the interest of creating a strong front. Last is the narrative model, which emphasizes shared meanings and social practices that bind people together in the process of creating identity. The act of narration reinforces the durability and permanence of who and what we are.

The identities explored in this book owe their evolution to one or more of these models, either in isolation or interacting with each other. This chapter proceeds to elaborate on the deficit and cultural difference models. Chapter 6 explores the influence of the social group dominance model, while the narrative model is employed throughout the book.

Medical and Functional Frames of Hearing Difference

The role of medicine in preventing or curing disease, treating symptoms, and improving or maintaining one's functional ability (Jonsen, Siegler, & Winslade, 1998) has given rise to the framing of hearing difference as a medical problem or deficit that is intrinsic to the person's impairment (Landsman, 2002) and demands curative approaches. Failing that, the focus is on enabling access to sound via hearing aids, assistive listening devices, or cochlear implants. Intensive auditory and speech training is instituted to facilitate the use of spoken language, the medium most connected with society's perception of the ability to reason (Brueggemann, 1999). "In this way, the hope is that the disability of deafness may be overcome and deaf people can function 'just like everyone else'" (Leigh, 2003, p. 324).

By virtue of the search for cure and advances in improving access to sound and spoken language, medical and allied health professionals have become the authority for determining treatment for hearing differences, whether remediation, habilitation, or rehabilitation. This has been a significant boon for people who want ease of interaction with those who hear. They find comfort in speaking as their hearing peers do.

However, there is an implied message, namely that to be disabled in terms of hearing status is unacceptable. Overtly or covertly, disability tends to be equated with powerlessness, incompetence, a violation of society's idealized norm, burden, forced dependency on others, or, a specific condition to be overcome by sheer will and motivation (Davis, 2001; Leigh & Brice, 2003; Linton, 1998; Olkin, 1999). To distance themselves from being identified as having a disability, individuals may strive to be as much like "hearing" as possible in order to blend into the spoken language environment. To do so often involves "passing for hearing" or "overcoming the hearing loss." It increases the comfort level of the nondisabled as well (Blotzer & Ruth, 1995; Mackelprang & Salsgiver, 1999; Olkin, 1999; Reagan, 2002; Williams & Abeles, 2004).

So, if you ask deaf or hard-of-hearing persons whether they identify as having a disability, some may qualify their answer rather than giving a straightforward yes or no, asserting that the disability of hearing loss has not held them back. If communication poses few barriers, the disability will recede into the background. But if background noises interfere with communication, feelings of disability are bound to predominate.

The Social-Minority Model

A different perspective of disability is espoused by those who are comfortable with claiming their disability or "difference" despite frequent difficult experiences (Mackelprang & Salsgiver, 1999; Shapiro, 1993; Vash & Crewe, 2004), even to the point that when they are asked about taking a pill to eliminate that difference should it be available, the answer could easily be "No" (Hahn & Belt, 2004; Ladd, 1994; Lane, 1997; Shapiro, 1993; Solomon, 1994). This can be bewildering to the average person. Who wants to be abnormal? Yet it has happened to me. I have been asked countless times about taking a pill to erase my deafness, and I say, "No way! I can't imagine being awakened every night by ambulance sirens racing to the nearby hospital." My deaf self is who I am. In contrast, Jim, who has a progressive hearing loss, would jump at the opportunity for a magic pill to regain what he is losing (Harvey, 2001).

So we approach the social-minority model, which posits that life with a "difference" reflects a different way of being, not a deficit, that confers minority group status. For such groups, the problem lies not with the hearing difference but rather with barriers created by parameters of expectations for functioning as hearing peers do (e.g., Corker, 1998; Fougeyrollas & Beauregard, 2001; Hahn, 1999; Landsman, 2002; Lane, 1997; Mackelprang & Salsgiver, 1999; Olkin, 1999). For example, theaters are built to enhance auditory dialogue, thereby creating a barrier to entertainment for those who need text, amplification, or sign language interpretation. Social and policy determinations about communication in theaters do not tend to permit access for those who rely on vision and are therefore oppressive for those individuals. The responsibility is placed squarely on the environment to facilitate a positive person–environment interaction.

The social-minority model incorporates a collective consciousness consisting of shared experiences and customs as deaf and hard-of-hearing persons deal with their individual issues in the face of social exclusion and marginalization (Barnartt & Scotch, 2001; Mackelprang & Salsgiver, 1999; Olkin, 1999). This collective consciousness view has spawned a cultural perspective related to Deaf ways of being, as elucidated below.

Deaf Culture

Despite ongoing debate about the definition of culture per se (Côté & Levine, 2002), it helps to have a frame for understanding this elusive construct in order to link it to Deaf culture. Culture consists of public standardized values of a group representing specific meanings, beliefs, and practices that guide social institutions, the creation of social products, and individual development (Triandis, 1996; Woodward, 1997). Culture incorporates beliefs about the nature of the person, the ideal person, and the person's life purpose. Cultural identity is constructed through contact with particular groups that reinforce a sense of belongingness. As such, culture has a powerful influence on how individuals organize their lives.

"Deaf culture" is a relatively recent term for the phenomenon of "a conspicuous social group" exclusively for deaf people (Rée, 1999, p. 231). This phenomenon, traditionally described as "the deaf community" or the "Deaf-World" (Higgins, 1980; Lane, Hoffmeister, & Bahan, 1996; Rée, 1999; Woll & Ladd, 2003), has been around for at least two centuries or more (Burch, 2002; Miles, 2000; Rée, 1999; Van Cleve & Crouch, 1989; Woll & Ladd, 2003), possibly even in Athens as far back as the fifth century BC, according to Bauman (2008b).

Rée (1999) comments that as deaf people were initially coalescing into deaf communities, the focus was on whether people were deaf or could hear. If deaf, this created a shared sense of bonding in opposition to a world of hearing people that afforded minimal opportunities for full immersion because of language and communication barriers (Bauman, 2008a; Davis, 1995; Higgins, 1980; Miles, 2000; Rée, 1999). In time, the concept of deaf community broadened to incorporate various people, including users of signed languages, oral deaf, hard of hearing, and hearing, who share and attempt to achieve common goals, such as communication access and respect for individual needs among others (Padden, 1980, 1996; Singleton & Tittle, 2000). In contrast, the Deaf-World includes only those who identify as members of Deaf cultures (Lane, Hoffmeister, & Bahan, 1996).

The concept of a Deaf culture began to be popularized with the publication of books such as *Deaf in America: Voices from a Culture* (Padden & Humphries, 1988). This seminal work explores how Deaf people view the world, not from a center of "cannot hear," "hearing loss," or audiological constructs, but rather from a Deaf center, one that reflects a different normality. For example, parents might report their baby as having "passed the deaf test" when screened for hearing after birth, as opposed to the standard "failed the hearing test." As the authors describe it, this Deaf center subsumes Deaf ways of connecting with others based on language and thought grounded in vision and the use of American Sign Language (ASL) rather than audition and spoken English. The process involves deaf people visually relating with each other utilizing eye contact, body movement, and the bona fide linguistic principles of ASL (initially endorsed by Stokoe [1960] and Stokoe, Croneberg, & Casterline [1965], and confirmed by extensive scholarly study). The end result has been an evolving standard of cultural and linguistic beliefs and values that focus on social relations with Deaf people, whether through school, social groups or organizations, within families, or on an informal basis. The common understanding of how to lead lives as Deaf people is often expressed through stories, literature, theater, and visual art (e.g., Lane, Hoffmeister, & Bahan, 1996; Padden & Humphries, 1988, 2005).

Considering the existence of older, comfortably familiar terms, such as "deaf community," why add this Deaf culture label? In exploring the "modern deaf self," Tom Humphries (1996, 2004, 2008) examines the discourse of culture as a process involving a concerted focus on self-definition rather than being defined by hearing observers as had previously been the case. Simply put, this process is a search for the Deaf voice and Deaf identity through analyzing similarities and differences related to the meaning of completeness, the value of being, the concept of wellness, and the nature of solidarity.

In the eyes of many hearing people, Deaf people appear incomplete because of the lack of auditory connection to spoken language, whereas for Deaf persons themselves "Deaf" asserts a state of being that reflects completeness. This Deaf completeness conveys the value of being as reflected in living full, rewarding Deaf lives instead of struggling to compensate for being "incomplete." As for the concept of wellness, the biological interpretations of inadequately functioning hearing mechanisms create impressions of ill health in need of attention, an impression denied by the healthy Deaf body. The Deaf person is not a marginalized "nonhearing person" (Humphries, 1996, p. 109) but rather one who is centered in wellness and a nondisabled self-schema.

The perception of the deaf self as responsible for communication failure, misunderstanding, and language problems has evolved into a stance that attributes responsibility for inadequacy to the hearing person's inability to understand the signed language or Deaf ways of being. As a result, the ideal of solidarity, connection, and self-definition between Deaf people was reinforced. This shift in self-perception among the Deaf community led Humphries (2008, p. 41) to frame the current task as one of moving on from "How are we different?" to "How are we being?"

This task has involved debates among Deaf people themselves and with hearing people about issues of membership, encompassing how to conceptualize practices that reflected bona fide Deaf culture ways of being (Humphries, 1996, 2008; Ladd, 1994). This is critical, considering that when hard-of-hearing parents are excluded, an estimated less than 5% of deaf parents have deaf children (Mitchell & Karchmer, 2004). There is debate about whether hearing children born to culturally Deaf parents are true inheritors of Deaf culture simply because they are not deaf (Hoffmeister, 2008; Shultz Myers, Myers, & Marcus, 1999; see Chapter 3). Most "members" who are deaf become culturally Deaf through exposure. This can occur during the school years if they interact with significant groups of deaf peers or as they join Deaf organizations or meet Deaf people and become exposed to Deaf ways of being (Andrews, Leigh, & Weiner, 2004).

Since there is no fixed pattern of entry into and adaptation to Deaf culture, Padden and Humphries (2005) prefer to avoid the concept of specific culture parameters that "suggest a fixedness of place and time" (p. 142). They choose to focus on a more fluid picture of how Deaf people experience and express life through a confluence of history and recent sociological influences. However, the essentialist paradigm of Deaf culture with specific expectations and identity has become increasingly part of the "establishment."

Deaf as Ethnicity

Lane (2005) argues that while Deaf people represent not a disability but rather a linguistic minority group within the constellation of language minorities, they also represent an ethnic Deaf group based on internal properties, including a collective name, shared language, feelings of community, behavior norms, distinct values, culture knowledge and customs, social/organization structures, the arts, history, and kinship, all of which support a Deaf identity. Kinship emanates from a sense of tribal connection (even without territorial ownership as claimed by many ethnic groups) and solidarity related to the use of visual communication pathways. Adding to this, Baker (1999) claims that disempowerment, low status, and discrimination based on being deaf entitle Deaf people to ethnic minority status.

Trevor Johnston's (2005) review of the ethnicity paradigm focuses on the premise that ethnic groups do not have inherently disabling characteristics like hearing loss. The lack of hearing is a biological characteristic that crosses ethnic boundaries. While Johnston acknowledges some similarities between deaf communities and ethnic minorities, he endorses the linguistic and cultural minority paradigm as more appropriate, although disability remains relevant. However, in many contexts, being deaf is not disabling nor is disability always relevant (e.g., when deaf persons interact with each other). Disability emerges primarily "within the contact zone between hearing and deaf worlds, between auditory and visual modalities ..." and not within the deaf world (Bauman, 2005, p. 314).

Lennard Davis (2007, 2008) sees the use of "ethnic" as also involving the biological domain, with reference to race, and as a precursor to racial profiling, with its attendant potentially negative consequences, including discrimination. He questions whether the ethnicity is lost for those who choose to speak and refers to contested boundaries about who is in and who is out. While acknowledging the issue of contested boundaries, Krentz (2007) argues for the empowering aspect of ethnic identity and the safe haven nature of the signing-Deaf community. He views boundaries to be critical in the presence of rampant discrimination against members who are "not hearing enough" and claims the boundaries are not rigid for those who respect the use of signed languages. It is comforting to be within a safe enclave, even to the point of attempting to preserve it (Page, 2006). However, Page envisions this becoming treacherous if the insularity of such enclaves separates members from the larger hearing world.

While minimization of "hearing and speaking" values related to audition has been an ongoing theme within Deaf perspectives, the actuality is that Deaf people nonetheless have had to coexist with the dominant hearing society, just as multicultural minority groups do with dominant national cultures. According to Paul Preston (1994), it is impossible to completely extract Deaf culture from hearing culture, since they exist in relationship to each other. Most deaf people have hearing family members, deal with hearing persons in employment settings, and depend on the hearing environment for daily essentials (Davis, 1995; Higgins, 1980).

How to find appropriate interfacing has been an ongoing dilemma because of communication and discrimination issues. Baynton (1996, p. 158) writes: "Integration has become a powerful symbol of fairness and decency, and segregation a powerful symbol of injustice. When deaf people try to make the case for separate education on the basis of their 'ethnic' or cultural identity, they struggle against a powerful current." Simply put, ethnic identity is an insufficient argument when the perception is more of access to language and communication to counteract a sensory disability. Whether the concept of ethnic identity is applicable for Deaf people remains an ongoing debate yet to be resolved in the face of paradoxes not easily reconciled.

Deaf and Disability: Uneasy Coexistence

The literature indicates that deaf and disability have had an uneasy coexistence (e.g., Barnartt & Scotch, 2001; Barnes & Mercer, 2001; Branson & Miller, 2002; Corker, 1998; Davis, 1995, 2008; Johnston, 2005; Ladd, 1994, 2003; Lane, 2005; Reagan, 2002; Skelton & Valentine, 2003), but only since the 1970s. Prior to that time, Deaf persons typically acknowledged their disability as the inability to hear (Baynton, 2008). The normalization of the Deaf experience has resulted in the counterargument that not deafness, but the linguistic issue, has fueled oppression and the demeaning of deaf people for centuries; therefore, the minority group appellation is appropriate (Barnartt & Scotch, 2001; Barnes & Mercer, 2001; Bauman, 2008a; Baynton, 2008; Branson & Miller, 2002; Lane, 1997). Deaf persons will often say that their barriers are communication barriers and not the type of barriers that hearing persons with various other disabilities face, thereby differentiating the two groups.

If I function comfortably within the constraints of my body, whatever its limitations, and am able to love, work, and play, am I truly disabled? If I as a deaf person go to a theater and follow the play by means of text captions, am I truly disabled? Not if I am getting the same information as my fellow attendees, albeit through a different medium. But if I see everyone abandoning my airport gate because of an audio-based announcement and have to scramble to find out where I need to go to catch my plane, then I have a disability. In essence, the environment informs me whether I have a disability:

> ...the distinction between the biological reality of a disability and the social construction of a disability cannot be made sharply, because the biological and the social are interactive in creating disability...not only in that complex interactions of social factors and our bodies affect health and functioning, but also in that social arrangements can make a biological condition more or less relevant to almost any situation." (Wendell, 1996, p. 35)

The results of a survey involving over 200 Deaf participants in Great Britain revealed that slightly more than half agreed they had a disability, thereby acknowledging the disabling component of not hearing (Dye, Kyle, Allsop, Dury, & Richter, 2001 as cited in Johnston, 2005). Yet Skelton and Valentine (2003) note that while the d/Deaf people they interviewed disavowed disability identity, they unknowingly endorsed it by having received help as a person with a disability, more out of pragmatic considerations for dealing with hearing issues as a fact of life rather than a belief in the self as disabled. This suggests that they acknowledge the problems and limitations engendered by not hearing and society's unwillingness to facilitate visual access to auditory information.

Lane (1992, p. 206) mentions the appropriateness of the "infirmity model" for the late-deafened contingent, thereby attempting to differentiate disability based on age of onset. But there are many late-deafened individuals, including I. King Jordan, the former president of Gallaudet University, who have repeatedly disavowed the infirmity concept. Corker (1994) indicates that Lane does a disservice to the late-deafened contingent, since the experiential process of deaf identity formation and self-perceptions as disabled are individualized and varied, not subject to generalization. This observation can be generalized to the case of hard-of-hearing persons and deaf users of spoken language as well. In the end, Davis (2008) highlights the notion of disability as a complex construct that does not exist when accommodation takes place. This notion has yet to be embraced in the consciousness of societies conditioned to the infirmity model of disability.

Deafhood: An Emerging Concept

Deafhood was coined by Paddy Ladd (2003) as a Deaf consciousness concept that involves process and reconstruction of Deaf traditions related to becoming and maintaining "Deaf." The term encompasses the ongoing discourse of sign language peoples (Ladd's term) in the journey to elucidate individual and collective shared beliefs and values and a sense of normality, pride, and confidence in the face of an oppressive society that holds on to the demeaning construct of a people who need to have their hearing fixed in order to be "normal." Ladd argues for a critical examination of Deafhood within venues such as Deaf culture forums, not necessarily to fragmentize Deaf culture, but rather as an act of deeper exploration of "the multiplicity and range of viewpoints and dispositions within Deaf culture" to make the concept stronger and more valid in terms of identity (Ladd, 2003, p. 430). In this way, he attempts a distance from essentialist and potentially exclusionary boundaries that implicitly oppress those who appear not to meet specific Deaf criteria while simultaneously scrutinizing which aspects of essential Deaf identity constitute Deafhood. This scrutiny is particularly timely as individuals increasingly become Deaf in various ways, with the residential schools for the deaf receding in prominence as incubators of Deaf cultures, and as people examine what might result if their signed language culture is allowed to flourish, particularly in the education sphere (see Chapters 4 and 5 for historical and current aspects).

Deaf Studies

The struggle to define the nature of the community of Deaf people forces attention on the unique social and cognitive abilities of "sign language peoples." The focus on culture and an increasing Deaf consciousness demands scholarly examination and consequently has resulted in the development of Deaf Studies as a discipline (Bauman, 2008a; Jankowski, 1997; Sanders, 1986). This discipline focuses on the study of the language, community, and culture of Deaf people, rather than hearing-loss prevention or cure. Its goal is to influence theory and practice in mainstream fields that deal with questions of human interaction, language, and cognition by adding vision to audition (Centre for

Deaf Studies, 2006). This endeavor is a reaction against the disability-based definitions of deaf put forth by people who hear. Ladd (2003) proposes a Deaf Studies framework of counternarratives by Deaf persons that explore medical, social welfare, human rights, linguistic minority, and Deafhood dimensions in the search for an in-depth understanding of the Deaf experience.

Deaf Culture: Linchpin for Identity

The issue of how "Deaf" one has to become to authentically qualify for Deaf culture membership has increasingly become more salient, thus leading to "the separatism that today divides us over language issues and issues of identity and self esteem" (Stewart, 1992, p.142). While Humphries (1996, 2004) describes this separatism as necessary to facilitate the analysis of what Deaf means, this process has exacerbated tensions about identity by reinforcing the distance between culturally Deaf members and those deaf and hard-of-hearing individuals comfortable with using spoken languages who may or may not use a sign language (Davis, 2008; Skelton & Valentine, 2003), distances that were far less prominent when I was growing up.

In turn, the groups being distanced from are simultaneously distancing themselves from Deaf groups. For example, on the Hearing Loss Web site, those who are hard of hearing, late-deafened, or oral deaf and prefer to use spoken language are described as being part of the oral hearing loss community. This community, which decries the typical expectation that sign language interpreters will provide appropriate access to auditory communication for all deaf and hard-of-hearing people, is slowly beginning to demand text-based and auditory enhancement services for the significantly greater majority of persons with hearing differences heretofore neglected (Hearing Loss Web, n.d.). They are specific regarding their distinction from the Deaf community as a way of emphasizing "them" and "us," as if the common bond of deafness and the deaf experience no longer hold for the two groups.

This two-way separation has created tension in identity affiliation related to language and communication choices:

> I was born with normal hearing and I grew up hard of hearing from the age of 7 until I became deaf at 19. Even though I was labeled hard of hearing, I had minimal ability to hear via auditory means alone...I transferred to Northern Illinois University (which has a contingent of deaf students) and it was there that I had a clash of identities. I was no longer hard of hearing, but I was labeled hard of hearing because I could talk well and didn't know how to sign. Suddenly I was surrounded by peers who were signing; some were native ASL users and some used simultaneous communication. I started making friends in this new world of mine. Five years later,

I was substitute teaching in sign classes at the university. It was at that point that the Association of Late-Deafened Adults (ALDA) formed and I attended their conference in Chicago. For a while ALDA fit. Here were people who also became deaf and were learning to communicate in a whole new way, just as I had done at 19. But I had moved on and into the Deaf community at that point. I was done grieving.

Then came the big D, little d identity crisis. Was I Deaf, or was I deaf? I had friends who used ASL, friends who used sim-com,* friends who were oral and I could code-switch with relative ease. Today I've moved beyond the identity crisis and simply tell people, I'm Karen. Yes, I'm deaf. Yes, I can sign. Yes, I can speak. I have a variety of interesting people in my life and they happen to communicate in a variety of ways. But most of all I'm just Karen—a wife, a mom, and a person who does a variety of things. Get to know me as Karen first, the rest falls in place. (K. Putz, personal communication, March 25, 2006)

Putz has decided to center herself on the personal self-definition, but the social definition as defined by "the other" is all too often omnipresent. As indicated in a study of oral deaf adults, those who wanted to connect with Deaf adults reported being rejected by those who objected to oral values (Leigh, 1999a), thereby reinforcing separatism and forcing further self-definition about who they were as opposed to Deaf culture members. I myself have been subject to this push and pull. Specifically, while I perceive myself as sufficiently competent in Deaf ways and as capable of participating within Deaf culture, I can also communicate adequately with users of spoken English. Because of this, I have at times been labeled as "hearing-mind," not truly Deaf, similarly to the Oreo label attached to African Americans who go by "White" rules.

However, there are intimidations that the Oreo crème filling that I've been likened to at times is going through an evolution (Brueggemann, 2008). Simply put, deaf can be simultaneously deaf (audiological/medical) and Deaf (cultural/linguistic) despite these separation efforts, depending on how the person navigates the fine line and how the "betweenity" space between the two is framed (Brueggemann, 2008). This amorphous in-between spectrum has not been extensively studied but is of great significance for those walking that fine line. While the push toward separatism has been dominant in terms of Deaf identity formation, the positive interconnections with the "hearing" part of oneself in the guise of speaking continue to reinforce the possibility of multiple deaf identities.

* Sim-com refers to the use of spoken English accompanied by signs.

THE IMPORTANCE OF DEAF IDENTITIES

The labels we choose are outward manifestations of our multiple identity roles, each of which comes to the fore depending on the situation
we find ourselves in. Clearly, identity is a much more complex construct
than immediately apparent. We need to move from the singular to the
plural and think in terms of the variability of our identities, their permutations, and their interactive effects (Mishler, 2004). Psychologists
and sociologists have struggled to examine the identity construct, how
it develops, and how the self and environment interact to reinforce or
negate specific individual identities. Within our personal selves, we
can internalize what we think or want our identities to be. When it
comes to our social selves, our identities may be supported or questioned, depending on which social group is salient at given times. In
the case of deaf identities, the onset of the methodological controversies
(Chapter 5), the evolution of the Deaf culture construct, and the advent
of technology (Chapter 8) have created complexities in the affirming or
balancing of deaf identities. The rest of the book will explore some of
these complexities.

2

Deaf Identities: Perspectives from Theory and Research

Frameworks and theories are, in my view, meant to assist and develop our thinking, not restrict it.
　　Mairian Corker (1998, p. 9)

Psychosocial literature covering theory and research on identity evolution in deaf and hard-of-hearing persons is relatively recent. This chapter presents conceptual and theoretical perspectives on the formation of diverse deaf identity categories and how individuals may transition into and out of categories. Supporting research and anecdotal evidence are included as well.

CONCEPTUAL AND THEORETICAL EXPLORATIONS

Ben Schowe's (1979) *Identity Crisis in Deafness* appears to be the first book that specifically documents how deaf people define their various deaf selves in response to negative perceptions from "outsiders." For example, Schowe describes a man who insisted on being called "deafened" rather than "deaf" in order to identify with hearing persons. In his book, he presents three patterns of adjustment developed by Lee Meyerson, a renowned mid-twentieth-century psychologist and professor who happened to be deaf. *Adjustment Pattern 1* represents those who search for connections with other deaf persons and reject the world of hearing; *Adjustment Pattern 2* covers those who aspire to the hearing world and reject the "world of impaired hearing" (Schowe, 1979, p. 50). This pattern acknowledges the reality of walking a tightrope between both worlds due to the lack of acceptance by the hearing world as manifested by marginality, self-hate, anxiety, and debilitating resentment. Finally, *Adjustment Pattern 3* reflects joyous acceptance of the commonality between those with impaired hearing and those with normal hearing. Schowe cautions that the boundaries between the patterns are not rigid.

Based on discussions with Deaf adult groups in Australia, Breda Carty (1994) suggests six stages of Deaf identity development that encompass the psychological distance deaf persons travel "to explore and embrace Deaf identity" (p. 42). First is *Confusion,* which emerges as deaf children recognize their hearing difference within their hearing family of origin. This in turn results in *Frustration/Anger/Blame* as these children respond to the lack of understanding or acceptance in their environment through outbursts or self-hate. If there is exposure to information about Deaf people at some point, the *Exploration* stage creates the possibility of associating with either hearing or Deaf groups. As the individual starts exploring these groups, tentative *Identification/Rejection* takes place depending on early experiences and level of acceptance. For example, if a deaf person feels rejected by hearing peers, the desire to join the Deaf community may become more salient. If exposure creates negative stereotypical perceptions of the group one is trying to identify with, feelings of *Ambivalence* may emerge. All Deaf people may be seen as rejecting of the newcomer if there are communication barriers due to nonfluent signing. Finally, there is the *Acceptance* stage, which encompasses becoming comfortable with personal and social identities, the reactions from both the in-group and others, and with functioning effectively in the chosen social setting. This identity exploration process is exemplified by Hilde, who realized in late adolescence that even though she wanted to be part of her hearing environment, she could not pass as a hearing person. She did not accept herself as deaf and vacillated until she finally attended a deaf event and began to embrace a Deaf identity (Breivik, 2005).

These six stages are essentially a guideline for eliciting Deaf stories that will clarify Deaf identity development (Carty, 1994). However, without theoretical foundations that buttress the identity constructs being labeled, it is difficult to make sense of the Deaf identity development process and the social context within which this development takes place. Researchers have relied on diverse theories to elucidate the meaning of identity constructs. We start first with the disability-based perspective utilized by Weinberg and Sterritt (1986).

Disability Framework

Weinberg and Sterritt (1986) define deaf children as having a disability, with parents striving to encourage their children to appear and behave as "able-bodied" as possible, apropos of the medical model. In providing an example of deaf children not being encouraged to use sign language to minimize identification as deaf, which then might doom them to feelings of inferiority because they cannot really achieve able-bodied status (hearing status), the authors acknowledge the potential negative impact of such an approach. The purpose of their study was to better understand how deaf persons identify themselves and how this may be associated with academic placement, social relationships, personal adjustment, and perceived family acceptance. Their choice to describe the more commonly phrased "state school for the deaf" as a state school for "people with hearing impairments" (p. 96), where they recruited 111 deaf adolescents for their study, appears to reinforce the focus on disability in the guise of impairment.

The authors constructed a Deaf Identity Scale (DIS) consisting of three subscales: *Hearing Identification*, which was comparable to able-bodied; *Deaf Identification*, which meant disabled; and *Dual Identification*, which covered identification with both the able-bodied and the disabled worlds. Their results indicated that 54% of the sample fell into the Dual Identification category, while 24% chose Deaf Identification and 18% Hearing Identification. Those deaf adolescents categorized as Dual Identification achieved the best outcomes in academic placement, social relationships, personal adjustment, and perceived family acceptance, followed by those with Deaf Identification and then the Hearing Identification adolescents. Since the participants came from a state school for the deaf where signing predominated, it might have been logical to assume stronger Deaf Identification than was the case. However, the desire to indicate comfort with both hearing and deaf worlds appears to have been relatively strong for this group of participants, keeping in mind this study was done prior to public awareness of a Deaf culture and Deaf pride. The authors interpreted their findings as reflecting the rejection of able-bodied/hearing identity because of its implied perception of disability identity as inferior, while combining the two identities increases positive connection with both hearing and deaf identities as well as better psychosocial outcomes. From a psychometric perspective, the reliability of the DIS was problematic, meaning that it was not clear whether the measures really reflected what they were supposed to measure.

Racial Identity Development Paradigm

It has been suggested that as members of a minority group, deaf individuals share experiences of oppression similarly to members of other minority groups (Glickman, 1996a; Ladd, 2003). They are not perceived as "normal" and are "damned for their difference" (Branson & Miller, 2002; Davis, 1995). Paralleling the theoretical progression of racial identity stages based on recognition of differences and experiences of oppression (see Chapter 7), deaf persons acknowledging their discriminatory status in life theoretically progress from a self-construction as "hearing identified" or marginal toward a more Deaf-oriented stance. Table 2.1 presents the categories Glickman developed to support this theory and help psychotherapists and allied professionals better understand the deaf–hearing dynamics that influence how their clients identify themselves.

Glickman (1996a) categorizes deaf people who are most comfortable with spoken language as culturally hearing. This is the first stage of

Table 2-1. Theory of Deaf Identity Development

Stage	Reference Group	View of Deafness	View of Deaf Community	Emotional Theme
Hearing	Hearing	Pathology	Uninformed & stereo-typed	Despair, Depression
Marginal	Switches	Pathology	Shifts from good to bad	Confusion & conflict
Immersion	Deaf	Cultural	Positive, non-reflective	Anger/"in love with Deafness"
Bicultural	Deaf	Cultural	Positive, personal, integrated	Self-acceptance & group pride

Source: From "The Development of Culturally Deaf Identities," by N. Glickman (1996). In N. Glickman & M. Harvey (Eds.). *Culturally Affirmative Psychotherapy with Deaf Persons* (pp. 115–153). Mahwah, NJ: Lawrence Erlbaum Associates. Copyright 1996. All rights reserved. Reprinted with permission.

his Deaf Cultural Identity Development theory. The goal of the hearing identified or culturally hearing stage is to be "as hearing as possible" by conforming to norms for people who speak and hear. As such, it parallels the conformity stage of the racial identity development models. It also begs the question: What does it mean to be as hearing as possible? How can individuals who are deaf have a hearing identity or be perceived as "hearing"? Is this the same as being part of the "hearing world" or "hearing culture"?

The concept of a hearing identity is alien to the majority of people who hear. Since "hearing" is perceived as the norm by virtue of its being a ubiquitous phenomenon, persons who hear tend to be unaware of "hearing" as an identity until they confront a deaf person or lose their hearing. I have had to enlighten naïve groups of hearing people totally mystified about how they are labeled by deaf people. This is analogous to White people being unaware of their being white until the perception of white as a norm is shaken by individuals outside this "norm" (e.g., Helms, 1994; Sue & Sue, 2008), or to people being unconscious of their heterosexuality until they are exposed to gay men and lesbians (Glickman, 1996a), or to able-bodied individuals who are oblivious to their status until they see persons with disabilities (Leigh & Brice, 2003).

The "hearing world–deaf world" dichotomy makes apparent intuitive sense. But when confronted with the notion of a standard hearing culture, hearing persons often react with puzzlement (Andrews, Leigh, & Weiner, 2004). For d/Deaf people, this phrase is taken to mean an auditory environment consisting of culturally sanctioned ways of communicating through spoken language, related gestures and facial expressions, attention-getting techniques, and vocal qualifiers, such as tone of voice (Stokoe, 1989). This hearing cultural environment is most typically the environment of mainstream culture but also can reflect the specific ethnic and cultural societies worldwide. Such environments are contrasted with Deaf cultural ways of being in which people respond through visual means, including body language, facial expressions, signs or mouthed words, tapping one's shoulder for attention, and so on, although there are in fact ethnic Deaf variations of Deaf cultural ways (e.g., Corbett, 1999; Eldredge, 1999; Hernández, 1999; Wu & Grant, 1999).

Now, how can the notion of a hearing identity apply to deaf people? While typically defined as one of the five body senses, hearing can also be defined as a state of mind that thinks in spoken language, maximizes auditory ways of functioning, and feels an affinity for spoken language users. The common representation for hearing identity is "think hearing," "passing as hearing," or behaving as a hearing person does (Bat-Chava, 2000; Cole & Edelman, 1991; Padden & Humphries, 1988).

According to Glickman (1996a), late-deafened individuals who lose their hearing after internalizing hearing-based identities are the prototype for the culturally hearing stage. For these individuals, becoming deaf is a major disability as manifested in the loss of meaningful connections with others and subsequently the exacerbation of emotional loneliness and isolation. Their biological deafness can create a dissonance with their hearing identity status (Graham & Sharp-Pucci, 1994; Harvey, 2003; Meadow-Orlans, 1985). Learning American Sign Language (ASL) often represents a huge psychological hurdle, since not only does this involve a new language but also a new and strange community to which the late-deafened person often cannot connect. The preference is to maintain contact with the familiar hearing world through hearing ways of speaking, understanding, and behaving. This typically entails a search for medical cures to eliminate the pathology of deafness and failing that, availing oneself of technology, such as hearing aids or cochlear implants, pressing the caption button on the television set, relying on text-based telecommunication devices for phone contact, and so on.

The culturally hearing stage also applies to those individuals who grow up deaf and exhibit preference for spoken English (Glickman, 1996a). They often interact primarily with hearing peers, may belong to organizations advocating spoken language for deaf children, and do not necessarily seek out contact with other deaf people.

> I tell people I consider myself a hearing person...no, not normally hearing, but hearing nonetheless. While I recognize that I have always and will continue to hear imperfectly, I do hear...well enough to use the phone and well enough to speak with ease. Therefore I wish professionals would stop referring to "the hearing" and "the hearing

impaired." I think when we use these two categories we limit our expectation of what can be done for deaf and hard-of-hearing people, at least on a functional level. (E. Rhoades, personal communication, October 22, 2007)

According to Glickman, this stage tends not to be a healthy one emotionally for those growing up deaf, because they are essentially "denying their deafness" and can never be truly hearing. Bonnie Tucker (1995) lists her numerous identities, including mother, lawyer, lover of books, and *deaf*. She defines deaf as a state of feeling, thinking, and experience, all a part of her being as she lives her life in the hearing world, only occasionally coming into contact with deaf people. She is up front about hating that deaf part. She *wants to be hearing*. Is it denial to acknowledge "deaf" and not embrace it?

In contrast, there are people with roots in the hearing world who declare they are at peace with themselves, choose not to transition to Deaf culture, and do not countenance negative perceptions of themselves as rootless or denying their deafness (e.g., Golan, 1995; Kisor, 1990). When asked whether he is happy, Henry Kisor (1990) exclaims that he is of course happy and is exasperated by the question. He is as happy as anyone else who has gone through a mixed plate of blessings and curses. Kisor acknowledges how difficult it is for many educators of deaf children and many deaf people themselves to recognize that he in fact does not live a melancholy life just because he communicates solely through spoken language. They tend to view him as an outcast from the hearing world or the deaf community, a "poor shadow of a hearing person, not a contented and fulfilled deaf person" (Kisor, 1990, pp. 242–243). And Karen Kirby writes that over the years, she has met some deaf people who see that she can speak and so they say to her, "Oh, you're hearing." But she replies: "I'm not. I'm deaf" (Kirby, 2002, p. 80).

Maxwell-McCaw (2001) suggests that members of this group could be psychologically healthy depending on how they frame their deaf self. To determine that individuals in this group are in fact denying their deafness requires a careful analysis of what denial of deafness means, particularly when there is more than one way to be deaf. The question then becomes that of which "deaf" is denied, the one reflecting Deaf cultural values, the one pretending to fit in, for example in noisy situations, the one who rejects the deaf label, or the one reflecting certain culturally ethnic ways of being deaf that reinforce mingling with hearing counterparts.

The second stage of Glickman's theory refers to cultural marginality, which parallels the dissonance/appreciating stage of racial identity development models. In this stage, deaf persons do not fully identify with either Deaf or hearing groups, are conflicted or ambivalent about membership in either group, exist on the fringe, and shift loyalties depending on degree of acceptance/rejection. They may not demonstrate appropriate social behavior or communication patterns expected within each group.

Cultural marginality may be the first identity stage for deaf children born into hearing families who are not fully assimilated into their hearing environment because of inadequate access to spoken language and simultaneously have no experience with deaf peers. Their social marginality can lead to psychological marginality in terms of identity confusion, poorly differentiated understanding of self and other, and emotional/behavioral difficulties. Deaf individuals with limited language development and limited access to appropriate education will exhibit more acting-out behavior that exemplifies their confusion about their internal sense of self and identity and exacerbates their marginality (Glickman, 1996a).

Cultural marginality can also occur for linguistically competent individuals who may be exploring where they belong on the deaf–hearing identity dimension if they feel caught between the deaf and hearing worlds and are struggling with feelings of belongingness and acceptance (Glickman, 1986; Leigh, 1999a). In studies of the relationship between deaf identities and self-concept/self-esteem, respondents who were classified as marginal scored lowest (Cornell & Lyness, 2004; Hintermair, 2008; Maxwell-McCaw, 2001). Additionally, a study of eating disorder symptomatology and Deaf cultural identity in deaf women demonstrated that being categorized as marginal correlated positively with eating disorder symptomatology (Moradi & Rottenstein, 2007). Hintermair (2008) cautions, however, that some of those identified as marginal may have personal resources other than connecting with hearing/deaf groups and may do well in life.

Late-deafened individuals often struggle with both the loss of their hearing self-image and the need to develop a new personal and social identity (Meadow-Orlans, 1985). Depending on their resiliency, however, it is possible to get through this stage and affirm a more clear-cut identity. This is supported by Maxwell-McCaw's (2001) finding that none of the late-deafened participants in her sample scored as marginal on the Deaf Acculturation Scale (see p. 34). In fact, it was difficult to predict acculturative styles for this group, possibly because they had resolved their issues and moved on to hard-of-hearing, hearing, or d/Deaf identities.

The third stage is that of immersion in the Deaf world, which is analogous to how racial and ethnic groups immerse themselves within their relevant groups as they become disenchanted with their treatment by the dominant group. There is an exuberant love affair with Deaf identity and Deaf cultures at the same time that hearing cultural values, including spoken languages, are disavowed. Immersion-stage deaf persons want to be surrounded by everything Deaf and avoid the compromises they see oral deaf persons making in accommodating to hearing environments. Anger may be directed at hearing persons for creating barriers to desired connections with Deaf people (e.g., Breivik, 2005). Political militancy related to, for example, taking control of their institutions (schools, places of employment serving deaf people, etc.) may emerge.

Individuals outside the fold who are trying to find common areas with immersion-stage Deaf persons may run the risk of finding this to be an exercise in futility. As mentioned in the Leigh (1999a) study on the personal development of oral deaf adults (see Chapter 3 for a brief description), several participants reported being rejected by those Deaf culture members they encountered. Some who may desire immersion in Deaf culture can end up on the margins because they are viewed as having intractable "hearing" thoughts and characteristics (e.g., Brooks, 1996).

Characteristics reflected by the introspective and integrative aware-ness stage of racial identity development models are incorporated into the fourth and final stage of the Deaf Identity Development Model. As deaf people begin to recognize the strengths and weaknesses of both deaf and hearing people and more fully integrate the values of both hearing and Deaf cultures, they enter this bicultural stage. There is an increasingly balanced perspective of what it means to be Deaf that incorporates mutually respectful collaboration with hearing people. They are at ease in both Deaf and hearing settings. This stage reflects the most optimal psychosocial adjustment compared to the other three stages (Cornell & Lyness, 2004; Hintermair, 2008; Jambor & Elliott, 2005; Maxwell-McCaw, 2001).

Glickman (1996a) acknowledges that Deaf identity development is not necessarily linear in terms of progressing from conformity or mar-ginality to commitment and integration. Rather, recycling through the stages occurs, depending on individual circumstances and one's attri-butions about the meaning of various identities and their associated positive or negative valences. A deaf child of hearing parents initially may accommodate to hearing ways and not experience marginality until later, when assuming a Deaf identity may become more attrac-tive. In turn, there are native culturally Deaf persons who eventually identify as culturally hearing (e.g., Bertling, 1994). Other Deaf children of Deaf parents who learn to be comfortable in hearing environments may project a bicultural identity early on even if they do not describe themselves as such. Having grown up in a signing environment where written languages are also respected although the spoken version may not be primary, and where they are taught how to relate positively with hearing outsiders, there is less reason for anger and more openness to balanced perspectives. However, there are anecdotal stories of how these children may demonstrate rejection of peers who are not suffi-ciently culturally Deaf within specialized schools for the deaf, at least until greater maturity is achieved (see Chapter 4). This may support Glickman's (1996a) suggestion that the immersion stage of close and uncritical identification with Deaf cultural values is a prerequisite for bicultural comfort as these children's perspectives evolve.

Extensive literature on identity status progression confirms the erratic nature of identity status formation (Côté, 2006). For example, Marcia's (1993) popular identity status categories: diffusion (no commitment and no crisis forcing exploration of identity), foreclosure (commitment without crisis or considering alternatives), moratorium (in crisis, going through active identity exploration), and identity achievement (commitment to identity choices after exploring different alternatives) were originally thought to represent a transformative developmental sequence. While Lytle (1987) has provided some empirical support for the similarity in Marcia's identity status categories between deaf college women and their hearing peers, whether the similarity in patterns reflects a stable developmental progression remains subject to challenge.

Glickman's four identity categories were incorporated into a 60-item Deaf Identity Development Scale (DIDS) (Glickman, 1996a; Glickman & Carey, 1993) to be filled out by deaf, late-deafened, and hard-of-hearing individuals. The Hearing Scale has items such as "I only socialize with hearing people," while the Marginal Scale is exemplified by items such as "Neither deaf nor hearing people accept me" (Glickman, 1996a, p. 149). "Deaf people should only socialize with other deaf people" is representative of items found in the Immersion Scale (p. 149), and the Bicultural Scale incorporates statements such as "I enjoy both Deaf and hearing cultures" (p. 150). While Glickman and Carey (1993) reported acceptable reliability and construct validity using 161 participants, follow-up studies found the Bicultural Scale to be less reliable in differentiating research subjects, possibly due to social desirability factors emphasizing biculturalism (Friedburg, 2000; Leigh, Marcus, Dobosh, & Allen, 1998). Fischer and McWhirter (2001) shortened the DIDS to 48 items and demonstrated acceptable reliability for all four categories. Interestingly, the Bicultural Scale demonstrated the lowest, albeit acceptable, reliability score.

The categories described in Glickman's Deaf Identity Development theory appear to be prescriptive in terms of idealized ways to be deaf and of stages that are predetermined or natural and therefore essential. Stein Erik Ohna (2004) recognizes that the politics of recognition related to identity demarcations require more of a prescriptive blueprint of what it means to be a deaf person, but he critiques this essentialist approach for not incorporating variations in cultural context and the communicative nature of the environment as these interact with the individual and vice versa. As tensions emerge during daily lives and different roles that juxtapose hearing–deaf issues at home, at work, and in the social context, it becomes more difficult to justify strong boundaries between the four categories (Ohna, 2003). For example, a Deaf adult may become more hearing-oriented or "hearing identified" when at work with hearing peers and still be a strong Deaf activist fighting against hearing domination of the nearby state school for the deaf. Boundaries between identities are really about the nature of interactions with people, and they can be either porous or rigid depending on context.

Social Identity Paradigm

The social identity theory, largely developed by Henri Tajfel (Tajfel, 1981; Turner, 1996), focuses on the relationship between individual and group membership processes for identity. There are three components: *(1)* the individual psychological dynamic that propels persons lacking a satisfactory social identity in the direction of assigning positive attributions to their relevant group memberships, including minority or stigmatized groups; *(2)* shifting in behavior from the interpersonal to the intergroup level, which involves complex social and psychological processes that result in the involved individual behaving similarly to those within the shared group; and *(3)* social categories associated with group affiliation becoming psychologically internalized and used to describe the subjective self. How effective this process is depends on the specific social context that provides meanings to the groups involved, whether highly valued, stigmatized, or somewhere in between. Decisions about group affiliation reflect how we evaluate information relevant to us, how we evaluate others, and how we create positive views of the groups with which we affiliate.

If a deaf or hard-of-hearing person sees a specific Deaf, deaf, or hard-of-hearing group as positive, she or he may identify with that particular group, depending on circumstances, even if in the public eye it is stigmatized. If the person perceives a specific group negatively due to stigmatization by more dominant or majority groups or societies, connections with that group will be minimized or disavowed in the interest of identifying with the dominant group.

Using social identity theory as a foundation, Yael Bat-Chava (2000) identified three identities through an analysis of cluster items based on four criterion variables related to communication and socialization, specifically the perceived importance of signing, the importance of speech, group identity, and attitudes toward deaf people. Data were obtained from 267 deaf adults who responded to a brief questionnaire covering language, attitudes toward deaf people, and level of involvement with Deaf people. Approximately one-third of the sample identified themselves as culturally Deaf, representing those who work to bring about social change that will decrease stigmatization due to minority status; another third identified themselves as bicultural in terms of maintaining access to the majority hearing group while also identifying with deaf peers and confronting majority group stigmatization. One-fourth of the sample was categorized as culturally hearing due to identifying with the majority hearing group and harboring negative attitudes toward deaf people, while the rest of the sample reflected negative identities, valuing neither sign language nor speech and not identifying with either group, similarly to Glickman's (1996a) marginal category. There was some support for the presence of higher self-esteem in those identifying as culturally Deaf or bicultural in comparison to those identified as culturally hearing or having negative identities. In terms of social identity theory, the focus was not primarily on the hearing disability. Rather, the importance of language and communication, socialization, and social perspectives about what it means to hear or not to hear in forging deaf-related or hearing-related identities was paramount.

In a series of projects that involved high school adolescents, Michael Stinson and his colleagues examined the social identities of deaf children and youth using social orientation as a parameter (e.g., Stinson & Foster, 2000; Stinson & Kluwin, 1996; Stinson & Whitmire, 1992). Social orientation is based in part on perceptions of relationships that involve self-appraisals of participation in activities, feelings of relatedness (self-appraisals of emotional security of relationships) toward peers, and perceived social competence. As such, social orientation can be viewed as an aspect of social identity because it involves cognitive, motivational, and social processes associated with group and intergroup behaviors (Hogg, 2003).

In a longitudinal study of 451 deaf adolescents in 15 public high school (mainstream) programs for deaf students consisting of anywhere from 70 to 540 deaf students, three cohorts of deaf participants were followed for 5 years, from ninth through twelfth grade or prior to dropping out (Kluwin & Stinson, 1993). Social orientation was derived from the Social Activity Scale. This scale provided information on participants' social competence and their perceptions of their social relationships in and out of school, who the participants felt most comfortable with related to social identity, and self-rated communication aspects.

Results indicated that the majority of the sample (37.1%) was oriented toward both deaf and hearing peers; 30.3% were socially oriented toward primarily deaf peers; 12.4% were oriented toward primarily hearing peers; and 20.2% exhibited no social orientation to either group. Students with more profound hearing losses and preference for/skill in using signs had stronger social orientation toward deaf peers, while the opposite was true for those with strong peer orientation toward hearing students; they had less severe hearing loss and preferred speech. The participants who were marginal as well as those who were socially oriented toward both deaf and hearing peers self-rated their signing skills roughly in between the highest and lowest mean for the entire sample.

In a study of 64 deaf adolescent participants at a summer camp who responded to a questionnaire soliciting preferred mode of communication and self-perceptions, those who preferred oral communication indicated preferences for hearing peers, while those preferring ASL or simultaneous communication (spoken English accompanied by signs) assigned higher ratings to deaf peers (Stinson, Chase, & Bondi-Wolcott, 1988 as cited in Stinson & Whitmire, 1992).

These findings as well as numerous studies in the literature cited by Stinson and colleagues and an additional study of deaf adolescents in segregated, partially integrated, and mainstreamed settings (Musselman, Mootilal, & MacKay, 1996) buttress the importance of language/communication competency in social connectedness with specific groups. Shared ways of communicating with peers, whether based on signed or spoken language, and effectiveness in communication will influence social relationships and in turn social identity.

Acculturation Paradigm

According to Deborah Maxwell-McCaw (2001), Glickman's (1996a) racial identity development approach focuses on internal dimensions of identity that facilitate progression toward self-actualization and a positive sense of self to counteract oppression. Minimal attention is given to behavioral components that support specific identities or to the possibility of shifting identity categories. Maxwell-McCaw (2001) prefers the concept of acculturation as a vehicle for explaining the deaf identity types defined by Glickman (1996a), each of which will become more salient depending on the extent and level of interactions between the person and various cultural environments.

This concept reflects not only psychological identification but also behavioral competencies that acculturation models (see Chapter 7) take into account to explain the fluidity in one's identity categorization. Specifically, acculturation patterns vary in terms of the level of psychological identification with Deaf culture and the cultures of the relevant hearing societies with which the individual is in contact. The ethnicity and/or other characteristics of these cultures, such as religion, as well as the degree of behavioral involvement and the level of cultural competence in these cultures also influence acculturation patterns.

Maxwell-McCaw (2001) developed the Deaf Acculturation Scale (DAS) as a means of applying the acculturation concept to deaf identities. The DAS consists of a Deaf Acculturation Scale and a Hearing Acculturation Scale, each of which has five relevant subscales that parallel each other and measure acculturation across five domains as follows:

1. *Cultural identification.* Psychological identification with deaf or hearing people, use of self-labels, and level of comfort

within each culture (e.g., "I am most comfortable with other deaf people" and "I am most comfortable with other hearing people")

2. *Cultural involvement.* The degree to which deaf and hard-of-hearing persons participate in various cultural activities (e.g., "How much do you enjoy attending deaf events/parties/gatherings?" and "How much do you enjoy attending hearing parties/gatherings?")

3. *Cultural preferences.* Preferences for friends, lovers, spouses, and educational and work colleagues to be either deaf or hearing (e.g., "I would prefer my lover/spouse to be deaf" and "I would prefer my lover/spouse to be hearing")

4. *Language competence.* Expressive and receptive competence in ASL as well as competence in spoken and written English (e.g., "How well do you sign ASL?" and "How well do you speak in English, using your voice?")

5. *Cultural knowledge.* Knowledge of the Deaf and hearing cultures (e.g., "How well do you know favorite jokes from Deaf culture?" or "How well do you know nursery rhymes and children's stories?")

Based on scoring parameters, respondents can be categorized in four ways: Hearing Acculturated (high scores in Hearing acculturation and low scores in Deaf acculturation), Marginal (low scores in both Hearing and Deaf acculturation), Deaf Acculturated (high scores in Deaf acculturation and low scores in Hearing acculturation), and Bicultural (high scores in both Hearing and Deaf acculturation). While acceptable reliability and validity were demonstrated for this 78-item DAS version based on 3,070 participants, Maxwell-McCaw and Zea (submitted) reduced the DAS to 58 items and strengthened its psychometrics based on exploratory factor analysis and validation.

In terms of psychological well-being, Maxwell-McCaw (2001) demonstrated that for deaf and hard-of-hearing subjects, Deaf acculturation and biculturalism were more equally associated with a healthy sense of well-being compared to those who were hearing acculturated. Marginalism was found to be the least adaptive (see also p. 29). In essence, being comfortable as a Deaf person and the ability to comfortably switch between Deaf and hearing cultures are conducive to psychological well-being.

In his critique of the work done in acculturation psychology, Rudmin (2003) takes issue with the concept that two cultures allow for only four types of acculturation, as incorporated in Maxwell-McCaw's approach. He argues that two cultures, two attitudes, two identities, or two languages result in 16 possible types of acculturation, not four. This is based on the logic that there are 16 possible combinations of these constructs reflecting different levels of acculturation. As cultures are added to create multiculturalism, the combinations reflecting various types of acculturation will increase exponentially. Rudmin claims that situational variables are more critical than individual attributes in the process of acculturation, thereby complicating research conclusions. For example, a deaf individual who identifies as oral deaf (reflecting hearing identity) but is open to learning a signed language may or may not gravitate toward a Deaf cultural identity depending on the extent to which Deaf cultural settings feel welcoming.

An additional example of the importance of context is provided by Rudmin's question regarding whether biculturalism and marginalism have clear boundaries. This is implied in the theoretical perspectives presented in this chapter, since these boundaries can be quite fluid depending on context. A speaking deaf person fluent in a signed language who internally feels positive about hearing and Deaf cultures could be made to feel marginalized if perceived as "fake hearing" by Deaf adherents. As Ladd (2003) emphasizes, Deafhood and the ways in which it coexists with hearing contexts are evolving constructs still undergoing scrutiny, and consequently boundaries should not be absolute.

Going even further, hearing–deaf boundaries may dissolve in some contexts. In Josh Swiller's evocative autobiography, *The Unheard: A Memoir of Deafness and Africa* (2007), he describes how he, as a deaf, limited-signing person, felt out of place and marginalized in a Deaf space (Gallaudet University). To his Deaf peers he was hearing, but to hearing peers he was deaf. To escape this limbo, he journeyed to Zambia to find a place where his hearing status was irrelevant compared with his foreigner status. There, he felt for the first time fully himself: not hearing, not deaf.

Terminology adds further complexity. In various research projects, the terms used reflect different meanings, so that comparability between projects may not be that hard and fast (Rudmin, 2003). Considering the term "culturally hearing" as applied to deaf persons, Bat-Chava (2000) and Glickman (1996a) incorporate negative attitudes toward Deaf people in their definition of this term. In contrast, Maxwell-McCaw and Zea's (submitted) DAS items rely on degree of comfort with hearing people, not on negative attitudes toward deaf people per se. This approach does not assume rejection of deaf people, as personified by Ken Levinson (2002), who is clearly hearing acculturated but also values contact with deaf persons.

The Narrative Approach

Narration has become a vehicle through which to examine the processes of identity formulation and changes. This process-oriented approach focuses on examining themes from life stories to describe individuals and how their interactions with others influence identity construction. This approach endorses the need to move identity categorizations beyond the veneer of obvious labels to consider the effect of situational and interactional variables, which reflect the interplay between individuals and communities.

Using data obtained from interviews with 22 deaf Norwegian young and middle-aged adults, Ohna (2004) focused primarily on alienation and affiliation interaction experiences (based on daily interactions between deaf and hearing persons) and the language used to reflect these experiences (self-history) to decipher how the dialectical relationship between both reported experiences and language used differentially framed the deaf identities of his interviewees. Relying on a dialogical constructional approach to extrapolate themes from the narratives that clarified critical junctures in identity development, he identified four phases of development in deaf identity construction for deaf interviewees with hearing parents. The phases start with a *taken-for-granted* phase (taking for granted I am like hearing people, even if I have met deaf persons) and then proceed to an *alienation* phase (acknowledging breakdown of communication with hearing persons and not being understood by them). Next is an *affiliation* phase, in which deaf as identity is viewed through the prism of affiliation and mutual understanding while hearing persons become different. Finally, there is *deaf-in-my-own-way*, with ambivalence toward hearing people being resolved depending on the level of mutual understanding or whether the hearing person understands deaf people collectively. The need to be with both deaf and hearing people in a "deaf in my own way" state of mind is expressed. There is more challenge in getting others to understand how one is as a deaf person than in terms of accommodating to hearing people.

Deaf persons with deaf parents will show different patterns in that their *taken-for-granted* phase will more likely engender feelings of similarity with deaf people as well as hearing people who are visible in their environment until there is recognition that interactions with hearing people can be problematic. This leads to the *alienation* phase, which involves ambivalence at recognizing one's difference from hearing persons while recognizing mutuality with deaf people. In the *affiliation* phase, being oneself as a deaf person is affirmed, and the *deaf-in-my-own-way* phase is similar to what deaf persons with hearing parents experience. In short, alienation, affiliation, language and communication, and hearing and deaf environments all interplay in structuring individual perceptions of deaf identities.

Based on ethnographic narrative interviews with 15 Flemish deaf role models, Goedele De Clerck (2007) identifies a progression from the "sleeping" stage (reflecting the deaf as a medical identity) through a stage that involves dialectical encounters with individuals from other countries who provided information on deaf cultural rhetoric and representations of a *deaf dream world*. That stage metamorphoses into an insurrection and empowerment phase encapsulated in the "waking up" process, during which interviewees experienced changes in their lives in the direction of a reframed deaf identity and become deaf activists. This deaf identity change process is cyclical in nature, with the waking-up phase re-enacted and new dimensions added at various times.

Using what they describe as life story interview methodology to elicit critical Deaf identity aspects from a group of Deaf interviewees, Deaf Studies specialists Benjamin Bahan and H-Dirksen Bauman (2005) note a recurring pattern involving construction, deconstruction, and reconstruction as stories are narrated to reveal the autobiographical "I" and the ideological "I" as components of the self. In the construction phase, Deaf lives are herded by social ideology encouraging mislabeling of the individual, for example, using "hearing impaired" with its attendant focus on speech and medical treatment rather than "Deaf." In the deconstruction phase, stories begin to reflect transition as the storyteller realizes the extent of ideological control related to communication in particular, assumes more visual ways of being in contrast to reliance on audition to enhance communication, journeys toward an ideologically Deaf space, and "wakes up" to the Deaf self. In the process of reconstruction, the self begins to internalize the new aspects through a move from being "unhomed" to being "at home" within a more comfortable space in the world, and passes the torch to the next generation. These phases parallel Glickman's (1996a) description of the process by which deaf persons not born to culturally Deaf families transition to a culturally Deaf identity as they get exposed to different possibilities of being. Martha Sheridan (2001, 2008) and Tom Humphries (Padden & Humphries, 2005) exemplify this process as they describe their "awakening" in the course of deciding to come to Gallaudet University (the world's only liberal arts higher education setting for deaf persons). They grew up as "a hearing person who didn't hear" (Padden & Humphries, 2005, p. 145). When they arrived at Gallaudet, they realized they were no longer in a world that viewed their difference as a hearing problem and began to internalize their identity as Deaf people who belonged.

Jan-Kåre Breivik (2005) devotes his book on deaf identities in the making to an analysis of narratives by 10 Norwegian adults that reveals how phenomenological understanding of the deaf self emerges through diverse experiences and perspectives. He identifies themes of being, becoming and longing, liminality, transnational connections, and deaf ethnification to illustrate how different forces converge to extract different manifestations of self and identity as situations change.

CORE IDENTITY AND SELF-CATEGORIZATION

The theories covered in this chapter illustrate various perspectives about deaf identities and their formation. The concept of a deaf or hearing-related identity begs the question of whether this can be considered a core identity for deaf and hard-of-hearing individuals. In Mairian Corker's (1996) eyes, "core identity" is most comparable to personal identity. Personal identities are formed through internal absorption of heritages starting within the family of origin, in particular ethnic heritages.

For a deaf child growing up in a culturally Deaf family, Deaf identity is a natural evolution based on family of origin. "Deaf" is not typically part of the hearing family heritage to be passed on to deaf children. Consequently, Corker argues that "deaf" is *not* necessarily a core identity for those who grow up within hearing families. She views the integration of a deaf identity into one's psyche as an additional developmental task very much dependent on family, school, and other environmental opportunities, including exposure to other deaf persons, in attaching positive or negative valences to hearing–deaf aspects. When experiences related to the deaf dimension are perceived as positive, deaf identities gain in value. If negative, such as when children make fun of a peer's "deaf speech" or awkward signing, the deaf identity may become an uncomfortable mantle to be shed, unless the child takes pride in being "different" because of the family's positive reinforcement or because of exposure to deaf role models.

As Karen Kirby (2002, p. 73) writes, "Of course I knew I couldn't hear as well as others. But I didn't grow up with the label 'deaf' or 'hard of hearing.'" And Ken Levinson (2002, p. 89) states that "All the time I was growing up, even through attending graduate school at Columbia University, I didn't think of myself as being deaf." Kirby and Levinson did not meet a deaf person until after childhood and eventually internalized their own deaf identities (Kirby, 2002; Levinson, 1990, 2002).

But we cannot ignore the opposite possibility that "deaf" can be a core identity for deaf children of hearing parents. I had hearing parents with whom I communicated easily and I always knew myself to be deaf. It was comfortable for me. From early on, I was surrounded by deaf peers. "Deaf" was a natural part of my environment, reinforced positively in the early years by my parents, who made sure I was connected with deaf friends and a deaf cousin.

Kannapell (1994) explores the role of language identity in influencing the choices of personal identity and social identity. The concept of language identity encompasses the specific language a person feels most at home with. Consequently, if a person prefers a signed language, the personal identity will be Deaf and the social identity will be with Deaf people, while the personal identity of combined signed and spoken language users will be hard of hearing and the social identity will be mixed between Deaf and Hearing. Finally, those with a preference for spoken language will personally identify as oralist, hearing impaired, or deafened and will socially identify with hearing people. Kannapell's prescriptive description of personal identity appears to be grounded not in Corker's (1996) core identity framework but rather in terms of self-awareness pertaining to language and related social choices. Additionally, the vagaries of experience and context in influencing language choice or self-labeling are not sufficiently captured within Kannapell's prescriptive sociolinguistic framework.

In thinking about the core aspects of deaf identities, it is helpful to consider Robert Pollard's (2004) frame of reference. He considers the deaf experience to be sensory (relative to how vision and audition are manipulated for environmental access), linguistic, social, and cultural. Each of these aspects coalesces into a phenomenological understanding of self, with much variability depending on individual strengths and diversity in functional and linguistic capabilities, family attributes, educational benefits, and social experiences. For example, based on specific combinations of these factors, combined signed/spoken language users, whether deaf, hearing, or hard of hearing, may consider themselves to be phenomenologically and socially bicultural or d/Deaf, depending on their immediate environment, rather than the hard-of-hearing classification coined by Kannapell (1994).

In her book, *Inner Lives of Deaf Children* (2001), Sheridan discusses the phenomenon of overt and covert identities. This is a crucial phenomenological concept, considering the variations in comfort with revealing desirably-perceived versus non-desirably-perceived identities. Covert identity is actual internalized identity, not necessarily visible, and as such could be construed as a core identity if internalized early in life, while overt identity reflects externalized labels or visible attributes. In responding to selected magazine characters, some of Sheridan's seven young American deaf interviewees attributed deaf, hard-of-hearing, or hearing identity status to the presence or lack of visual indicators, including the use of visual electronic devices and signing versus speech. Such overt identity decisions did not always jibe with the actual covert identity of the individual the children were responding to. For example, a person was labeled as hearing because of mouth movement when the person actually was hard of hearing. Hearing aids may signify that someone is hard of hearing, when in fact that individual has a Deaf identity that is covert unless the person starts signing.

When these seven children were interviewed again as adolescents, the original indicators remained (visual alerting and electronic devices, use of sign language, hearing aids), but new indicators were added, such as *gestures, stance, emotional affect, and academic subject matter* as visual cues to hearing status (Sheridan, 2008). Interestingly, none of the participants suggested that the picture might indicate an oral deaf person as a possible identity. In any case, these visual cues do not necessarily correlate with internalized identity status. Identity mislabeling of perceived attributes has the potential to affect how relationships are formed, depending on how these are handled and on the congruence between the individuals involved once the covert identity is revealed. Sheridan considers attempts by professionals to determine deaf persons' identities through measures or listings of criteria to be an infringement of one's basic psychological freedom to project specific identities depending on the situation. For her, narratives and phenomenological understanding of processes are critical for identity determination.

Dymaneke Dinnel Mitchell (2006), a deaf African American female, vividly personifies how covert and overt identities convey messages about the phenomenological self. She uses the metaphor of flashcards to illustrate the visibility or invisibility of specific identities within whatever reality she is currently experiencing. As she was growing up, the flashcard of deaf as invisible was primary, reflecting her knowing of "deaf" as a distancing concept, something to be made invisible so that it could disappear and therefore enable her to "pass," to function within her hearing family or in the mainstream. It was not until she entered college and was exposed to the various meanings of d/Deaf that she began to acknowledge and identify with being deaf, though not necessarily embracing it. She appreciates how her family treated her by disregarding her deafness, because it meant essentially that "the deafness was not me" (p. 140), thereby enabling her to develop as a person. Additionally, it meant that there was less opportunity to be devalued by an oppressive society. Essentially, she describes herself as not becoming the deafness but rather that the deafness with time became a part of her. For her, this required a process of renegotiation of her sense of self in terms of when and how parts of her self, the deaf part in particular, colored as it was by her being female and African American, became visible or invisible. This is a journey she sees as continuing throughout life, a journey that encompasses integrating "deaf" into her core identity.

ISSUES TO CONSIDER

Attempting to crystallize the complexities of life into theoretical concepts, categories, and labels can lead to a simplistic understanding (Rudmin, 2003). Without taking into account the phenomenological and narrative aspects that expose subtle nuances and currents of meaning to an individual's life, we cannot gain a true understanding of one's Deaf or hard-of hearing identity. Furthermore, each time the narrative is told, the story can vary (Mishler, 2004). Mishler asks whether this becomes unreliable data, or whether we should move toward more complicated multiple, partial identities that depend on context. The process of establishing congruence between the evolving personal identity, fraught with covert meanings, and the seemingly infinite social identity categories imposed from outside the individual is one that is necessarily unique to each person (Corker, 1996; Sheridan, 2001). The next chapter will scrutinize some of the attributes and experiential aspects that make for additional fascinating, albeit frustrating, conceptualizations about the complex nature of d/Deaf and hard-of-hearing identities.

3

Beyond Category: The Complexities of Deaf-Hearing Identity

There is a tension in identity commitment. It is the tension between the individual's needs and proclivities on the one hand and the demands of society on the other.
Dan McAdams (1993, p. 94)

For me, being deaf is not audiological, but rather a way of life. I sign. I speak. I comfortably navigate my environment using a hearing aid to back up my eyes. Internally, I identify myself as a person navigating the continuum between Deaf and deaf. The tension in identity commitment reveals itself when my self-perceptions collide with how others perceive me. Being labeled as hard of hearing (because I speak and use a hearing aid), "hearing," oral deaf, culturally Deaf, academically Deaf because of my association with Gallaudet University, or whatever, poses a challenge to my internal identity. I cannot compress myself into one basic identity as I navigate my varied environments, nor can I wholly accommodate the external perceptions of me. I cannot be boxed in by the various prescriptive deaf identity categories reviewed in Chapter 2.

Reagan (2002) goes to the heart of the matter by describing the process of identity constructions as occurring along two interacting axes, the first differentiating personal and social constructions and the second distinguishing between emic constructions (those of participants) and etic constructions (based on external observers). He highlights the tensions that emerge between both poles when incompatibilities between identities are revealed. Ultimately, however, people shape their identities "in their own way" in their attempt to integrate life experiences into coherent identities depending on how situations, individual responses, and external perceptions align (e.g., Corker, 1998; Cross & Gore, 2003; McAdams, 1993; Ohna, 2004; Raggatt, 2006; Woodward, 2002). The narrative approach as introduced in Chapter 2 encompasses the notion that "We are all storytellers, and we are the stories we tell" (McAdams, Josselson, & Lieblich, 2006, p. 3).

These life stories incorporate multilayered levels of interplay between the self and social contexts that reflect disparate voices and identities residing alongside each other which are involved in a dialogical conversation about the meanings of each disparate component (see McAdams, 2001; McAdams, Josselson, & Lieblich, 2006; Raggatt, 2006 for a review). Exemplifying this, Brenda Jo Brueggemann (1999) claims deaf, hard of hearing, and hearing as her identities, depending on the day. And she shifts stances often. So there is the possibility of integrating the multiplicity into a coherent yet evolving self, comfortable with incorporating different facets of deaf and hearing as the situation may warrant, rather than adhering to the binary or essentialist concept of Deaf and hearing.

To elucidate the complexities outlined thus far, we will be looking at the multifaceted aspects of the following identities: culturally hearing, culturally Deaf, bicultural, child of deaf parents, and hard of hearing.

CULTURALLY "HEARING"

Do the oral deaf, those apparently "hearing people who do not hear," really want to be fully immersed in the hearing world? Do they see other deaf people in their lives? Are they comfortable internalizing "deaf" as an identity? Do they have a cultural home?

Growing up as Deaf Persons Relying on Speech and Audition

Interviews with 28 deaf adults raised using spoken English (Bain, Scott, & Steinberg, 2004), as well as some of the comments made by respondents in Oliva's (2004) study of individuals who were the only deaf person in their schools, reveal positive values surrounding contact with similar deaf peers. In a study of British deaf young people and their families, half of those who preferred spoken communication were likely to attend a Deaf club (Gregory, Bishop, & Shelden, 1995). "Veronica" reports having many hearing friends and seeing her deaf friends occasionally, "but with deaf people I know I am with my own people" (Gregory, Bishop, & Shelden, 1995, p. 163). Many of the 14 role models Jim Reisler (2002) selected for his book on voices of the oral deaf happen to know some sign language as well.

In the Leigh (1999a) study of 34 oral deaf adults who responded to a questionnaire asking about personal development, everyone valued contact with hearing peers. While the majority of participants (25) identified as belonging to the hearing community, half of the respondents expressed feelings of affinity with similar deaf peers. This speaks to the presence of some kind of oral deaf ethos that brings some of these individuals together. The term "oral deaf culture" has even come up, although not everyone agrees on what it means or its existence. As described by a hearing spouse of a deaf person at an AGB* convention:

* The Alexander Graham Bell Association for the Deaf and Hard of Hearing (AGB) is an organization that advocates for the use of spoken language.

The convention was a great cultural experience for me, in that I had never before had a chance to experience deaf culture. I found that most of the people at the convention (both hearing and deaf) were very friendly and it was easy to meet people and get involved in conversations...It probably took me about half an hour after getting to the convention center to get adjusted to having to make eye contact and speak clearly to people other than just my wife. After that, it was smooth sailing. (J. LeBoy, personal communication, February 19, 2006)

Janger (2002) describes this culture as one that allows for both deaf and hearing interaction through spoken language in contrast to the sign language centrality of Deaf culture. Clearly, the choice to interact with hearing persons does not automatically equate internalizing a hearing identity and distancing from interactions with deaf peers.

...I bluffed my way through while growing up. As I got older I realized how foolish it was to pretend I could "hear." It took a long time for me to accept being deaf. Part of this acceptance process took place when I learned sign language when I was in my early 20s. Then I had to sort of re-program myself when I figured out I wasn't much of a signer—but all along I developed better strategies for communicating and coming out with the fact I couldn't hear what was said...My signing deaf identity was fun—and I met a lot of people through sign language but I find myself more comfortable being orally deaf. (J. Tochterman, personal communication, February 15, 2006)

...while I can sign enough to have a conversation (when I'm not under extreme pressure!), I am a terrible sign-reader! But I do give signers credit, because more often than not they have been perfectly happy to sign something again and again, slowly, teaching me the language and trying to get me to understand them (usually this is a one-on-one conversation). (S. Pollack, personal communication, February 15, 2006)

Referring back to the Leigh (1999a) study of 34 oral deaf adults, 24 respondents reported feeling a sense of "betweenity" (Brueggemann, 2008; see Chapter 1), of being caught to varying extents between the deaf and hearing worlds, and needing to be comfortably at home in both worlds. While a majority of the respondents recognized the advantages of Deaf culture, with some reporting sign language abilities and an interest in the culture, they avoided those Deaf culture adherents who were negative about oral deaf people.

In turn, within Deaf culture, "oral" has traditionally been a derogatory term that implies a malevolent desire to decimate sign language people on the part of oralists who want to strengthen the power of the audist* establishment (Padden & Humphries, 1988). To be oral is to be

* See Chapter 6 for a definition of audism.

of the opposition. To be welcomed into the Deaf community, the oral deaf person may have to subdue the primacy of speech in order to gain the trust of the community.

Clearly, the existence of rapprochement between deaf individuals comfortable with speech and those who are culturally Deaf is a matter of debate. The foundation of acceptance appears to be the willingness to respect cultural assumptions on both sides, an untenable position for those who take a righteous essentialist approach. This begs the question of how acceptance, whether wholehearted or superficial, is defined and perceived by various individuals, taking into account the fact that the American Deaf community consists mostly of deaf persons who enter the culture rather than those born into the culture. Be that as it may, the "culturally hearing" deaf person is not necessarily a rigid construct.

Late Deafened

For many late-deafened persons, losing their hearing after they have accommodated to the sounds of life is something to be mourned. They feel cut-off from their normal channels of communication and may express ongoing dismay and sorrow, or determination to make the best of it and forge ahead (Harvey, 2003; Meadow-Orlans, 1985; Rutman, 1989). How they shift their self-perceptions as they accommodate new communication needs and interrelationship patterns will influence how they internalize a "late-deafened" identity status. Initially, the "late deafened" label will emerge as an alien identity that forces them to acknowledge their need to learn how to be "deaf." Often, they are unwilling to connect with other deaf people, a group outside their sphere of experience (Harvey, 2003). Repudiation of any indicator of their hearing difference, including hearing aids, is in part an attempt to preserve some semblance of their former selves and avoid the implication of a "spoiled identity" (Kent, Furlonger, & Goodrick, 2001). However, communication difficulties may exacerbate their sense of isolation.

Those who acknowledge that they have moved to a different phase and need to get on with life may be amenable to seeking out contact with other late-deafened persons through venues such as the Association of Late-Deafened Adults, Inc. (ALDA) (http://www.alda.org, 2008) in their search for a sense of fellowship. At ALDA meetings, attention to diverse communication needs, including signed English,* spoken language with speechreading and assistive listening devices, note writing, and CART⁺ (http://www.alda.org, 2008), draws these late-deafened

---

* Signed English is a term representing speech accompanied by matching signs.
    ⁺ CART stands for Communication Access Real Time Translation using court reporting technology.

individuals together. Conclusions from data obtained from 97 late-deafened participants in 12 focus groups confirm that while hearing community affiliation remains strong, meetings with ALDA members are valued (Goulder, 1997).

Getting to this stage in identity evolution may involve confronting feelings of marginalization as the late-deafened person fluctuates between the former pre–hearing loss status and current status (Goulder, 1997). After exploring Deaf culture in an attempt to deal with her acquired hearing loss and being attacked for "thinking hearing" by some Deaf individuals, Amy described herself as marginal and "in a class of my own" (Harvey, 2003, p. 95). In contrast, none of the late-deafened adults in Maxwell-McCaw's (2001) acculturation study using the Deaf Acculturation Scale (see Chapter 2) scored as marginal in their identity. They were equally apt to score as hearing, Deaf, or bicultural. Admittedly, this sample may have been skewed in favor of those who have positively internalized their current state and were comfortable enough to participate in a deaf-acculturation research project. But we can recognize the fallacy of automatically assuming that the late-deafened contingent remains culturally hearing.

CULTURALLY DEAF

Padden and Humphries (1988) conceptualize a Deaf center as the heart of Deaf culture. But what exactly are Deaf people supposed to personify apart from reliance on a signed language, visual avenues of relating, and preference for the company of signing people? While Paddy Ladd (1994) credits deaf offspring of Deaf parents with shaping Deaf culture, he and others acknowledge that this Deaf center is not immune to the variable permutations of Deaf identities (Breivik, 2005; Johnston, 1994; Padden & Humphries, 2005; Reagan, 2002; Turner, 1994). The existence of multiple Deaf groupings in the United States and abroad, with various evolving behavioral expectations influenced by social, political, cultural, linguistic, religious, regional, and ethnic dynamics complicates attempts to define Deaf culture in addition to the fact that most members are not born to the culture (Christensen, 2000; Corker, 1994; Humphries, 1993; Lane, Hoffmeister, & Bahan, 1996; Leigh, 1999b; Monaghan, Schmaling, Nakamura, & Turner, 2003). It is self-evident that new entrants from the mainstream are critical to ensuring the vitality of Deaf culture, even if they will be uniquely reshaping the culture in diverse ways. Consequently, belief systems are not standard and ideology can be powerful enough that diverse constituencies and even Deaf culture experts contradict each other regarding Deaf culture (Grosjean, 1996; Hoffmeister & Harvey, 1996; Solomon, 1994). But the concept of spread is so ubiquitous that the inherent diversity is swallowed by the umbrella of Deaf culture.

How use of a signed language and eagerness to achieve fluency translates into one's acceptance or rejection as Deaf has implications for identity. At its crux, language is "a symbol of social identity, a medium of social interaction, and a store of cultural knowledge" (Lane, Hoffmeister, & Bahan, 1996, p. 67). Despite the ideal of a hegemonic signed language, the reality is that language is fluid, its components transformed by the people using and interpreting the language (Gesser, 2007). Within any Deaf community, variations of its signed language are par for the course as long as the use of hands and vision are the medium (Gesser, 2007; Woll & Ladd, 2003). The American Sign Language (ASL) used at Gallaudet University likely differs somewhat from the ASL used at a Deaf gathering in the heartland of North America. These linguistic variations are analogous to the spoken language variations typical of hearing communities, where the overarching notion of hearing culture plays out differently in practice depending on the specific hearing community or group being referred to. At which point specific variations of language fluency qualify one for Deaf culture membership is quite situation-specific.

Typically, membership is achieved through identification, shared experiences, and participation in activities, facilitated by having conversational sign skills (however these are defined) (Higgins, 1980). For mainstreamed or isolated deaf persons, there is often a sense of coming home, a sentiment going at least as far back as 1828 when Edmund Booth knew he was "at home" among strange deaf peers in his new school (Lang, 2004, p. 5).

But during a pre-college orientation program at Gallaudet University, Dianne Brooks' (1996) Deaf roommate exhibited no patience with Dianne's fledging signing skills and called her a "fake." Bill Graham became desperate to learn sign language after losing his hearing and feeling dissonance with his hearing friends (Graham & Sharp-Pucci, 1994). But several visits to a Deaf club reinforced his "outsider" status. Amy (see p. 47) struggled with "coming home" as do many outsiders who wrestle with learning the language in trying to achieve a sense of belongingness. As indicated earlier in this chapter, oral deaf persons have been rejected by Deaf culture adherents (Leigh, 1999a). All of them may have felt the message that they were "not Deaf enough." This phrase was touted by the media during the Gallaudet University 2006 protest as one reason why the deaf president-designate was unacceptable to the campus community (see Chapter 9 for further discussion). But again, what it really means depends greatly on context, perception, and attitude.

Why may the path to immersion appear treacherous for some when there are no firm guidelines for being Deaf? Anecdotes of anger at hearing people for not validating Deaf choices for language and communication access and education, for not giving Deaf persons autonomy, status, and respect, for misrepresenting what Deaf people say because of language barriers, and for idealizing interaction with hearing people rather than with deaf peers reinforce mistrust of those deaf individuals who appear "hearing" (e.g., Breivik, 2005; Hoffmeister & Harvey, 1996; Humphries, 1996; Ladd, 1994; Searls & Johnston, 1996). At what point new entrants appear sufficiently Deaf depends not only on their linguistic skills, but also their ability to shift from a hearing-dominant stance to a Deaf-centered approach in interacting with others and whether they can find mentors to lead the way. It also depends on which Deaf group they are attempting to enter, whether religious, sports, social, or otherwise, since group boundaries vary according to internal dynamics.

Increased access to the larger society is bound to influence Deaf ways. The expanding availability of sign language classes for hearing students and sign language interpreters, accessible telecommunications and Internet venues (see Chapter 8), as well as the shift from private (e.g., Deaf clubs) to temporary public spaces (e.g., convention centers) for Deaf functions, have resulted in increased intermingling between Deaf and hearing people and opportunities for varying acculturative experiences (e.g., Andersson, 1994; Murray, 2008; Padden & Humphries, 2005; Woll & Ladd, 2003). In light of this trend toward hearing spaces, any attempt at a definitive framework of Deaf culture and Deafhood is bound to result in further evolution.

BICULTURAL ISSUES

We live in a multicultural world. But for discussion purposes, we will examine biculturalism as it pertains to deaf/hard-of-hearing identities. Multiculturalism will be explored in Chapter 7 when we examine how deaf and hard-of-hearing identities interface with other individual identities.

In my experience, the term "bicultural" is not typically used to describe one's cultural affiliation. If deaf or hard-of-hearing persons are asked directly how they identify themselves regarding the hearing–deaf dimension, they tend to use standard labels, such as late deafened, Deaf, deaf, oral deaf, hearing impaired, or hard of hearing. Is it because biculturalism dilutes allegiance to a specific identity, or is it because the meaning of biculturalism within a deaf–hearing context has yet to be clearly defined?

Grosjean (1996) suggests three traits that characterize biculturals: (1) living in two or more cultures, (2) adapting, at least in part, to specific cultural attitudes, behaviors, values, etc., and (3) blending aspects of these cultures such that some aspects of one culture will emerge within the other culture, depending on individual and context. The typical expectation is for one to retain the culture of origin while adapting to or acculturating to the second culture, and by extension to additional cultures as well. As people become exposed to different cultures, starting with families of origin and proceeding through life stages, they can internally shift cultural belief systems in a way that indicates how new cultural self-representations take their place with the previously learned cultural self-representations, which themselves are also metamorphosing over time (Cross & Gore, 2003; Phinney, 2002).

No one can be fully 100% in one culture and 100% in the other culture. While most biculturals are tied more closely to one culture than the other, it can be possible, depending on context, to maintain a positive relationship with both cultures without having to choose either one (Grosjean, 1996; LaFromboise, Coleman, & Gerton, 1993). Grosjean (1996) views most Deaf persons as Deaf-dominant biculturals, with the extent of their hearing culture acculturation ranging from low to high depending on variables, including d/Deaf-hearing family characteristics, mastery of the dominant language, education level, and level of exposure. These variables also influence how spoken-language dominant biculturals acculturate to Deaf culture. The level of adaptation to each culture will fluctuate, depending on the salience of variables such as language and friendship as well as the vitality of the community being acculturated to or because of feelings of discrimination in the dominant society versus the nondominant society (Phinney, 2002; Sue & Sue, 2008).

Some claim that greater orientation toward a host or dominant culture does not necessarily weaken connections with the nondominant culture (Phinney, 2002). The reality is that in such situations, it can be stressful to figure out how and when to exhibit certain behaviors in order to maximize acceptability, how to manage situations when behavior unacceptable within one culture is witnessed, and how to avoid the impression of dominance (e.g., spoken-language values) when acculturating to the nondominant (e.g., Deaf) culture (Côté & Levine, 2002; Grosjean, 1996; Ohna, 2003; Padden, 1996; Skelton & Valentine, 2003). Consequently, to become bicultural requires sensitivity in juxtaposing cultural paradigms and knowing when to use certain cultural attributes, especially if cultures have apparent irreconcilable values and, as in the case of Deaf culture, lack a marker indicating that one has met a satisfactory degree of acculturation (Grosjean, 1996). Whether the culture in question accepts one as bicultural depends not only on cultural competency but also on the extent to which being a member of the other culture is acceptable (Sue & Sue, 2008) because of perceptions about exclusivity, loyalty, and authenticity in terms of membership.

Based on the anecdotes reported in the previous section, those who explored Deaf culture but could not gain a sense of acceptance may have fallen prey to misperceptions in the ways they adjusted their communication and behavior in Deaf situations. In turn, how apparent these individuals were in exhibiting the values of the dominant hearing society may also have been a complicating factor. Essentially, acceptance is in the eyes of the beholder who determines what degree of behavioral involvement and level of cultural competence in the relevant culture is acceptable.

From the perspective of a Deaf person, it is plausible that a fluent Deaf signer who writes well might easily be perceived more optimally compared to a fluent Deaf signer who speaks well. While both may appear "normal" in terms of Deaf behavior, if the latter is caught speaking, it can appear that the language of choice is spoken language. This may cause suspicion that the speaker is trying to pass for hearing (Aiello & Aiello, 2001) rather than simply shifting between cultures. For example, accusations of hypocrisy were targeted at a well-known Deaf activist who decried spoken language but was caught talking on the phone in an anonymous public space. Even a Deaf child of Deaf parents who is fluent in both signed and spoken languages can be an object of suspicion among Deaf persons (Solomon, 1994).

Theoretically, biculturalism can lead to marginality if the cultures are seen as incompatible with each other due to their essentialist nature, or switching/mixing languages is marginalized despite this process being ubiquitous (Bishop & Hicks, 2005; Bochner, 1982, as cited in Rudmin, 2003). However, marginality can reflect a positive attribute in that one can maintain dualistic orientation and be individualistic, even unorthodox, not tied down by cultural constraints (Emerton, 1996; Hintermair, 2008; Rudmin, 2003).

The viability of a "true bicultural stance" based on the hearing–deaf dimension has been subjected to debate. Paddy Ladd (1994, 2003) questions such a stance while the nature of Deaf culture and levels of competency in the various areas constituting Deaf culture still require clear definition. With recent generations of deaf people becoming less constrained by Deaf–hearing divides and more flexible in terms of identity pathways, Ladd fears an undermining of the clarity of Deaf culture per se and the diluting of resistance to full majority culture assimilation. He accuses those crossing the divide as complicit in the weakening of Deaf communities worldwide and proposes an essentialist counternarrative to biculturalism: deaf people simply cannot be "hearing" when they still have functional limitations even with the assistance of "top of the line" technology. Therefore, to idealize biculturalism is counterintuitive when deaf persons cannot be truly bicultural.

The reality is that people do shift to fit both Deaf and hearing contexts, either consciously or unconsciously. Carol Padden (1996) views this process as a shift from the cultural to the bicultural, from Deaf culture to traversing both Deaf and "hearing" societies, based in large part on increased interaction due to advances in civil rights and technology.

This is not an additive state, to be of two cultures as commonly represented in the literature. It is more about "states of tension" in the process of traversing the two cultures (Padden, 1996, p. 95).

From an identity perspective, being able to navigate both cultures will satisfy the biculturally inclined person who will not have to split off culturally syntonic aspects of the culture being denied. For example, a competent Deaf signer comfortable with speaking can continue to use spoken language within appropriate contexts rather than splitting it off. A study of 78 deaf students at California State University, Northridge, a university with a significant deaf student contingent, indicated that either identifying with the Deaf community or demonstrating greater bicultural skills is correlated with higher self-esteem (Jambor & Elliott, 2005). The authors hypothesize that such individuals are less likely to deny their hearing loss, more likely to accept themselves, and take pride in their ability to negotiate the dominant society while benefiting from the social support of their Deaf community. During an interview study of 41 d/Deaf persons, dynamic identities were demonstrated by, for example, one participant who acknowledged the pragmatic aspect of an oral education as well as the attractiveness of sign language (Skelton & Valentine, 2003). In exploring identity changes, Bat-Chava (2000) found that interviewees with culturally hearing or Deaf identities reported no major shifts, while those who affirmed both Deaf and "hearing" values made the shift from a culturally hearing background upon contact with sign language or Deaf role models, mostly at normative transition points, such as entering a high school with a program for deaf students.

The issue of language preference and communication ability functions as a critical determinant in the degree of bicultural comfort (Foster, 1996; Stinson, Chase, & Bondi-Wolcott, 1988 as cited in Stinson & Whitmire, 1992). Individuals with limited access to or limited skills in spoken and/or written language versus a signed language may have greater difficulty demonstrating bicultural competence compared to those with better access, considering the importance of linguistic proficiency in either culture. In terms of preference, while a British interview study of young deaf adults demonstrated a significant relationship between one's preferred communication and preference for deaf or hearing friends, a majority claimed both deaf and hearing friends and many reported knowing either British Sign Language or Sign Supported English (Gregory, Bishop, & Sheldon, 1995). Half of those who preferred spoken language attended a Deaf club as well, suggesting a bicultural orientation.

What can we conclude about the compatibility of Deaf and hearing cultures? With interactions between Deaf and hearing persons increasing, there is room, depending on what is acceptable to the "center" of the Deaf person, to trust individuals, either deaf or hearing, who have developed skills for navigating cultures such that they look like they can "pass for hearing" or behave fully as "Deaf."

CHILDREN OF DEAF ADULTS

The most typical mode of cultural transmission is that of generation to generation (Phinney, 2002). Therefore, it is self-evident that Deaf parents pass their Deaf cultural ways of being to their Deaf children. These children of deaf Adults (Codas) are true inheritors of Deaf culture.

But approximately 90% of the children born to Deaf parents are hearing (Schein, 1989). Despite the fact that they are typically acculturated to Deaf ways within their families, their hearing status creates uncertainty as to whether they are true inheritors of Deaf culture (Bishop & Hicks, 2005; Lane, Hoffmeister, & Bahan, 1996; Preston, 1994; Shultz Myers, Myers, & Marcus, 1999; Singleton & Tittle, 2000). They may not even see themselves initially as hearing within their family of origin; this dawns upon them as they get older (Bishop & Hicks, 2005; Hoffmeister, 2008). Some may even view the hearing world as the enemy, the "other" (Davis, 2000, p. 13), pass as Deaf (Hoffmeister, 2008), and wish they could puncture their eardrums to become deaf (Harvey, 2003).

The Australian videotape *Passport without a Country* (Davie, 1992) graphically portrays how such children, even in adulthood, will resort to culturally Deaf ways of behaving and communicating when they want to "be themselves." Jenn, a hearing undergraduate student at Gallaudet University where Deaf undergraduates are the norm, states that she expresses herself more easily with sign language than words (Fernandez, 2005). Robert H. Miller's (2004) memoir of his experiences as a hearing child of Deaf parents is titled: *Deaf Hearing Boy.* Not only is the first description that of "Deaf;" this book is part of a Deaf Lives series under the aegis of Gallaudet University Press.

However, these individuals tend to be ascribed an unusual and separate status by the culture (Hoffmeister, 2008; Padden & Humphries, 1988) and may be at times covertly marginalized (Higgins, 1980; Mudgett-DeCaro, 1995). Even while they are absorbing their parents' Deaf identity, they are simultaneously learning that they are not Deaf, but hearing, with all the overtures their parents ascribe to the meaning of "hearing." When interacting with Deaf persons they have just met, they will be welcomed as Deaf. Once they disclose that they are hearing, there may be a subtle change in the dynamics of the interaction that reinforces the outsider status (Mudgett-Decaro, 1995). Yet in the larger society they may conceivably also be dealing with subtle outsider status attributed to being a native signer dependent on vision and/or the discriminatory marginalization of their Deaf parents. This can create internalized feelings of marginality related to both hearing and Deaf identities (Bishop & Hicks, 2005; Hoffmeister, 2008; Preston, 1994). Codas constantly have to negotiate both worlds, often with varying degrees of vacillation (Bauman, 2005; Hoffmeister, 2008). Their answer to the question, "Are you Deaf or hearing?" can create a potential minefield of identity choice.

A modified form of Glickman's Deaf Identity Development Scale (see Chapter 2) was administered to 244 deaf, hard-of-hearing, and hearing respondents in an effort to analyze the nature of their deaf/hearing cultural identities (Leigh, Marcus, Dobosh, & Allen, 1998). Of the 88 hearing respondents, 45 reported having deaf or hard-of-hearing parents. This subgroup was likely more connected with the Deaf community by virtue of their having heard about the study. Results indicated that they were more marginalized, less immersed (lower Deaf identity), and similarly "hearing" in comparison to deaf respondents with deaf parents. The authors suggested that the respondents were experiencing relatively more conflict between hearing and deaf values.

In Preston's (1994) seminal study of 150 interviews with hearing Codas, he notes that the most frequently discussed feature of identity was being hearing or Deaf. Some felt the real Deaf person was inside the hearing façade. Being able to identify as either hearing or Deaf was a form of "coming out" in that it meant one was dealing openly with Deaf-hearing issues and trying to grapple with the sense of cultural marginality.

This unique group satisfies the definition of bicultural in that they are hearing-Deaf, or Deaf-hearing. Their formative years may involve acculturating in variable ways to two conflicting sets of values, one related to the Deaf environment of the home, the other to the hearing environment of the school and neighborhood. Often there is code-switching between signed and spoken languages depending on the situation. Cultural switching happens when, for example, Codas have to minimize eye contact with hearing peers and strictly adhere to eye contact rules with Deaf persons. As they transition between the Deaf home and hearing environments, they begin to realize that even if they conform to the cultural values of either world as a bicultural person does, their hearing makes them different: hearing in the Deaf world, and hearing but still "Deaf" in the hearing world. This feeling of difference was frequently mentioned by many of the interviewees in Preston's (1994) study.

With this in mind, how do hearing Codas interpret their unique biculturalism? Preston (1994) identifies four basic constructs to encapsulate this uniqueness: Deaf and hearing (side-by-side); being a chameleon (changeable as the occasion demands); being the bridge or link between Deaf and hearing; and being in the gap between the deaf and hearing worlds. In his treatise on Coda lives, Hoffmeister (2008) describes their experiences as an amalgam of Deaf-hearing derived from dwelling in the borderlands of the multiple boundaries between Deaf and hearing that center on language, communication, education, political control, and social viewpoints, among others. These borderlands are a territory that Codas themselves have difficulty exploring in part because of their experiences of being the same and yet not the same whether the context is hearing or Deaf. Therefore, Hoffmeister inveighs against the tendency to code Coda issues into binary Deaf-hearing issues when the amalgam of centering and decentering Deaf-hearing experiences is in fact the reality of their lives.

In their effort at reconciliation, Bishop and Hicks (2005) consider a "third identity" (p. 193), specifically one that manages both deaf and hearing "parts," each of which emerges depending on environmental and emotional context. This third identity represents a constellation incorporating the Codas' desire to be Deaf as their parents are, to be hearing in a way that differs from the surrounding hearing society, and simultaneously wanting both aspects to reflect a unique hearing–deaf dimension (Preston, 1994) and not a binary conceptualization of the Coda identity as implied by the bicultural. CODA International, Inc. is an organization that was formed to help with this process of identity clarification in the search for a cultural home (Bull, 1998).

The saliency of this unique bicultural identity diminishes but does not disappear if life partners are not Deaf or if employment does not involve working with Deaf people. Vestiges can remain, as witness the Coda who needs to be faced by the hearing partner in order to affirm love and closeness, even when the hearing partner's declaration of love is clearly articulated. While many Codas do work in some capacity with deaf people, including sign language interpreting, teaching deaf children, or functioning as cultural mediators in other professions (nearly two-thirds of the 150 hearing adult children of deaf parents in Preston's [1994] study worked with deaf people), others who drift away from their Deaf background by virtue of choice or circumstance acknowledge the impact of their Deaf-related experiences (Davie, 1992; Hoffmeister, 2008; Miller, 2004). Having long since left his Deaf community to explore, work, and marry, Lennard Davis (2000) confesses that part of him "wants to go home to it" (p. 7).

The culturally Deaf parents of those hearing children have their own adjustments as well. Even when a signed language is the language of the home, the hearing component cannot be ignored. As reported in Ohna's (2004) Norwegian narrative study of deaf adults, one Deaf parent who grew up in a culturally Deaf home and continued signing with her hearing children reported that they often spoke with each other at the table and comfortably switched to signing when asked to do so. Despite the context of a culturally Deaf environment, this parent recognized the presence of cultural tension and the need for family resolution. Rather than demand 100% signing in the home, she decided to juxtapose her own respect for her identity as a Deaf person with her respect for the hearing identity component of her children. Such a process could become complicated if she were to allow hearing oppression to overcome the home signed language, but she has had to figure out a respectful balance in her home.

There are some Deaf parents who believe that spoken language has to be primary for their hearing children and consequently do not sign with their children even though their speech might sound unnatural (Hoffmeister, 2008). Hoffmeister believes that this causes distance between parent and child such that these children cannot identify with other Codas or with Deaf people because of the lack of signing experience; eventually they flee the borderlands to the safety of a hearing identity that represents less conflict and greater access to social connection.

Some hearing children have deaf parents who prefer and competently manage spoken language. Their connections with the hearing environment may be more frequent. While there may be little or no code-switching between spoken and signed languages, these hearing children may end up mediating possible disconnects if their parents miss environmental information. They may also manage the ensuing stigma if their deaf parents are perceived as objects of pity, scorn, or strangeness (if they misunderstand or their speech quality is somewhat off) (Shultz Myers, Myers, & Marcus, 1999). While Deaf cultural identity issues may not be paramount for this group, they will be aware of a hearing identity that differs from the unconscious hearing identity of their peers. For example, their ways of relating with others may be shaped by their relatively greater reliance on vision for face-to-face contact to facilitate communication with their parents, even if the parents also rely on auditory amplification. Such prolonged eye contact can be discomfiting for hearing peers.

In conclusion, Codas are multifaceted in terms of articulating their d/Deaf/hearing parts. Deaf, deaf, hearing, and bicultural are filtered differently depending on their experience and context. While many will recognize the uniqueness of their culture and community, others will gravitate toward hearing culture affiliation and distance from, but never entirely lose, the d/Deaf part of themselves.

HARD OF HEARING

As a child participating in my Chicago elementary school deaf program, I remember seeing the hard-of-hearing students in separate classes as odd, more allied with our hearing classmates. I know where my deaf friends went after elementary school, but I have no idea what happened to the hard-of-hearing students. Today, I wonder how these long-lost classmates dealt with their identity issues. I wonder why as a user of spoken language (albeit still evolving considering the relatively primitive state of hearing aids back then), I kept away from them except for an occasional "hi." In turn, perhaps they were also maintaining that distance, not wanting to be identified with me and my group. Clearly, issues of labeling, boundaries, and bias were simmering beneath the surface.

U.S. demographics indicate that the hard-of-hearing contingent is far greater compared to those who are audiologically deaf (see Appendix). Paradoxically, the hard-of-hearing group has received minimal attention in terms of needs and definitions as well as theories regarding hard-of-hearing identity development, having been overshadowed by Deaf academic studies and advocacy efforts. The phrase "deaf and hard of hearing" often used by agency or telecommunications service providers perpetuates the myth that the two groups and their accommodation needs are similar (Collins, 2005a; Ross, 2005). Frequently, the focus is on the sign language interpreting needs of Deaf persons rather than the text captioning services or FM* systems preferred by the great majority who do not sign.

Even though the audiological criteria for the hard-of-hearing category specifies it as falling between the mild hearing loss and the severely to profoundly deaf categories (see Appendix), this category has begun to incorporate individuals who use primarily oral-aural communication methods and rely on their residual hearing, whether moderate or severe to profound, supplemented by speechreading and auditory aids (Israelite, Ower, & Goldstein, 2002; Laszlo, 1994; Punch, Creed, & Hyde, 2006; Ross, 2001; Warick, 1994).

> I still call myself and think of myself as being hard of hearing, even though I know I am totally deaf due to my two implants. (E. Rhoades, personal communication, October 2, 2007)

On the surface, these individuals can appear to "pass for hearing." Their needs and existential realities most typically center on being participating members of and culturally identifying with the larger society rather than coalescing into a recognizable hard-of-hearing group, even if they identify as hard of hearing (Collins, 2005b; Harvey, 2003; Ross, 2005; Sorkin, 2000). All four hard-of-hearing respondents in the Leigh (1999a) study of 34 oral deaf respondents to a survey questionnaire on self-perceptions reported feeling more connected with their hearing community because of communication preference and feelings of naturalness. Several of the hard-of-hearing adolescents in the Kent and Smith (2006) New Zealand qualitative study of hearing aid users

---

* Frequency-modulated (FM) systems transmit a person's voice directly to the listener above the level of background noise. A microphone and transmitter ensure that sound is conveyed to a receiver connected to the hearing device.

explicitly affirmed their ability to speak, distinguishing themselves from the stereotypical notions of what "deaf" means, basically that deaf people cannot talk and use sign language. If the public responded to them by signing, as might happen in a store, they would make it clear they were speakers, not signers (identifying with "hearing"). In Japan, increasing numbers of young people undergoing mainstreamed education are increasingly identifying themselves as hard of hearing/hearing disabled/not-deaf in an effort to dissociate themselves from what they view as the negative connotations of "deaf" (Nakamura, 2003).

Erin Geld (2005), a hard-of-hearing college student, reveals that she tried to hold out as long as long as possible before telling someone about her hearing difference, because it was somewhat like admitting a bad secret. Even wearing a hearing aid could be problematic when one was trying not to be identified as having a hearing difference (Arnold & MacKenzie, 1998; Geld, 2005; Kent & Smith, 2006). The Kent (2003) study on hard-of-hearing adolescents in mainstream settings (see Chapter 4) emphasized their reluctance to self-identify and avoid being stigmatized. As Paul Jacobs (2007) wrote:

> I grew my hair long when I was nineteen. It provided a veil for my hearing aids—one of many subterfuges I adopted to give the impression of normal hearing. (p. 70)

Attempts to dissemble by looking as though one is "hearing" will belie the fact that participation in the greater society can be tenuous at times (Punch, Creed, & Hyde, 2006; Ross, 2001; Woodcock, 2001). Depending on the exact nature of the hearing difference, whether the difference is disclosed, and the extent of background noise, hard-of-hearing individuals are at significant risk for missed auditory-based information because they, for example, may tolerate inadequate lighting or insufficiently take advantage of face-to-face communication. Such situations may make them look "stupid" when in fact they are not. Missed information can result in educational lags and problems at work if appropriate individualized accommodations are not instituted (Harvey, 2003; Hétu, 1994; Laroche, Garcia, & Barrette, 2000; Scherich & Mowry, 1997). A survey involving 373 members of a European hard-of-hearing association indicated that members have worse social relationships than signing deaf people and are disadvantaged compared to hearing peers in quality of life, general health, and psychological symptoms (Fellinger, Holzinger, Gerich, & Goldberg, 2007). Mark Ross (2005), a premier authority on the subject, consequently claims that hard of hearing is not some lesser manifestation of the more visual "deaf" but a disability entity in its own right.

There are hard-of-hearing individuals who even avoid associating with nonsigning/oral deaf peers, whom they perceive as having a distinct identity: not hard of hearing but rather "deaf" (Harvey, 2003). A possible rationale is that such encounters might stir up fears of becoming "more deaf," meaning more "impaired" (Harvey, 2003). Erving Goffman's (1963) landmark book on the management of spoiled identity touches on the turmoil of hard-of-hearing individuals who strive to disavow what they perceive to be a more stigmatizing deaf identity by stratifying themselves on a higher plane. Such discomfort reflects difficulty with self-acceptance, an issue that can drive some to seek therapy. Years ago, I was assigned to provide psychotherapy for one such adult who had been ridiculed in childhood for appearing stupid until the hearing difference was identified. This adult desperately continued to conceal the hearing difference status in order to reinforce the appearance of "normalcy," even with friends in a car with the radio blaring. After several productive sessions, upon noticing my hearing aid, the client indicated great discomfort with my being deaf, claiming that it was impossible to continue therapy with me.

While many hard-of-hearing adults perceive signing Deaf adults as comparatively more impaired in communication and avoid any association with them (Harvey, 2003), some will be motivated to enter the Deaf community and call themselves Deaf. Kathy Vesey and Beth Wilson (2003), both hard of hearing, learned sign language as adults and feel fortunate to be part of the richness of Deaf culture while also being accepted in hearing society. For such individuals, revealing their deaf part can facilitate far better communication access based on awareness of situational communication needs and, in turn, a better sense of connections with others. Vesey and Wilson view the attempt of hard-of-hearing individuals to "pass for hearing" as sad. Mindy Huebner (2001) is up front in stating that being ashamed or hiding the fact that she has a hearing loss will not help her in life.

But some of those individuals who attempt to enter Deaf communities can be overwhelmed by the linguistic and communication requirements as well as the potential of being rejected if they appear to unacceptably "think hearing." Within the Deaf community, the hard-of-hearing person may confront expectations of being too much like a hearing person, even in an unclear auditory environment (Padden & Humphries, 1988). "Hard of hearing" is not necessarily seen as a positive attribute in Deaf culture, implying as it does identification with the "other," that is, with hearing people and their spoken language (Grushkin, 2003; Padden & Humphries, 1988). From a Deaf-centered perspective, these individuals may be called very hard of hearing, meaning "too hearing," rather than a little hard of hearing, which is perceived as being closer to "Deaf." In contrast, the more typical perspective is that very hard of hearing means "more Deaf" and a little hard of hearing means more like hearing (Padden & Humphries, 1988, pp. 39–42). Thus individuals trying to enter the Deaf community who appear very hard of hearing may land squarely on the fringe, feeling alienated and isolated (Harvey, 2003).

What are the implications for identity? None of the theories described in Chapter 2 consider "hard of hearing" as an identity per se, thereby implying either the amorphous nature or invisibility of this specific identity. Sometimes hard-of-hearing individuals themselves do not even know what hard of hearing is, and they appear not to have a clear identity (Laszlo, 1994). This is reinforced when they are told by deaf people that they are hearing, while hearing people label them as deaf. Nini Silver (2003) describes the hard-of-hearing category as neither deaf nor hearing, but also both deaf and hearing, because they do not hear, but they do hear. Such mixed messages can create "a sort of zombie land" (Heppner, 1992, p. 99), quite discombobulating and marginalizing when one is trying to secure Deaf, hearing, or bicultural identities and find a viable social community to identify with (Grushkin, 2003; Harvey, 2003). Those who maintain affiliation with both hearing and Deaf communities while acknowledging their hard-of-hearing status are indeed engaged in a delicate balancing act (National Association of the Deaf, 2006), an act that requires internal strength to manage.

The vagueness in hard-of-hearing identity and distance from d/ Deaf identities is buttressed by the Leigh, Marcus, Dobosh, and Allen (1998) findings in their study of deaf/hearing cultural identity paradigms (mentioned earlier in the Children of Deaf Adults section) based on 40 hard-of-hearing respondents with hearing parents and 22 hard-of-hearing respondents with Deaf/hard-of-hearing parents. Results indicated that there were no significant differences between deaf and hard-of-hearing respondents with hearing parents. Specifically, these respondents tended to be more hearing and more marginalized than their counterparts with deaf parents and not as immersed in deaf values similarly to hearing respondents with hearing parents, meaning they perceived themselves as aligned with hearing values. Additionally, hard-of hearing respondents with deaf parents endorsed more hearing values, fewer deaf values, and more marginalization in comparison to deaf respondents with deaf parents. Warick's (2004) study of 14 hard-of-hearing university students in Canada revealed identity constructions that were complex, partly based on these students striving to be part of the hearing world but simultaneously encountering differences because of their hearing difference.

Brenda Brueggemann (1999), who is hard of hearing, adds a twist to the complexity of hard-of-hearing identity. She confronted the inevitable "Are you deaf or hearing?" question head-on when she first arrived at the Gallaudet University campus. She had not thought of herself as hearing or as deaf and answered, "Hard of hearing." As she rhetorically puts it, this answer called for a foul from the umpire. This in-between state did not clinch it with the negative implications of being hard of hearing in a Deaf setting. But over time she achieved a sense of rap-prochement: she is neither Deaf nor hearing, but both, sort of a "stuck between" and okay with it. The same was true of Paul Jacobs (2007), who in his autobiography describes his efforts to come to terms with being neither Deaf nor hearing, which he defines as a "neither-nor." For him, this was a social identity yet to be invented.

In contrast, Susan Searls decided with her husband to call her children deaf despite their audiologically hard-of-hearing diagnosis to avoid this "stuck between" sense of marginality (Searls & Johnston, 1996). Others view "hard of hearing" as a term to be eschewed due to its perceived negative association with old people (Oliva, 2004) or confirmation of deficiency as a hearing person (Laszlo, 1994). While Bernard Hurwitz's (2004) audiogram proclaims his hard-of-hearing status, he emphasizes that what he is depends on whom he is with. He reveals his hearing identity with colleagues at work and his d/Deaf identity with his Deaf wife and Deaf social circle. He views these identities as the sum of his parts: hard of hearing, deaf, and hearing.

Keep in mind that this variable depiction of hard of hearing is *not* functionally equivalent to the "third identity" of Codas. Simply put, for the hard-of-hearing person, there is an actual functional hearing difference that complicates the pathway to a hearing identity in addition to the typical distance from the Deaf community in educational and neighborhood settings. In contrast, the hearing children of Deaf parents do hear and are immersed within Deaf families in the early years of life. So what might a hard-of-hearing identity constitute? The "hearing" identity claimed by those immersed in the mainstream, the "stuck in between" state Brueggemann describes, the marginality that Searls wants to avoid, or the combined deaf-hearing components described by Hurwitz? Each one is viable.

Laszlo (1994) supports the notion of a hard-of-hearing identity based on increased self-awareness, acceptance of hearing status, and shared experiences. If there are individuals who comfortably accommodate the hard-of-hearing person's needs, the potential for becoming comfortable with a hard-of-hearing label increases (Heppner, 1992; Vesey & Wilson, 2003). Affirming "hard of hearing" takes a certain amount of resiliency and comfort with difference. Erin Geld (2005) acknowledges she probably should be more open about her hard-of-hearing status but needs to move more into this comfort zone. A study of seven hard-of hearing students in classrooms specifically for hard-of-hearing students indicated it was possible for them to be comfortable with this in-between identity when it was reinforced by positive connotations based on unique differences between them and hearing as well as Deaf peers (Israelite, Ower, & Goldstein, 2002).

Grushkin (2003) recommends immersion in Deaf school programs to deal with hard-of-hearing identity issues by exploring connections with Deaf people. Contrary to expectations, his research on four hard-of-hearing participants attending a Deaf residential school indicated that receptive and expressive spoken-language skills were not negatively affected. These interviewees demonstrated an amalgam of Deaf/hearing identity components, which led Grushkin (2003) to suggest the possibility that these constitute a third culture. However, even among his four participants, this was a debatable concept because of the nebulous nature of the "hard of hearing" label.

Mark Ross (2005) claims that the transition to signing environments happens primarily when the hard-of-hearing students are not provided with the services they need to fully access mainstream education. With appropriate services, this group will meld into the hearing society. This of course renders them increasingly invisible. Laszlo (1994) confirms that there is little evidence that the large majority of hard-of-hearing individuals seek each other out. The label itself may turn people off because of the lack of positive association and multiple negative experiences that detract from the possibility of "coming out" and finding a comfort zone labeled "hard of hearing" (Harvey, 2003). To broaden its appeal, Self Help for the Hard of Hearing, a well-known advocacy organization, changed its name to Hearing Loss Association of America (http://www.hearingloss.org/aboutus/history.asp).

The pronounced desire to meld into hearing society, the perceived stigma of the hard of hearing label, the variety of hearing levels, variable ability to access hearing environments, and, moving to the other end of the spectrum, variable ability to connect with hard-of-hearing/deaf peers or to ally with Deaf culture, all mitigate the possibility of clustering "hard of hearing" into an easily defined and acceptable identity constellation. Paralleling the notion that there are many ways to be d/Deaf, there are also many ways to be hard of hearing. To understand this requires not necessarily creating a theory of "hard-of-hearing" identity but rather close scrutiny of how individuals and environments interact to create unique hard-of-hearing social identities.

THE FLUIDITY OF IDENTITIES

"Deaf," "hard of hearing," or "hearing" labels do not exist as sole entities. We need to acknowledge the interfaces between the various identities we own within ourselves, including that of our particular deaf/hard-of-hearing/hearing identities, each of which are colored by life experiences and emerge when stimulated by specific situations. This book focuses on deaf and hard-of-hearing identities per se, but that does not discount the existence of other aspects of life that contribute to the coloring of these identities. For example, "I am a Deaf woman" conveys different hues about identity when juxtaposed with "I am a man who is hard of hearing," even while we recognize the need to analyze the individualized meanings of Deaf and hard of hearing. Not only gender but also ability, religion, nationality, sexual orientation, career and employment, stage of life status, family role, ad infinitum all influence identity expression. The interfaces between deaf and ethnic/racial identities, sexual orientation, and disability are discussed in Chapter 7.

4

Family and School: Creating Identities

...I was raised belonging to both the deaf world and the hearing world...
My mom always made sure I was exposed to both sides.
  Kristin Buehl (2002, pp. 7–8)

Among my favorite childhood memories is one of a stranger prais-
ing my speech and then deflating my ego by questioning what I said.
Instead of insisting I needed to improve my speech, my hearing mother
ascribed fault to the stranger for not being initially honest about my
speech. That boosted my ego. Additionally, my deaf friends consistently
referred to my mother's genuine interest in them even though she did
not sign, not having been encouraged to learn to sign when I was a
child. My parents never insinuated that I should date hearing guys and
encouraged me to socialize with both deaf and hearing groups. Clearly,
my family significantly validated my deaf identity.

My educational experience also molded my identity as a person
comfortable with "deaf/Deaf" and capable of traversing hearing-
d/Deaf worlds. The elementary and high schools I attended were
not local, thereby diluting the possibility of neighborhood affiliation.
Both were typical urban schools with large programs for deaf and
hard-of-hearing students. The only alternative was the state residential school for the deaf, an unacceptable option for my parents who
wanted their only child at home. There was flexibility in hearing-deaf
class placement based on academic and social needs. I had deaf and
hearing friends and could navigate the deaf–hearing divide without
fear of being ostracized by either group. These experiences reinforced
my comfort in my deaf identity.

THE ROLE OF THE FAMILY

It all starts with the family. The processes whereby children evolve into
adults involve the interaction of cognitive, emotional, and social characteristics with multiple environmental influences, initially within the
family and subsequently within the community and school. This fuels

the ongoing creation of internal identities that reflect the children's life-worlds (Sheridan, 2008). These life-worlds include all elements of the self, environmental exposure, values, relationships, interaction dynamics, and the reciprocal influences of various systems (i.e., individual, family, small groups, cultural, organizational, and political systems). The deaf or hard-of-hearing person's life-world may stimulate narratives throughout the life span that entail ideological struggle in juxtaposing hearing values with d/Deaf values, particularly during adolescence, based on imageries culled from family background, school experiences, and ongoing life experiences.

Family Influences

Susan Harter (1999), a premier developmental psychologist, highlights the early attachment/bonding experiences provided by parents or caretakers as influences that shape the security of emerging self and self-representations. This is followed by ongoing social comparisons that others make about the child. She defines the self as a cognitive construction based on evolving meanings of one's experiences as these interact with individual differences in self-understanding.

The development of positive attachment between caretaker and child frees the child to securely explore the environment and competently face challenges with relative confidence, thereby radiating self-confidence and a secure sense of self (Sarason, Sarason, & Pierce, 1990). For an insecure child, depending on individual strengths and vulnerabilities, the process of internalizing identities can be fraught with conflict and confusion based on shifting types of bonding experiences with caretakers who do not provide consistent positive feedback. Memory-based schemas of experiences fueled by linguistic interactions with caregivers/family help expand the meaning and valences of labels reflecting categories such as gender, ethnicity, and disability and form the basis for the life story, a narrative that provides coherence and meaning for one's sense of self (McAdams, 1993; Peterson & McCabe, 2004). Cultural perceptions can influence how families realign themselves in response to the presence of a difference (Cuéllar & Glazer, 1996; Stone, 2005).

Whether the child internalizes a normative or stigmatized type of identity depends on how the family attributes meaning to having a "different" child and conveys that to the child. For example, in an interview study of 60 mothers of children with disabilities identified at birth, Landsman (2002) found that most mothers initially used the mainstream medical model of disability to frame their experiences of having a child with a disability. Eventually, they began to see their child's disability as normal within their life contexts and transitioned from minimizing the disability to maximizing the child's quality of life. This type of transformation altered the mothers' linguistic discourse.

At age 3, children typically can describe themselves in concrete, disparate terms related to cognitive and physical abilities, behaviors, emotions, possessions, preferences, looks, and friendship aspects, based on family and social input (Harter, 1999). Their perceptions of their competency levels in the domains they attach importance to will be reflected in their self-descriptions. As the children improve their ability to integrate information about themselves, their self-descriptions will increasingly incorporate both positive and negative self-representations.

In adolescence, the role of the social environment heightens in importance (Erikson, 1968, 1980), with adolescents dwelling on the opinions and expectations of others. As they increasingly focus on building stories about themselves that attempt to answer questions about who and what they are (Dunbar & Grotevant, 2004), they are increasingly able to abstractly juxtapose and integrate various and possibly contradictory aspects of their selves into multiple connected identities. Belief systems in the guise of themes and ideology aspects emerge (McAdams, 1993). Themes refer to human intention in terms of desires and how these are pursued, while ideology relates to a systematic body of values and beliefs. Motivation is the fuel that propels the development of themes and ideology.

Based on work done with adolescent adoptees who lack biological connections with adoptive families and are motivated to create meaning out of their beginnings, Dunbar and Grotevant (2004) illuminated how examining the reasons for adoption resulted in stories with themes, ideology, and affective tone created through family responses and interactions as well as peer and media influence. These stories allowed for the extraction of adoptive identity status (including unexamined, limited, unsettled, and integrated). Internalizing an adoptive identity status required thematically coming to terms with the unique differences in relation to family and culture, a process that can also influence deaf and hard-of-hearing children born to hearing families (see later discussion in the section on Families with Deaf and Hard-of-Hearing Children). The authors additionally noted the juxtaposition of three levels: the intrapsychic, relational, and social. The first one includes the internal cognitive and affective processes involved in creating identity; the relational level involves family relationships within which negotiation about adoptive identity happens. Finally, the social level involves the influence of relationships and contexts beyond the family. These levels contribute to the creation of an adoptive identity that accompanies the larger process of identity development.

Harter (1999) expands on the relational level mentioned above through her use of "the construct of relational self-worth" (p. 64), a construct that becomes even more salient in adolescence. It covers how the levels of self-worth vary across relational contexts. For example, the adolescent may feel great when thinking about parents but not so great when focusing on school peers. Support within these specific relationships can contribute to positive self-worth/well-being as indicated by Kef and Dekovićs (2004) study, which found that for both sighted adolescents and adolescents with visual disabilities, peer and parental support was important for their well-being. Further examination indicated that peer support was secondary to parental support for sighted adolescents, while the reverse was true for adolescents with visual disabilities. Perhaps this is because additional energy may be expended in attempting to fit in with peers without disabilities, thereby reinforcing the greater salience of peer support for this group of adolescents. This is one example of how specific social supports may differentially influence self-image (see Sarason, Pierce, & Sarason, 1990 for further discussion).

If there are contradictory messages about one's attributes from family members and peers, the adolescent may experience confusion about which self-descriptions to adopt. This can be compounded by the need to create selves or identities that bridge various "worlds" as is the case with diverse ethnic groups and groups that adopt different deaf-related identities. The less developed these self-identities are, the more confusion these adolescents may experience in terms of balancing their uniqueness from and similarities to others. Parental support and acceptance can facilitate the adolescent's ability to navigate this balancing process.

Families with Deaf or Hard-of-Hearing Children

In the past, normalizing hearing differences within family contexts was subverted by the trend toward sending very young deaf children to residential schools or relegating parents to the sidelines as observers during teaching sessions (Luterman, 2004). Parents were rarely given the opportunity to work through the emotional process of integrating their special child into the family. With a few notable exceptions such as the John Tracy Clinic in California, a 1950s pioneer in parent-centered programs and correspondence courses designed to facilitate parent–child communication (John Tracy Clinic, 2003), family-centered models are a relatively recent and growing phenomenon (e.g., Luterman, 2004; Sass-Lehrer & Bodner-Johnson, 2003). The supportive intervention provided by such programs provides opportunities for families to process feelings and ameliorate stress (Calderon & Greenberg, 1999; Pipp-Siegel, Sedey, & Yoshinaga-Itano, 2002).

Stating that parents need to accept the deaf or hard-of-hearing child is an overly simplistic mantra without clear-cut operational descriptions of how acceptance is manifested throughout various family life events. Each developmental window, starting with identification of the hearing difference and proceeding through linguistic and psychosocial development levels, lends itself to influences that will affect identity development; this depends greatly on how families experience the hearing difference (Pollard, 2004). The child's individual characteristics (temperament, cognitive abilities, personality, communication responsiveness, etc.) will also influence how the hearing difference is treated within the family context and beyond (Harvey, 2003).

Though hearing parents typically are faced with the process of adjusting to their deaf children's communication and learning needs (Hintermair, 2004; Koester, Papousek, & Smith-Gray, 2000), the absence of significant differences in secure attachment between young deaf children with hearing parents and hearing children with hearing parents suggests that the influence of childhood deafness on hearing mother–deaf child social relationship quality is not necessarily negative for attachment, maternal affection, and maternal control (see Lederberg & Prezbindowski, 2000 for a review) Parents often are resilient and, with adequate support networks, can adjust while maintaining positive parent–child relationships unless they do not handle their stress well (Hintermair, 2006; Meadow-Orlans & Steinberg, 1993).

However, the benefit of multigenerational sameness is absent for deaf and hard-of-hearing children with hearing parents (Calderon & Greenberg, 2003; Sheridan, 2001). Consequently, these children may very well go through a process analogous to that earlier described for adoptees. When they ask questions such as "Why am I deaf and not you?" or "Why am I different?" how the families frame their answer, whether as a positive or negative difference, as an affliction, an irritant, or as normal/special, will create imageries within the child's conscious and unconscious outlook of self and world. Such questions may typically emerge between the ages of 7 and 9, when children begin to recognize the permanence of their hearing difference or notice differences as well as inadequacies in themselves (Montoya, Camberg, & Rall, 2005).

Deaf and hard-of-hearing children in hearing families may express a wish to be hearing, more so in childhood when they are struggling with their difference, as demonstrated by various studies. Out of 71 deaf young people interviewed, 97% described wanting to be hearing in childhood, sometimes to ameliorate that difference and sometimes for practical reasons, such as the lack of visual monitor boards at train stations (Gregory, Bishop, and Sheldon, 1995). At the time of the interviews, just over half did not wish to be hearing and the rest wished they were hearing, in part to communicate more easily in the local scene. Nonetheless, the majority of this sample saw being deaf as an integral part of their identity.

At a school for the deaf, 43 students aged 7 through 15 were asked questions about their identity as part of a structured interview (Stone & Stirling, 1994). Fifty percent of the children with deaf parents and 64% of those with hearing parents used "deaf" to identify themselves, while 43% of those with deaf parents and 28% with hearing parents used "hard of hearing," even within the context of a strong deaf setting. Compared to children of deaf parents, more children with hearing parents predicted their identity would change in the direction of becoming hard of hearing or hearing. Identity satisfaction was affirmed by 86% of children with deaf parents and 56% of those with hearing parents. Since deaf children of deaf parents were more often satisfied with their identity status, the authors concluded that parent hearing status and related attitudes may shape how deaf children portray themselves. As the children were not separated by age into children and young adolescents, it is not possible to determine the extent to which developmental stage might have affected the results or the extent to which the parents have resolved their own feelings about having a deaf child.

Based on exploratory research with 58 sets of participants (parent and hearing-impaired child), Warren and Hasenstab (1986) highlighted the critical role of parent child-rearing attitudes in predicting the child's self-concept, with indulgence, protection, and rejection negatively correlating with self-concept, while acceptance and parental discipline showed positive correlations. Hadadian (1995) noted that young deaf children's security of attachment scores were correlated with their parents' attitudes toward deafness in terms of more negative attitudes correlating with less secure attachment. In Sheridan's (2001) narrative study of seven deaf and hard-of-hearing children, the children described being deaf as an insignificant obstacle in their lives; furthermore, they tended to see their parents as consistent in providing love and acceptance, which overrode communication difficulties at home. These studies reinforce the importance of parental attitudes in the child's sense of self (see also Bat-Chava, 1993; Harvey, 2003; Hintermair, 2006; Kent & Smith, 2006; Leigh, 1999a).

The book *We CAN Hear and Speak!* (Parents and Families of Natural Communication, Inc., 1998) contains examples of narratives that can subtly shape the child's self-perceptions about being deaf. As Kristina's mother states, Kristina is "a true hearing child" (p. 31). Jillian leads "such a normal life" that her parents think of her as hearing, not as deaf or hard of hearing (p. 45). Vera says she lives a normal, barrier-free life, and Chris says, "Mom, I'm not deaf" because he has hearing aids (p. 90). These statements reinforce the perception of hearing as normal and implicitly suggest the inferiority of "deaf." In contrast, Peters (2000) writes that his 4-year-old daughter "is not broken and she does not need to be fixed...She is deaf, that's all" (p. 265).

Parental acceptance issues are likely to be re-enacted during life transitions when deaf-related issues, such as the often-noted adolescent shift from a primarily hearing social orientation toward increased contact with deaf peers, surface (Gregory, Bishop, & Sheldon, 1995).

The level of security in the parent–child relationship and the family's ability to normalize the situation of having a "different" child through providing confirmatory overt and covert positive messages can enhance the child's comfort in internalizing *and* disclosing deaf or hard-of-hearing labels as well as in exploring connections with d/Deaf groups (Kent & Smith, 2006; Leigh, 1987; Oliva, 2004). Focus group discussions with orally educated young adults and their parents emphasized the importance of maintaining open communication in the interest of fostering independence, self-actualization, and family inclusion (Eriks-Brophy et al., 2006). This open communication is critical when adolescents express interest in the Deaf community, since parental ambivalence about the social safety of the Deaf community does exist (Christiansen & Leigh, 2002/2005, Higgins, 1990; Luterman, 1987). The fear that parents will lose their children to the culture wrestles with gratitude for the community as a place for their children. Children will sense that dilemma and discomfort, which can create internal conflict; however, it can be readily resolved if the parents can arrive at a comfortable level of rapprochement and recognize that the bonds between them and their children will not be broken.

Moving into adulthood, there is evidence of resiliency in connection and attachment. A study of 50 deaf adult Amercian Sign Language users with nonsigning parents suggested that deaf adult attachment classifications based on the Adult Attachment Interview (AAI) were similar to a normative distribution of hearing adults (Chovaz McKinnon, Moran, & Pederson, 2004). Somewhat more secure attachment on the part of deaf women with hearing parents compared to those with deaf parents, also based on the AAI, was reported in a study of 32 Deaf women (Leigh, Brice, & Meadow-Orlans, 2004). Despite narratives that included dealing with communication frustrations in their family of origin, these women were able to make coherent sense of their past frustrations and reflect on who they were, thereby revealing in part a solid sense of their identity as Deaf women.

However, based on two scales from the Individuation-Attachment Questionnaire that involve Likert-type ratings, Weisel and Kamara (2005) found that fear of attachment and individuation as well as lower self-esteem and well-being were more evident in their 38 deaf and hard-of-hearing adult sample of mostly spoken language users compared to hearing peers. Less than half defined themselves as deaf, while the rest of the participants described themselves using functional hearing abilities. In explaining their findings, the authors consider histories of greater social isolation due to mainstream education. Other explanations for why the present findings differed from those reported earlier include differences in measurement approaches as well as the possibility that parental attachment and relationship attachment (based on friendship and love) are different constructs, with security in the former not necessarily predicting security in the latter (Cowan & Cowan, 2007; Weisel & Kamara, 2005). The role of attachment security in the consolidation of deaf identities clearly requires further investigation.

Communication Aspects

The role of communication in conveying the family's comfort with the child's difference cannot be gainsaid. For hearing parents or caretakers adjusting to the existence of the child's hearing difference, communication tends to be painstakingly created once decisions are made about language, communication mode, intervention approaches, and auditory aids in addition to the typical decisions on child-rearing approaches. Family involvement in the communication process plays a critical role in the development of psychologically healthy deaf children who are communicatively competent (Luckner & Muir, 2001).

Based on data from parents of 192 deaf adolescents, the mother was identified as the determining factor in choosing the family's communication mode (Kluwin & Gaustad, 1991). The mother's education level, the child's level of hearing loss, and preschool communication mode all influenced the mother's decision. Interestingly, higher education level was related to the likelihood of selecting a signing option. Whether that is currently true in view of improved hearing technology remains open to question, though many parents of children with cochlear implants participating in the Christiansen and Leigh (2002/2005) study reported signing with their children, at least prior to the implants. Bat-Chava's (1993) meta-analysis of studies on self-esteem in deaf individuals indicated that those with higher self-esteem had parents who used sign language. This finding suggests that these parents have internalized some degree of comfort with visual communication and could convey that level of comfort to their deaf child, thus affirming the child's sense of self as Deaf. The decision to learn sign language represents a significant parental level of commitment that the child may indirectly value in terms of self-validation. Going further, while the seven adolescents interviewed by Sheridan (2008) acknowledged the ongoing support of their parents, they reported feelings of disconnection in hearing family gatherings due to lack of communication access. They emphasized the importance of shared linguistic modes of communication in terms of "deaf-like" communication rather than accessible communication at home. These feelings engendered wishes for greater deaf-like communication with immediate hearing family members.

On the other hand, mothers who choose the spoken language option also demonstrate significant commitment, since working on receptive and expressive spoken language requires exactly that. This commitment differs in that the focus is on easing the child into the hearing culture of the family. The crux is that of family motivation to get messages across to the child in ways that are inclusive and support- ing for the child. Current evidence indicates that it is not just the use of signs but rather the mutuality of communication between parent and child that is positively associated with positive self-esteem in deaf adolescents (Desselle, 1994), healthy socioemotional development (Hintermair, 2006), and mental health (Leigh, 1990; Wallis, Musselman, & MacKay, 2004).

While having a hard-of-hearing child is often perceived as being easier to incorporate into the family compared to having a deaf child, in reality communication can be as or even more stressful (Laszlo, 1994). This was demonstrated in a study that identified higher parental risk for significant stress when children had less severe degrees of hearing loss (Pipp-Siegel, Sedey, & Yoshinaga-Itano, 2002). When the child is presumed to hear "well enough" but frequently misses cues and con- stantly requests that comments be repeated, this eventually can create fatigue and avoidance on the part of hearing family members (Harvey, 2003). Such experiences may serve to reinforce the hard-of-hearing child's ambivalence about self-disclosure.

Role Models

The presence of deaf adults, whether within the family or external, is also associated with increased communicative responsiveness (Jackson & Turnbull, 2004) and better acceptance of the child's deaf identity (Hintermair, 2000). However, deaf adults are not a typical presence for many parents and their advice is rarely solicited (Benedict & Sass- Lehrer, 2007; Christiansen & Leigh, 2002/2005; Lane, Hoffmeister, & Bahan, 1996). This can compound the sense of loneliness, alienation, and vulnerability to negative self-perceptions for those who identify as the only deaf or hard-of-hearing child in the world (Oliva, 2004). In the absence of in-depth friendship with a hearing peer, such feelings can be counteracted when the life journey incorporates positive encounters with deaf or hard-of-hearing peers.

Extended Family

Research on families tends to focus on the parents/caregivers of deaf and hard-of-hearing children rather than on siblings and extended family members. Research covering how extended family members may contribute to the deaf child's identity development is lacking. Luterman (1987) has observed that siblings reflect parental cues and feelings about the deaf child. The parents' ability to demonstrate acceptance and comfort permeates the family system and provides additional validation and support for the deaf child. Studies of hear- ing siblings with signing or speaking deaf children document that positive sibling relationships were associated with fewer emotional and behavioral problems as well as more social competence (Bat-Chava & Martin, 2002; Verté, Hebbrecht, & Roeyers, 2006). An informal survey indicates that parents generally valued the support of grand-parents, who tend to provide love and attention similarly to both deaf and hearing grandchildren (Morton, 2000). Qualitative data from six sets of grandparents suggested that their involvement facilitated family adjustment (Nybo, Scherman, & Freeman, 1998). While the grandchildren wished their grandparents could sign, the presence of love and connection was noted.

SCHOOL AND PEER INFLUENCES

The Role of Schools in Identity Formation

As the child segues into the educational system, there is greater oppor-tunity for a broader span of influences that have a bearing on identity development. Daily school interactions involving peers and authority figures have been identified as a powerful force in the making and molding of identities (Davidson, 1996). How these interactions influ-ence individuals is based in part on ideology and politics, perceptions of social categories, and the juxtaposition of diverse groups with differ-ential status hierarchies.

Theoretically, education is the equalizer for diverse unequal groups by providing them with access to academic and social infor-mation through curricular and extracurricular activities, intellectual and social role experiences, and role models for students to emulate (Israelite, Ower, & Goldstein, 2002; Leigh, 1999a). Teacher and peer influences implicitly provide opportunities for nurturing, shaping, or resisting the identities students bring with them from home and community settings (Davidson, 1996). Conceptualizing identity influences within schools requires consideration of the interactive effects of educational placement with communication, motivation, individual attributes, relationships, and academic achievement.

The established social identities children bring with them structure their responses to the school environment, which then reciprocally influences these identities. Davidson's (1996) interview study of how 55 students of color asserted ethnic and racial identities within high school settings suggested salient factors for the ongoing construction of identities: *(1)* marginalization along demarcated social lines; *(2)* bar-riers to information reinforcing marginalization; *(3)* bureaucratic rela-tionships and practices that silence and thereby disempower; *(4)* distant and depersonalized relationships with authority figures, including differential treatment engendering resentment, and *(5)* interaction between peers, teacher expectations, and differential treatment leading to positive or negative group labels.

These factors highlight the atypicality of secure school environments for marginalized and stigmatized groups (e.g., Davidson, 1996; Kozol, 2005; Nash, 2000; Ramsey, 1997). Actual teacher and school administrator practices often do not include appropriate equalizing educational experiences and perpetuate grouping and hierarchical patterns that work against disadvantaged groups, including those with disabilities (e.g., Osgood, 2005; Sleeter & Grant, 2005; Stainback, 2000). The resulting inequities create lower status for these disadvantaged groups with repercussions for self-perceptions and identity. The potential implications for deaf and hard-of-hearing students require some understanding of current educational settings for this population.

School Settings

Historically, the education of deaf and hard-of-hearing children took place in residential and specialized day schools. Since 1974, the trend internationally has shifted toward mainstreaming/inclusion (e.g., Angelides & Aravi, 2006/2007; Hyde, Ohna, & Hjulstadt, 2006; Moores, 2001; Risdale & Thompson, 2002). In the United States, approximately 26% are educated in residential and specialized day school settings, while the rest are dispersed in various public schools (Gallaudet Research Institute, 2006), as well as private and parochial settings (e.g., Marschark, Lang, & Albertini, 2002; Stinson & Kluwin, 2003). In the nonspecialized schools, alternative placements can include resource rooms for selected subjects and separate designated classrooms for most or all of the entire time, larger regional programs for deaf students within public schools, and standard classroom settings with itinerant teachers providing individualized support services as needed. Less common are co-enrollment classes that incorporate groups of deaf, hard-of-hearing, and hearing students taught by general and special education teacher teams (Kirchner, 2004; Stinson & Kluwin, 2003). Hard-of-hearing children tend to be educated in the mainstream with minimal support services; this is based on perceptions that their access to audition with or without auditory aids guarantees access, despite evidence of academic disadvantages, including missed information (Punch, Creed, & Hyde, 2006; Ross, 2001).

A key philosophical concept of inclusion is that diverse students, including those with disabilities, are full members of school communities. The assumption is that when individual needs are met, everyone will have equal access to richer educational offerings and learning experiences through a broader spectrum of academics (Angelides & Aravi, 2006/2007). The provision of support services within the classroom theoretically reinforces classroom assimilation, thereby working against the social rejection of students with hearing differences through increased opportunities for hearing–deaf peer interaction (Israelite, Ower, & Goldstein, 2002; Stinson & Kluwin, 2003). The definition of social success becomes that of "making it" with hearing peers. Special education is viewed as separate and unequal, thereby reinforcing the stigmatization of disability (Osgood, 2005).

Special education advocates argue that inclusion, even with support services, detracts attention from the unique individualized needs of students with disabilities that nonspecialized instructors are unfamiliar with (Osgood, 2005). Communication barriers, including limitations in linguistic competence as well as limitations in auditory and linguistic access due to language/modality differences, subvert the goal of equal access (see e.g., Cerney, 2007; Stinson & Kluwin, 2003 for further discussion). Problematic aspects include the following: no similar peers to identify with; hearing students unfamiliar with peers who do not hear; being derided for using classroom amplification; and being taken out of classes for support services, which leads to missed social opportunities and being marked as different (Maxon & Brackett, 1992; Osgood, 2005). A series of focus groups involving 16 oral deaf young adults, 24 parents, and 14 itinerant teachers of the deaf identified external facilitators and barriers to the inclusion of deaf and hard-of-hearing children in schools. These included administrator atmosphere, parental involvement, student skills (e.g., self-advocacy), welcoming versus nonwelcoming peers, with the most critical being that of teachers who may provide positive or negative reinforcement (Eriks-Brophy et al., 2006). The essential long-term classroom interactive and equipment-based intervention strategies designed to increase academic and social interaction (e.g., Antia & Kreimeyer, 2003; Calderon & Greenberg, 2003; Oliva, 2004) rarely take place (Ramsey, 1997).

This negative atmosphere spurs the argument that true inclusion happens only in specialized school settings with minimal communication barriers; this facilitates access to social contact and educational input, thereby reinforcing positive d/Deaf identity development (Cerney, 2007; Foster, 1996; Schildroth & Hotto, 1995; Stinson & Whitmire, 2000; Thumann-Prezioso, 2005). Deaf parents with deaf children tend to select specialized settings where communication access and deaf peer socialization are readily available (Thumann-Prezioso, 2005), though there are concerns about low academic expectations and limited academic choices (e.g., Angelides & Aravi, 2006/2007; Leigh & Stinson, 1991; Nikolaraizi & Hadjikakou, 2006). While self-contained classes in public schools minimize opportunities for developing transitional social skills and more multifaceted identities, these classes alternatively provide opportunities for more focused attention to individual needs and socialization opportunities with similar peers (Ramsey, 1997). The ultimate outcome of the inclusion versus specialized school debate is that special education for deaf and hard-of-hearing children has yet to die a complete death, while the inclusion philosophy now predominates.

Socialization-Identity Issues

In school settings, succeeding stages of development will involve increased social pressure, an intensified need for social acceptance, and various social groupings based on academic, special interest, status, and ethnic parameters. Entering and exiting those groups requires social skills that evolve over time (Maxon & Brackett, 1992). Whatever the school placement, it is critical to recognize that both positive and negative experiences are possible (Sheridan, 2001, 2008).

The Role of Communication

The importance of communication competency and effective language/ communication access in the process of identifying with hearing or deaf groups is profound (e.g., Musselman, Mootilal, & MacKay, 1996; Spencer & Hafer, 1998; Stinson & Whitmire, 2000). Communication ease or difficulty will influence the possibility of experiencing positive social appraisals, group affiliation, and optimal peer social learning.

The importance of intelligible speech in facilitating comfort during interactions with hearing peers has been affirmed in various studies (Bat-Chava & Deignan, 2001; Musselman, Mootilal, & MacKay, 1996; Stinson & Antia, 1999; Wheeler, Archbold, Gregory, & Skipp, 2007). Intelligible speech, however, does not always compensate for inadequate audiological information. Because the effect of specific audiograms is rarely explained, students may not understand why information is being missed in the context of the classroom or interaction with hearing peers, even in the presence of intelligible speech. This can contribute to internal confusion and struggles to appear as though they understand. Harvey (2003) describes a hard-of-hearing adolescent as feeling "a bit off" (p. 51), even though teachers praised her academic achievement and social skills. Luterman (2004) attacks proponents of auditory-focused approaches for not recognizing potential social and emotional consequences of oral successes (see the section on Acceptance below), since these students are still "hearing impaired," even with good speech and language skills. Involvement with available deaf or hard-of-hearing peer groups that provide ease as well as depth in communication may reinforce comfort with deaf or hard-of-hearing identities.

Ohna (2003) describes the metamorphosis of a signing 12-year-old Norwegian girl who "knew" she was deaf. Her unproblematic communication in school because of sign language interpreter use reinforced her sense of sameness with hearing people until she attempted to join her hearing friends outside school and realized how excluded she was, how she was not like them. To her shock, "That was a great barrier."

(Ohna, 2003, p. 7). Her sense of alienation led her to search for affiliation with deaf peers.

A mainstreamed adolescent student sample with communication access to both deaf and hearing peers reported not only satisfactory relationships with hearing peers but also maintaining ties with deaf peers, which served as a buffer function (Musselman, Mootilal, & MacKay, 1996). Deaf and hard-of-hearing mainstreamed students recruited for a large-scale study generally preferred similar peers even with increase in hearing peer contact and communication capabilities (Stinson & Kluwin, 2003; Stinson & Whitmire, 1992).

Within specialized school settings that incorporate the use of a signed language, how one signs can have significant bearing on level of acceptance by deaf peers (Sheridan, 2001, 2008). This can become an issue if students move into the specialized school from mainstream settings and have a language learning curve to deal with in addition to overcoming their initial outsider status (Weiner & Miller, 2006). Identification with signing peer groups may depend on the extent to which these outsiders achieve signing competency.

In a semistructured interview study of 20 successful mainstreamed students selected by their teachers and evenly divided between signing and speaking students, communication mode did not appear to be a salient issue (Luckner & Muir, 2001). Students were comfortable with assistive technology and noted both the importance of hard work in response to high expectations and significant support from family, friends, and education personnel. Self-determination was a critical attribute. Though not stated outright, the importance of individualized support services was evident. In contrast, Cerney (2007) notes a divide between the five signing and five speaking deaf children and adolescents within inclusion settings whom she interviewed, with the former experiencing significant communication barriers and more loneliness. Cerney reports her group as demonstrating fewer positive ways of coping compared to Sheridan's (2001) interviewees. As Julie stated, "Sometimes I just give up" (Cerney, 2007, p. 93).

Athletics tend to create structured opportunities for interaction (Leigh & Stinson, 1991; Luckner & Muir; 2001; Martin & Bat-Chava, 2003). Stewart (1991) writes about the educational implications of Deaf sport, particularly as a vehicle for deaf–hearing integration. More recently, Stewart and Ellis (2005) argue for the inclusion of mainstreamed deaf children in a Deaf sports program, considering that in those venues communication barriers and academic concerns recede and opportunities for specialized social skill development and internalization of identity as capable deaf individuals increase. Since hearing athletic venues are competitive and opportunities for participation are not guaranteed, an increasing number of deaf public school athletes have been migrating to national Deaf teams.

Greater congruence in communication between deaf and hearing students will facilitate the development of bicultural identities if this occurs simultaneously with deaf–deaf communication congruence. In the specialized Deaf school setting, it is expected that Deaf cultural identity will be primary. Currently there is very little evidence that bicultural identities will be internalized within bilingual-bicultural programs as is expected unless the student possesses communication skills sufficient for comfort in interacting with both Deaf and hearing peers (Hadjikakou & Nikolaraizi, 2007). Hintermair (2008) reminds us that whatever the case may be regarding communication mode, good communicative conditions will enhance quality-of-life issues.

School Settings and Identity

A number of studies appear to support the presence of a relationship between school setting and d/Deaf-hearing identity formation. Using Weinberg and Sterritt's Deaf Identity Scale (see Chapter 2) with deaf adolescents in Turkish residential schools, Sari (2005) concluded that identities are reinforced by the nature of the school setting, with dual identity being more prominent in total communication schools, while the culturally hearing identity was endorsed by students attending an oral school. In addition, dual identity was consistently associated with better communication and the use of combined communication modes. Deaf Acculturation Scale (see Chapter 2) results indicated that adolescents educated in mainstream settings were more likely to be hearing-acculturated compared to those attending deaf schools who tended to be more Deaf-acculturated (Leigh, Maxwell-McCaw, Bat-Chava, & Christiansen, 2009). Semistructured interviews with 24 Cypriot deaf adults revealed the influence school setting types had on identity perceptions (Hadjikakou & Nikolaraizi, 2007). Those attending both oral and signing specialized schools affirmed a Deaf cultural identity, with oral interviewees having been exposed to sign language outside the classroom. Those in general education programs either claimed hearing cultural identification or gravitated toward Deaf identity, perhaps because of communication difficulties. Participants from either specialized or general settings who had positive experiences using spoken language reported being comfortable with both hearing and Deaf adults in a bicultural sense.

The influence of educational settings on deaf identity status was less evident in the Wheeler et al. (2007) study of twenty-nine 13- to 16-year-old adolescents with cochlear implants in mainstreamed and specialized educational settings. Most of the students endorsed a deaf identity that was neither culturally Deaf nor strongly hearing and were flexible in terms of communication mode. It would be interesting to know whether this would change in later adolescence. The Leigh et al. (2009) study mentioned earlier suggests the presence of a trend for adolescents in older-grade levels to be Deaf-acculturated compared to those in younger grades who were more hearing–acculturated (Leigh, Maxwell-McCaw, Bat-Chava, & Christiansen, 2009). Possible reasons include imperfect access to hearing peers as well as heightened interest in identity issues typical of adolescence. This can entail learning a formal sign language and accessing Deaf culture in transitioning from deaf to Deaf (Ladd, 2003; Valentine & Skelton, 2007). From a cross-sectional perspective, the pattern of residential school versus public school placement suggests that more deaf students may be migrating into specialized schools during the high school years than vice versa (Holden-Pitt, 1997), although this requires careful demographic scrutiny.

Acceptance

The mantra that deaf students will be accepted by hearing peers has been reinforced by success stories in which difficulties are overcome (e.g., Reisler, 2002). But the stories can be painful. One of the chapter titles in Gina Oliva's (2004) book on solitaires in the mainstream tells it all: "Academically It Was Better Than a Deaf School, but Socially, Well..." The book covers retrospective memories expressed in four essays and responses to a multiple-choice questionnaire by 60 participants who were the only deaf students in their school during some or all of their educational experiences. These memories reveal social difficulties and emotional turmoil in the effort to be accepted. There was a pervasive sense of shame associated with having a nonmainstream identity. Some respondents had positive experiences while disclosing their hearing status; others dreaded disclosing their "difference." This dread is supported by additional studies reporting on attempts by children in mainstream school settings to avoid embarrassment by hiding their deaf-or hard-of-hearing status (Davis, Elfenbein, Schum, & Bentler, 1986; Kent, 2003). Those who felt their mainstream experiences were worthwhile nonetheless have noted the pain of less than full acceptance, struggles against a typical hearing bias, either subtle or overt, and continual efforts to achieve a sense of equality and internal validation with hearing peers (Leigh & Stinson, 1991; Oliva, 2004).

Studies of acceptance reveal that deaf and hard-of-hearing students in preschool and elementary school received lower peer ratings of likeability and acceptance, were "neglected" or patronized rather than actively liked or disliked, or interacted less frequently with hearing peers (Antia & Kreimeyer, 2003; Cappelli, Daniels, Durieux-Smith, McGrath, & Neuss, 1995; Cerney, 2007; Nunes, Pretzlik, & Olsson, 2001; Ramsey, 1997; Risdale & Thompson, 2002; Yetman, 2000). However, in Ladd, Munson, and Miller's (1984) study, hearing peers found their deaf peers to be more considerate, and in the Wauters and Knoors (2008) social integration study conducted in the Netherlands, where extensive support is provided in inclusion settings, there were no differences between oral deaf (who had good communication skills) and hearing children within inclusion and co-enrollment programs in terms of peer acceptance.

Almost all of the 23 "successful" students from both residential and nonspecialized schools interviewed by Charlson, Strong, and Gold (1992) experienced some degree of isolation, with the mainstreamed students feeling isolated from hearing peers while the residential students complained about communication barriers at home. Most had developed positive coping strategies. The researchers normalize this within the context of adolescence and the tendency to focus on feeling different. This parallels the perceptions of the 28 oral deaf adult participants in the Bain, Scott, and Steinberg (2004) interview study, a number of whom reported dealing with the isolating social consequences of being "different" from hearing peers during adolescence and having to develop coping mechanisms involving assertively relating to these peers in venues such as organized social and athletic activities. Parents and friends often were instrumental in reducing social barriers through informational activities to minimize intolerance. In a case study of four fully mainstreamed young people who had great difficulty with social acceptance, contact with other deaf individuals outside of school was desired (Risdale & Thompson, 2002). Their teachers, who reportedly did not have time to provide positive support, felt these four students were less marginalized than they themselves felt.

The role of individual student characteristics, such as maturity, that might facilitate acceptance has not been well-researched, in part due to the complexity of teasing out various influences. Within kindergarten co-enrollment classes, self-report and nominations regarding peer preference indicated balance between deaf and hearing peers (see Stinson & Kluwin, 2003), suggesting age as one possible factor. This is supported by a Spanish study of 792 hearing students' perceptions of deaf peers, which found that younger students were more likely than adolescents to identify a deaf classmate as a friend, while the adolescents felt deaf peers might be better off at specialized schools (Cambra, 2002). However, from the perspective of 35 parents with "successful" deaf children, improvement with age was noted by approximately half of the parents who saw their children as increasingly confident in social situations with hearing peers. Only a quarter stated their children were comfortable requesting repetition from hearing peers because of reinforced perceptions that hearing peers were impatient (Martin & Bat-Chava, 2003).

Self-Esteem and Adjustment

Judgments of self-esteem or self-worth can be based on various constructs, including scholastic, athletic, behavior, and other functional competencies as well as physical appearance, social acceptance, close friendship, and romantic appeal (Harter, 1985, 1988; Shavelson,

Hubner, & Stanton, 1976) in addition to communication competence and individual attributes, such as resilience. The value ascribed to each construct by the individual may determine the extent to which it influences self-esteem. For example, if academics are of minor importance, mediocre grades will minimally affect self-esteem. So it makes intuitive sense that according to a variety of studies including children with diverse levels of hearing or in various school placements, self-esteem is not necessarily affected by hearing peers' level of acceptance (Kluwin, 1999; Stinson & Kluwin, 2003), depending on one's value system or if deaf peers are available.

However, other studies have documented lower levels of self-esteem in deaf and hard-of-hearing mainstreamed children who are neglected or rejected by their hearing peers, based in part on awareness of their lower social status (Cappelli, Daniels, Durieux-Smith, McGrath, & Neuss, 1995; Yetman, 2000). One possible explanation is that reference groups need to be considered in assessing social self-esteem (Tajfel, 1981). Yetman's (2000) study based on a sociometric approach using deaf children in suburban mainstream settings found that social self-esteem was rated higher if the comparison group involved deaf peers rather than hearing peers. Coyner (1993) noted a similar trend in that lower levels of acceptance by hearing peers were not related to self-esteem levels when high levels of deaf and hard-of-hearing peer acceptance were present. Based on a meta-analytic review of self-esteem studies, Bat-Chava (1993, 1994) found that Deaf adults who value sign language or compare themselves with deaf groups have higher self-esteem and concluded that stronger Deaf identity contributed positively to self-esteem in deaf adolescents and adults.

In terms of adjustment, teacher ratings of deaf British residential school adolescents who were classified as having hearing, deaf, and dual identities based on the Weinberg and Sterritt (1986) Deaf Identity Scale (see Chapter 2) indicated that those with dual identity had the fewest rated adjustment difficulties, while the deaf identity group had the highest problem ratings (Cole & Edelman, 1991). How dependent the results were on teacher levels of Deaf cultural awareness remains an open question, since the teachers were hearing. In contrast, a large-scale study of deaf adolescents and adults exhibited a stronger link between both Deaf/bicultural acculturation and satisfaction with life compared to hearing acculturation (Maxwell-McCaw, 2001). Hintermair's (2008) study of deaf and hard-of-hearing adults, while confirming the Maxwell-McCaw (2001) results, also emphasizes the importance of psychological resources, such as optimism and self-efficacy, not only for satisfaction with life but also for self-esteem.

Bullying

Children with disabilities, including hearing differences, are frequently victims of bullying (Dixon, 2006; Legge, 2004; Marschark,

Lang, & Albertini, 2002; Skelton & Valentine, 2003; Wheeler, Archbold, Gregory, & Skipp, 2007). The philosophy of inclusion presumes a belief that humans are inherently kind and that exposure to the disadvantaged will result in a kinder, gentler world (Ramsey, 1997), but the presence and pervasiveness of bullying (though based more on case reports than research evidence) belies that. Bullying is multifaceted, involving various forms of verbal and physical aggression (Smith & Sharp, 1994 as cited in Weiner & Miller, 2006).

In her autobiography, Bonnie Tucker (1995), a deaf law professor as well as an ardent advocate of living in hearing society, describes her hearing classmates and teachers as both kind and cruel. A hard-of-hearing woman working on her Ph.D. reported being the recipient of taunts and hurled rocks during her childhood because children are typically not tolerant of those who are "different" (Marschark, Lang, & Albertini, 2002). Peter Steyger (2004), an associate professor of otolaryngology, went through years of bullying in English mainstream schools. He implicates the tendency to deny hearing loss as a way of encouraging bullying by hearing peers. When defenses against bullying are weak, resiliency is low, and coping strategies are not effective, the student may be unable to confront antagonists who ridicule the student's auditory devices and communication, thus exacerbating inner pain. Having a positive self-image and identity that incorporates hearing difference as well as strategic coping with bullies will mitigate that vulnerability (Sheridan, 2008; Steyger, 2004).

Another approach is that of not self-identifying. A New Zealand study by Kent (2003) indicates that hard-of-hearing students who self-identify are more at risk of being bullied. The reluctance of the majority of his sample of 52 to self-identify also may reflect perceptions of negative stigma. The importance of administrator atmosphere and teacher expectations in transmitting positive or negative valences surrounding hearing differences and minimizing if not preventing bullying cannot be denied (Eriks-Brophy et al., 2006; McCrone, 2004).

Bullying is not exclusive to mainstream/inclusion settings. It also happens in schools for deaf children, where those who are vulnerable may be picked on (Fidler, 2004; Weiner & Miller, 2006). Some of Sheridan's (2001, 2008) interviewees told of rejection, rudeness, teasing imitations of sign language production, and conflict despite the proclivity to identify with deaf peers. They responded with creative solutions to cope with negative incidents, such as expanding social networks rather than withdrawing from them.

Hard-of-Hearing Identity Issues

A Canadian study involving open-ended group interviews and written questionnaires with seven hard-of-hearing adolescent participants who had been in hard-of-hearing classrooms for part or all of their elementary school years indicated they strongly identified as hard of hearing, not as hearing or deaf (Israelite, Ower, & Goldstein, 2002). Their hard-of-hearing identity was constructed based on how they differed from hearing and Deaf peers. Proximity to hard-of-hearing peers and social support facilitated this identity construction, though relationships with hearing peers continued to be important. Five participants viewed fitting into the mainstream as the biggest challenge because they were likely to be noted as "different" and had wanted to hide their hearing difference. They also felt mistreated due to lack of understanding on the part of regular education teachers. The other two had more positive experiences but did not appreciate being singled out as hard of hearing. When they were together in the hard-of-hearing class, they bonded with each other, showed comfort with their hard-of-hearing identity, and received positive support from their specialized teachers whom they perceived as sensitive. They were comfortably prepared to return to the mainstream after getting the necessary support in the hard-of-hearing class, indicating they wanted to learn the rules so that they could enhance relationships with hearing peers. All of them indicated they would select oral communication for their children, while five out of the seven also added exposure to sign language as a secondary choice.

Hard-of-hearing classes are the exception rather than the norm. Studies done of hard-of-hearing adolescents in New Zealand and Canada mainstream/inclusion settings indicate the majority avoid self-identifying as hard of hearing (Kent, 2003; Warick, 1994). Incidents, such as not responding consistently when peers call their names, reinforce the possibility that those who identify as such may be more prone to negative stigma from hearing peers and psychosocial stress. This can enhance the prevalence of behavioral and self-esteem concerns (Meadow-Orlans, Mertens, & Sass-Lehrer, 2003).

In Sweden, the integration of hard-of-hearing classes into Deaf school environments represents a relatively recent addition to the options of full mainstreaming and mainstream enrollment in hard-of-hearing classes and an acknowledgment of the unique educational needs of hard-of-hearing children (Bagga-Gupta & Domfors, 2003). The perception that this group should be included with Deaf students using a bilingual-bicultural approach has been suggested by Grushkin (2003; see Chapter 3). In support of this, Brunnberg's (2005) study using video-camera observations of school playground scenes showed that at a mainstream school the hard-of-hearing children played on the periphery while their hearing peers played in the central interaction areas. At the specialized school, the hard-of-hearing children played with their deaf peers in the central interaction areas, thus demonstrating that this group was socially included in the specialized setting and socially excluded in the mainstream setting.

THINKING POINTS

The role of teachers in facilitating social integration is critical. Student identities are devalued when classroom philosophy does not validate the deaf or hard-of-hearing student as a fully participating member. Classroom philosophy is framed by the practices teachers use, how they evaluate the influence of these practices on nonmainstream students, and how they re-evaluate their teaching strategies to improve relationships and create more inclusion (Igoa, 1995). Teachers are the ultimate arbiters of how "d/Deaf-friendly" their classrooms are. They are the ones who can ensure the child's full access to information, including incidental learning situations and access to deaf role models to minimize the deaf child being left out and stigmatized (e.g., Andrews & Covell, 2006/2007; Miller & Moores, 2000; Oliva, 2004; Risdale & Thompson, 2002; Stinson & Kluwin, 2003).

Unfortunately, teachers are not consistently equipped to ensure the deaf or hard-of-hearing child's inclusion. Donald Moores (2005/2006) attributes this to "institutional ignorance" on the part of administrators rather than deliberate discrimination (p. 400). However, such ignorance becomes a subtle stigmatizing of "difference." Ultimately, mainstreaming or inclusion could possibly have the ironical consequence of motivating migration into the deaf community to escape the continual frustrations of communication barriers when support and success become elusive.

Despite the research findings presented here, mainstream schools continue to focus on academics to the neglect of the deaf and hard-of-hearing child's socialization needs. A review of Davidson's (1996) factors relevant to identity construction (discussed earlier) suggests that in the case of deaf and hard-of-hearing students the following are often observed: *(1)* marginalization along demarcated hearing–deaf social lines is a risk factor for this population; *(2)* barriers to information in the nature of communication access reinforce marginalization; *(3)* bureaucratic relationships and practices on the part of administrators who limit their support for accommodating their deaf and hard-of-hearing student needs, often through ignorance if not discrimination, silences and disempowers these students; *(4)* distant and depersonalized relationships with authority figures accompanied by differential treatment creates resentment; and *(5)* speech acts produced by peers or school personnel label deaf and hard-of-hearing groups positively or negatively.

In his musings on mainstreaming and identity, Paul Higgins (1990) opines that schools can play an important role in the development of deaf identities, but the difficulties in doing so are greater today with the decrease in opportunities to develop feelings of closeness with deaf peers. To counteract this trend, the challenge of these schools is to create accessible pathways to deaf communities that deaf youth can choose to bridge as they see fit. Having a critical mass of deaf or hard-of-hearing peers for identifying with each other will provide increased opportunity for solidifying identities through encounters that often may be more satisfying than those with hearing peers (Israelite, Ower, & Goldstein, 2002; Leigh, 1999a). Kirchner (2004) advocates co-enrollment on the premise that equality in numbers of hearing and deaf/hard-of-hearing students will foster positive identity development. A popular solution is to have courses and programs on Deaf identity, history, and worldviews. Brooks (2006) provides a template for how schools can promote resilience through strategies such as developing social competence, increasing caring relationships with school personnel, communicating high expectations, maximizing opportunities for meaningful participation, strengthening school capacity for building resilience through positive treatment of school personnel, and creating partnerships with family and community.

How leaving the specialized deaf school setting for the "hearing world" affects deaf identity evolution will depend on how the transition is handled. Valentine and Skelton (2007) use the term "transition shock" to describe this process of suddenly having to cope most of the time with hearing people and deal with intransigent communication issues (p. 111). Family resources that facilitate understanding and bridging are a critical factor in easing this transition. The employment setting and persistence of underemployment may exacerbate frustrations (Backenroth, 1995; Gregory, Bishop, & Shelden, 1995). Even in the absence of direct questions posed by interviewers, participants narrated stories about being teased and bullied on the job (Gregory, Bishop, & Shelden, 1995). The role of communication and cooperation in validating the deaf person's working sense of self is critical (Backenroth, 1995).

While families and schools clearly play a role in identity evolution, the nature of their influence varies depending on a multiplicity of complex variables related to individual characteristics and environmental factors. Stinson and Kluwin's (2003) review of studies focusing on the relationship between various student characteristics and school placement concludes that attempts to relate each of these characteristics to school placement ultimately becomes an exercise in futility due to variances in personality, maturity levels, resilience, communication skills, social aptitude, cultural and socioeconomic issues, how classroom interaction is organized, the types of peers in each placement, and a multitude of other factors. There is no easy way to pin down specific influences.

However, despite the vagaries of growing up and confronting multiple challenges to their sense of self, more often than not we will find young deaf people who are resilient in confronting school/social barriers, believe in themselves, and have hopes for their future and their connections with significant social groups, whether d/Deaf, hard of hearing, or hearing. According to much of the research presented here, feelings of closeness to hearing peers are not easily developed, but they can result when effective communication exists. Closeness to hearing family members is typically sustained over time. Comfort with others who communicate like they do will encourage gravitation toward d/Deaf communities and the consolidation of d/Deaf identities to some degree. This trend is less clear for hard-of-hearing students who are often isolated in the mainstream and avoid internalizing even a hard-of-hearing identity in the face of social discomfort. Deaf students who tend to gravitate to each other are reflective of a historical pattern that will be discussed in Chapter 5.

5

The Influence of the Past

As historians probe more deeply into the past, as they ask new questions and discover new evidence, it is becoming apparent that deaf people have played a larger role in their own history than has been recognized.
John Vickrey Van Cleve (1993, p. x)

While deaf identities are an area of relatively recent scholarly interest, there is a long history of deaf identity evolution that indicates how historical contexts have affected the shape of these identities. Such historical contexts, containing national, ethnic, racial, religious, regional, and local components or perceptions, colored by culture, ideology, and politics, can have a powerful influence on identity formulations of sameness and difference (Baynton, 1996; Branson & Miller, 2002; Gilroy, 2004). In the earliest eras, deaf identities would have had to start with the physical manifestation of whether one heard and not necessarily with whom one socialized or how one communicated. Exactly what deaf identities have meant since that time depends on the specific historical era, since different periods reflect different perceptions of deaf identities based on different social, cultural, and political constructs created by deaf and hearing voices. There are elements of deaf identities that have been inherited from the past, thereby providing continuity as these identities continue to be reworked within the context of the present.

Here I focus on selected seminal historical events, of which there were many, that appear to have been pivotal in shaping the meaning of deaf identities.

EARLY BEGINNINGS

There are limited records of deaf people extending back to the times of ancient Egypt, Greece, and Rome, as well as the Old and New Testament periods (Abrams, 1998; Baumann, 2008b; Eriksson, 1993; Miles, 2000; Moores, 2001; Rée, 1999; Van Cleve & Crouch, 1989). Regarding how they fit into the societies of their times, the evidence indicates variable levels of acceptance and rejection. Ancient Jewish texts illustrate a gradual transition from neutral perceptions about the capabilities of deaf persons to more overt exclusionary rhetoric (Abrams, 1998).

Despite common perceptions that Saint Augustine, one of the earliest developers of Catholic doctrine, considered the spoken word to be the only way to salvation, he nonetheless viewed deaf people as capable of salvation because sign language was available to reach their souls (Branson & Miller, 2002; Eriksson, 1993; Van Cleve & Crouch, 1989). In the fifteenth century, the Turkish Ottoman Court relied on "mutes" to provide essential services, prizing their inability to hear state secrets (Miles, 2000). These individuals were able to receive their instructions through the use of signs.

During the Middle Ages in Europe, the predominant perspective was that possessing a deaf identity meant being outcast from society and thereby doomed because of the lack of a language and the appearance of disability (Branson & Miller, 2002). Such individuals were portrayed as uneducable and were not permitted to marry, inherit property, or be involved in legal transactions (Moores, 2001; Rée, 1999). Consequently, they ended up as beggars and objects of charity. Contradicting this dismal portrayal is the existence of records that note the presence of deaf people who could communicate through sign language and live functional lives, for example as painters, craftspeople, and farmers, and in the Ottoman era as members of the court. Whether they were excluded from laws governing individual rights depended on their ability to demonstrate comprehension of language. How they perceived themselves and their identity in comparison with hearing compatriots is lost to history.

Beginning in the 1500s, first in Spain, and subsequently in France, Great Britain, Germany, and other European countries, enlightened individuals began to acknowledge the possibility that deaf persons were capable of thought and therefore were educable. They started devising means to formally provide deaf children with language and learning opportunities, initially based on tutorial-type situations with deaf youngsters alone or in small groups before creating larger educational programs (see Branson & Miller, 2002; Groce, 1985; Moores, 2001; Rée, 1999; Van Cleve & Crouch, 1989 for historical reviews). These earlier initiatives were based on visual foundations incorporating manual alphabets or signs, frequently accompanied by ongoing efforts to institute speech.

Branson and Miller (2002) highlight how the political context was instrumental in formulating policy covering the education and treatment of deaf individuals during those early years. As they theorize, the influence of centralized monarchies giving way to more democratic forms of government, often through rebellion, served to promote the ideologies of egalitarianism and individualism. The famed "Paris Banquets," which took place in post-revolutionary France, exemplify the independent living and intellectual thinking of Deaf people at that time (Mottez, 1993; Quartararo, 2008). This proclivity toward lively intellectual discourse was most likely facilitated by the schools established for them prior to, during, and after the French Revolution. These were individuals who had a strong sense of self as Deaf people and were able to advocate to the public their perceptions of what it meant to be Deaf (Quartararo, 2008).

While the emergence of formal education for deaf children fueled a more enlightened treatment of deaf people and greater opportunities for satisfying lives (Lang, 2007), there also emerged a paradoxical movement that created legitimization of inequality for these individuals based on differences in ability and communication (Branson & Miller, 2002). This was created in part by setting deaf people apart from the expected diversity of the human population through labeling them as disabled. For the most part, it was the hearing authority figures, rather than deaf people themselves, who focused on curative treatment and educational approaches that reinforced the legitimization of disability.

THE ROLE OF DEAF SCHOOLS

In the 1700s, families with financial resources sent their deaf children to Europe to be educated, with the earliest schools for deaf children having been established in Britain, France, and Germany (Eriksson, 1993; Moores, 2001). The American Asylum for the Education of the Deaf and Dumb in Connecticut (now the American School for the Deaf), the first permanent formal school for deaf children in the United States, was established in 1817. The school focused on providing not only basic academic subjects but also vocational training, with sign language as the language of instruction.

The founding of successive schools for the deaf in the United States and Europe throughout the 1800s was not without variable levels of conflict, primarily over language and communication issues (Branson & Miller, 2002; Moores, 2001). In addition to disagreement about whether to utilize signed or spoken communication, there was disagreement over which signed approach to take, whether based on the natural language approach, following spoken word order, or utilizing finger-spelling (Burch, 2002). Baynton (1993, 1996) describes how the historical tempo of the times influenced American perceptions of the newly developing theory of evolution, which framed spoken languages as being of a higher order than signed languages. The ultimate outcome was to denigrate sign language as a primitive form of language preceding the more sophisticated oral language, which also insinuated the denigration of deaf people who signed. Spoken language was theoretically viewed as the pathway to a homogenous, assimilated citizenry within a strong nation. The prevailing "isolation" of deaf people from their surrounding hearing communities noted by society was not in line with the ideal of social homogeneity. Therefore, despite strong

objections from coalitions of Deaf people with a strong sense of their
identity and language (Ladd, 2008), spoken language increasingly
began to be idealized as the language to which deaf students should
aspire. This approach was promulgated by hearing propagators,
including Alexander Graham Bell, the inventor of the telephone and
the most famous historical figure supporting oral education. The 1880
International Congress on the Education of the Deaf in Milan, Italy,
where only one of the 164 participants was deaf (Van Cleve & Crouch,
1989), basically confirmed the spread of spoken language education
within schools for the deaf, more so in Europe than in the United States
(Moores, 2001; Rée, 1999; Van Cleve & Crouch, 1989).

In the United States, the majority of programs focused on spoken
English, yet various forms of sign communication unofficially continued to predominate on a variety of campuses (Burch, 2002). Essentially,
it was the educators who set the stage for the either-or dichotomy of
either spoken or sign language and perpetuated the controversy. Deaf
people who valued sign language fought for significant roles in this
controversy (see next section), but their views were marginalized by
authorities who used their professionalism, experience, and hearing
status to advance their positions. Baynton (1996) describes these positions essentially as "metaphorically constructed fantasies" constructed
to deny the Deaf identity and make deaf persons something that they
were not, that is, hearing (p. 11). The voices of deaf users of sign language were basically downplayed, even though they were the ones
who actually had experiences with which communication or language
worked best and in which surroundings.

Clearly, there had to be examples of deaf speakers in order to galva-
nize the supporters of spoken language. The most typical exemplars
were those who were adventitiously deafened after having mastered
spoken language as well as those who were hard of hearing or with
audiometrically sufficient hearing to capitalize on fragments of speech
with the assistance of mechanical devices, such as ear trumpets and
rudimentary predecessors of group amplification that emerged during
the late 1800s and early 1900s (Burch, 2002; Connor, 1992; Rée, 1999). This
group included such individuals as Mabel Hubbard, the future wife of
Alexander Graham Bell, who lost her hearing at age 4 and recalled her
discomfort when she first saw deaf people using sign language (Rée,
1999). She did not want to be called deaf, rejected deaf as an identity,
and avoided deaf people (Nielsen, 2006). Leo Connor (1992) notes that
in 1924–1925 roughly 50% of the pupils at the Lexington School for the
Deaf, a long-standing oral school in New York City, "would currently
be called 'hard of hearing' or 'mildly to moderately impaired'" (p. 53).
There were rare examples of those who were deaf before starting to
talk, keeping in mind their practically nonexistent access to the sounds
of spoken language except perhaps through tactile means. The most

notable of these rare examples included Helen Heckman, a success-ful dancer (Burch, 2002), and Helen Keller, who was deaf and blind (Nielsen, 2006).

These examples of oral success rarely if ever attained speech that sounded as if the speaker had normal hearing (Rée, 1999). Leo Connor (1992) acknowledged the difficulties in providing lipreading and speech development to Lexington School enrollees who were age 7 or older. School reports indicated progress in reading and writing more than in spoken language, though its success is implied by the increasing num-ber of pupils placed by satisfied parents. Despite the efforts of these pupils, ongoing barriers (variable quality of speech and speechreading skills) that limited the potential for meaningful interactions with hear-ing peers reinforced their tendencies to gravitate to and identify with others like themselves, reasons that were essentially similar to students in signing educational environments. There were some exceptions, such as Ernest Calkins, a successful writer who saw deaf people as socially inferior and attacked sign language (Burch, 2002). Baynton (1996) directs our attention to the finding that even oral deaf adults themselves did not wholeheartedly support the oral movement in the late 1800s. Specifically, they acknowledged the limitations of oral communication in facilitating easy interaction within larger hearing contexts. Many who were identified as hard of hearing were often caricatured and margin-alized because of their loud voices and the need to have people speak loudly to them. Consequently, they were likely more lonely than most. This probably was also compounded by their lack of connection with any similar constituency. However, there were a good number of hard-of-hearing as well as late-deafened individuals who associated with the Deaf cultural world and found a home where their hearing defi-ciency assumed far less importance as witnessed those who assumed leadership roles, particularly within the National Association of the Deaf (NAD, see the section on Socialization below) (Burch, 2002).

Deaf education in the 1800s was predominantly residential, primar-ily due to the lack of rapid travel and the dispersal of deaf students over wide areas, which made daily commutes to school impossible. The ostensible goal of these schools was to facilitate assimilation into mainstream society through providing students with the tools to do so (Burch, 2002). The result, however, was the opposite. The ongoing intimate interactions of the students within residential schools, both oral- and sign-based, became a major historical force in the coalescing of the deaf community (Burch, 2002; Rée, 1999; Van Cleve & Crouch, 1989). These students developed and reinforced socialization patterns with deaf peers and carried those patterns with them as they migrated out of the schools into areas where they could maintain their school social connections and affirm their identity as deaf people. This trend held even as urbanization spread and day schools with the mission of preparing their students for interactions with hearing peers opened to serve urban deaf students. Many urban students did not move far away after graduation or leaving school. Their proximity to each other and their well-forged school ties served to carry their cohesiveness beyond the school years. Such cohesiveness also enabled deaf people to pull together in the decades-long fight not only to organize political support for sign language in the schools (Baynton, 1996), but also to lobby against discriminatory laws and achieve social welfare goals, such as a home for the aged deaf constituency (Boyd & Van Cleve, 2007). As such, these long-term coalitions reflected how the schools were not only formative educationally but also culturally and socially in creating communities that met the need for social identity and converting deaf people into activists.

Even though there is a great deal of sentiment for the residential or specialized schools of the past, these settings were not always as romantic as they have been characterized. The closed nature of the residential school experience created opportunities for excessive regimentation, cruel treatment at the hands of harsh houseparents, sexual abuse, and hierarchies of status (Padden & Humphries, 2005; Plann, 2008; Valentine, 1993). All of these present the dark underside of Deaf cultural history, an underside that has received insufficient historical scrutiny until recently. Nonetheless, even with the negative experiences, imprinting of deaf identities was part of the school experience, reinforcing as it did a sense of belonging to a communal group, in contrast to the typical isolating experiences outside the school (Padden & Humphries, 2005). This early imprinting is now changing, however, due in large part to the social force of inclusion (see Chapter 4).

It is important to recognize that the schools did not function in a vacuum. They were greatly influenced by religious and social forces that shaped not only surrounding societal perceptions of deaf and hard-of-hearing people but also their identities.

RELIGIOUS AND SOCIAL FORCES

Religious Influence

The role of religion in fostering the emergence of deaf education and, in turn, the coalescing of deaf identities is considerable. Starting with Spanish Catholic monks in the 1500s and proceeding to European and American Protestant clergy, a major motivation for establishing educational programs was to provide deaf students with access to religion and redemption (Moores, 2001; Van Cleve & Crouch, 1989). Congregating in schools for the deaf and eventually in religious and social settings brought deaf people together in a search for mutuality and affirmation.

During the 1800s and well into the 1900s, residential school administrators required chapel services and religious classes for their deaf students (Burch, 2002). These services, often run by deaf ministers, were usually conducted in sign language. Specialized services were even endorsed by oral supporters to bring religion to their deaf constituents, particularly because it was impractical to speechread speakers on stage while sitting in pews. The prevailing ethos of the signed services was that deaf people had been created by God and sign language was a means of direct access to religious doctrine. These services also benefitted deaf adults outside of the schools not only by affording them religious participation but also by linking them with deaf students; in turn, this encouraged the perpetuation of deaf societies and strong Deaf identity centered on sign language. Furthermore, religious services conducted by influential congregations, such as the Chicago Mission for the Deaf, which was established in the late 1800s, counteracted the sense of marginality in communication many deaf people felt in other nonschool spheres of their lives. These services provided opportunities for connecting religious values with political initiatives related to, for example, the efforts to preserve sign language in the face of ascending oralism, thereby enhancing deaf community cohesiveness (Olney, 2007). The Chicago Mission for the Deaf was managed by deaf members of faith who were able to perpetuate the coherence of Deaf community identity and the relevance of sign language through their ability to attract a broad spectrum of deaf congregants (Olney, 2007). According to Burch (2002), such deaf religious organizations reinforced a sense of normality parallel with hearing religious offerings and simultaneously afforded deaf congregants a unique sense of identity. She defines this movement as part of organized resistance to hearing and oral value domination.

Socialization

Social functions organized by deaf people themselves provided opportunities for setting their own agendas and creating comfortable communication zones (Mottez, 1993). These functions included, for example, a plethora of banquets, deaf club activities, conventions, athletic events, and self-help and literary societies (Burch, 2002; Mottez, 1993; Stewart, 1991/1993; Van Cleve & Crouch, 1989). Oralists and manualists had their own organizations (Padden & Humphries, 2005; S. Robinson, 2006; Van Cleve & Crouch, 1989) that served as venues for deaf women and men to interact in comfort with "extended families" and find marriage partners. Even during the eras when schools turned to the oral philosophy as a way of assimilating into the hearing world, deaf people, whether oral or signing, continued to marry each other at a rate of approximately 90% (Baynton, 1996; Rée, 1999).

These organizations, which provide examples of affinity for "their own kind," whether signing or oral, represent a strong sense of identity and cohesiveness that goes beyond the basic physical needs for survival. Hearing participants were often excluded so that deaf members could maintain a sense of autonomy and control and could have a safe haven for sharing common experiences and concerns about hearing society (Burch, 2002; Lane, Hoffmeister, & Bahan, 1996; Rée, 1999; Van Cleve & Crouch, 1989).

In the United States, the founding of the NAD in 1880 was a national effort to articulate positions relevant to the various discriminatory social forces affecting the lives of deaf people, including but not limited to education, language choice, employment, and politics (Van Cleve & Crouch, 1989). The NAD and localized special interest organizations demonstrated that deaf people could advocate for common interests, particularly related to what they felt worked in their own lives.

Susan Burch (2002) has suggested that over and beyond the sense of affinity, these Deaf organizations centered on the use of sign language also can be viewed as an example of resistance to dominant hearing values. These groups reflected a Deaf sense of normality that contradicted the hearing push for assimilation framed within an oralist philosophy (Burch, 2002). Although access to spoken language with hearing families and peers tended to be limited during these times, due in part to inadequate technology, deaf people did not support the opposing view that their organizations perpetuated the narrowness of deaf people's lives by limiting their access to full participation in the larger society. However, the societal ideal of homogeneity in the interest of assimilation served to downplay the critical contributions of deaf coalitions to hearing outsiders, namely how identifying with their own groups actually expanded their worlds through communication access.

Sports organizations exclusively for deaf athletes became a passion for many, not only participants but also spectators (Burch, 2002; Stewart, 1991/1993). Not only did these provide venues to exhibit the athletic competency of deaf participants comparable to those of mainstream athletes; they also provided opportunities for socialization, camaraderie, and identity reaffirmation. Deaf sports countered the notion of bodily deafness as an infirmity often perpetuated by outsiders, most specifically by demonstrating skill and coordination in ways that defied the notion of broken bodies and broken ears. Additionally, deaf sports circumvented both the need to confront the typical hearing misapprehensions of bodily infirmity and the usual difficulties in communicating with hearing team members and coaches. Deaf sports reflected the self-determination of deaf people in organizing and participating in sports events and, in turn, pride in deaf abilities.

A significant exception to this trend of exclusive deaf communities, however, occurred on the island of Martha's Vineyard, Massachuesetts, where from the late 1600s to the late 1800s deaf people intermingled with their hearing counterparts (Groce, 1985; Lane, Pillard, & French, 2000). Apparently, hearing residents were bilingual in the local sign language and their native English and therefore could easily communicate with their deaf peers. Nora Groce (1985) could not find any evidence that the deaf were set apart as a group. Rather, because "everyone here spoke sign language,"* deaf people were treated as individuals, and their being deaf was typically described as an afterthought rather than as a primary identifier. However, whether this was consistently the case is subject to debate.

More recently, researchers have identified various hearing-deaf signing communities. For example, indigenous sign languages shared by hearing and deaf members have been found in the Al-Sayyid group, a Bedouin community in Israel's Negev Desert going back approximately 200 years (Kisch, 2003; Sandler, Meir, Padden, & Aronoff, 2005) as well as in Desa Kolok, a village in Bali, Indonesia, with deaf and hearing inhabitants going back multiple generations in living memory (Branson, Miller, & Marsaja, 1996). In these communities, there are no apparent significant boundaries to deaf–hearing social interaction. Deafness is perceived as a natural occurrence and therefore as part of life. Deaf members appear to be as equally valued as hearing members and are continually involved in communication. Social labeling in the interest of differentiating deaf and hearing members is not prominent, nor is concern about dealing with a child identified as deaf. In these situations, deaf identities do not come to the fore as much as they do in situations where differentness and "other" are more salient and hearing persons have minimal exposure to deaf persons.

Groce (1985, 2003) claims that the Vineyard experience buttresses claims that descriptions of deaf people as having a handicap or disability is an arbitrary social construct that emerges when deaf people are not perceived as equal. When the environment is accommodating, as indicated by the Martha's Vineyard, Desa Kolok, and the Al-Sayyid groups, deaf becomes a simple human characteristic that differentiates one from the other, similarly to the role of other characteristics, such as quickness in intelligence, rather than as a deficit to be stigmatized. Considering this, it seems that the predominant perspective of genuine equality may work against the need to assert any form of deaf identity.

The historical deaf organizations and Deaf communities of past years have given way to other forces creating associations for advocacy, recreational and social service, and professional interests. Padden and Humphries (2005) ascribe this evolution not only to technological changes but also to the increasing professionalization of deaf people,

* This quote is the exact Groce (1985) book title.

which created a deaf middle class, thereby creating new tensions between professional and nonprofessional individuals. Increasing crime in the vicinity of deaf clubs also contributed to this decline, since economics prevented a move to safer locations. Socialization is now mainstream in the guise of rented space and public places, such as restaurants and Internet chatrooms. Despite the changing faces of socialization, the gravitation toward d/Deaf venues continues, albeit in different ways (see, for example, Chapter 8).

EMPLOYMENT

In American society, jobs are a critical identity determinant. For deaf people, being employed meant assuming an egalitarian identity that demonstrated their normalcy as contributing citizens of society. However, Buchanan (1999) describes this as *Illusions of Equality* (the title of his book). Why is that?

Education is a critical key to job development, career mobility, and socioeconomic status. With the advent of post–Civil War industrialization, deaf advocates increasingly argued for more advanced vocational training to enhance not only the prestige but also the competitiveness of deaf graduates for existing skilled labor work. This was particularly critical to convince dubious hearing employers of the capability of deaf workers, thereby reinforcing attempts to achieve equality in the face of overt discrimination. Starting in the latter half of the 1800s, while schools for the deaf assumed responsibility for academic education, they also increasingly assumed responsibility for vocational training to ensure the employability of deaf graduates (e.g., Buchanan, 1999; Burch, 2002; Van Cleve & Crouch, 1989), particularly in the areas of farming, tailoring, shoemaking, and printing. This inadvertently further fostered the development of culturally Deaf cohesiveness, since most of the vocational teachers were deaf (Burch, 2002). Those with more advanced education obtained at Gallaudet College (now University, established in 1864) tended to end up in vocational teaching or support staff positions.

In 1906, with new Civil Service employment guidelines prohibiting the hiring of deaf applicants, deaf leaders successfully organized to have this discriminatory clause removed in the interest of fair treatment of capable deaf workers. This event presaged ongoing endeavors to minimize persistent exclusion from application pools, even one for a Depression-era public works project (Buchanan, 1999). Ironically, both World War I and II provided boom times for deaf employees due to the need for war material and workers to replace those on war duty, but paradoxically their employability continued to be questioned during and after war time, even with the documentation of impeccable work histories. There were always newly emerging naïve hearing employers who subscribed to stereotypical perceptions of deaf men, women, and minority individuals as less intelligent and less capable. The only recourse was that of ongoing pioneering advocacy efforts by deaf individuals eager to break barriers and affirm positive attributes to being deaf rather than subscribe to prevailing negative perspectives. That such barriers hold true to this day is reinforced by research indicating that employer attitudes continue to be seriously problematic, even in the face of qualified deaf or hard-of-hearing workers (Dobie & Van Hemel, 2005).

These barriers were true not only for blue-collar work but also for professional employment. Success stories of deaf pioneers breaking through professional barriers abound, with examples in medicine, law, science, academia, the arts, and so on (e.g., Gannon, 1981; Lang & Meath-Lang, 1995). This attests to the determination of deaf individuals who were eager to dispel the perceived limitations of deaf people and create more diversified job-related identities, thereby strengthening the positive attributes of having a deaf identity. These stories notwithstanding, barriers continued to be erected. For example, Philip Zazove (1993) applied to numerous medical schools. Despite the existence of eminent predecessors who were deaf, not one school accepted him, yet his friends with lower grades and test scores were accepted. At long last, with persistence, he was accepted into one school and is currently a successful medical doctor and researcher. Such struggles magnify the existence of inequality, which forces deaf people to repeatedly "prove themselves" despite the illusion of equality.

On the other hand, it is sobering to acknowledge the 44% high school drop-out rate for deaf students, particularly when this percentage is compared with the 19% drop-out rate for the general population (Blanchfield, Feldman, Dunbar, & Gardner, 2001). In addition to exacerbating socioeconomic disadvantages, this of course is a subtle de-valuator of deaf identity and capability. Students who do not complete their education form an underclass of individuals who are increasingly isolated from the opportunities available to the educated deaf. This difference of experience can divide these two groups and make finding areas of commonality increasingly difficult. This situation requires careful attention from an education field already struggling with language and communication methodology, mainstreaming strategies, and ever-increasing immigration populations of deaf students.

EUGENICS

In the late 1800s, studies on the breeding of animals and plants led to the formation of a new area of study: eugenics (see Branson & Miller, 2002; Burch, 2002; Arnos, 2002 for brief reviews). This field ultimately focused on human heredity and how to refine the genetic pool with the goal of increasing the "fitness" of the human race. In considering the implications for deaf people, both prominent oralist Alexander Graham Bell and Edward Miner Gallaudet, president of Gallaudet College during the time when Bell held sway, were concerned about deaf marriages and the potential for perpetuating the deaf condition and self-segregationist way of life (Branson & Miller, 2002; Winefield, 1987). Based on inadequate existing information about genetic transmission, various pieces of legislation that permitted the sterilization of "potential carriers," including the insane, feebleminded, or criminal, were passed in the United States during the early 1900s. These laws were further supported by two U.S. Supreme Court decisions, one in 1927 and the other in 1931 (Friedlander, 2002).

Despite efforts to demonstrate their abilities as good citizens, deaf people often were stereotypically labeled "deaf and dumb" and socially inadequate, thereby fueling their classification with the undesirable or unfit and reinforcing intimidations of shame at being deaf. One victim of this legislation was an African American deaf man, Junius Wilson, castrated in 1932 and involuntarily hospitalized for most of his life. He was deemed mentally defective and unable to comprehend that he was accused of rape . This was due, in part, to the fact that his unique signing dialect was unfamiliar to those working with deaf people at that time (Burch & Joyner, 2007).

Nonetheless, even at the height of the U.S. eugenics movement, deaf people generally were not subject to anti-marriage or sterilization laws due to advocacy and educational efforts. Bell did not support such laws to limit the freedom of deaf people. Rather, he preferred other means to limit increasing the genetic potential for deaf offspring, such as reducing the number of residential schools where deaf people learned to congregate with each other and supporting hearing–deaf rather than deaf–deaf marriages. Brian Greenwald (2004), a Deaf historian, argues that Bell may have indirectly helped the deaf community by not lending support to potentially drastic measures advocated by those supporters of negative eugenics. The NAD also passed resolutions pertaining to the right of deaf people to marry, but during one period they actually encouraged congenitally deaf people to avoid marrying each other (Burch, 2002).

The most adverse consequence of socially constructing disability as unfit and stigmatizing deaf identity emerged in the guise of Nazi Germany's ultimate solution (see Biesold, 1999; Ryan & Schuchman, 2002 for reviews). Subsequent to the 1933 Law for the Prevention of Offspring with Hereditary Diseases and a 1934 manifesto (Lietz, 2002), deaf Germans could never be full citizens "but merely German subjects" due to communication barriers. Because it was necessary to sacrifice for the good of the State, the stage was set for the secretly planned extermination of "lives unworthy of life" or, in other words, unfit people. Deaf people were forbidden to marry, and sterilization of deaf people was legitimatized. Deaf persons were collapsed with those with mental or psychiatric disabilities and subject to euthanasia as part of the notorious T-4 program, which was an experimental predecessor of the death camps. Health care professionals and teachers of the deaf colluded in reporting deaf people for sterilization and deportation to certain death.

German deaf people were a proud group who had been viewed as leaders by deaf international groups. The Nazi banning of a film depicting a strong German deaf citizenry that counteracted the defective image of deaf people (*Verkannte Menschen*, 1932, translated as *Misjudged People* [Schuchman, 2002]) and the subsequent sterilization policies conveyed a strong message that deaf Germans were genetically diseased and unfit to exist. This presaged a deep shame that continued after the war as the survivors entered into an unacknowledged and pained conspiracy of silence to perpetuate a façade of normalcy. Only when Biesold (1999), a professional deaf educator and sign language interpreter, won their trust and learned of their stories, was this silence broken. Their ongoing contacts within deaf groups speak to their affinity for their deaf identity and their comfort in associating with other deaf people despite the earlier shame visited upon them.

Many deaf persons perished in the maelstrom of the Holocaust, mostly because they were Jewish. Those who survived, including the Hungarian deaf persons interviewed by Ryan and Schuchman (2002), often found their way to deaf communities. Despite his horrendous experiences in Hungary, Harry Dunai, who ended up in California (Dunai, 2002), adamantly proclaimed, "I am deaf and I'm proud of it" (p. 176).

In the United States, the eugenics movement lost appeal as the results of the Nazi policy and its cruel aftermath became evident to the public. With the advent of genetic technology (see Chapter 8), however, the specter of eugenics has recently been revitalized. This time eugenics assumes the guise of eliminating perceived defects together with their associated and assumed negative quality of life.

Another consequence of eugenics, less often mentioned in the literature referring to deaf history, was that of immigration policy. Exclusionary policies in the United States dating back to 1882 with the intent of keeping out undesirable elements were gradually expanded to include persons with disabilities. The government framed these individuals as a threat to the physical and intellectual integrity of the American citizenry and deemed them as likely to become a burdensome charge (Baynton, 2005). This had a profound influence on deaf people wishing to enter the United States (Baynton, 2006). Deaf people with American sponsors who could guarantee financial support managed to be released from Ellis Island, the former immigration gateway to the United States and a holding station for those with questionable status; the rest were sent back to their home countries, never to be heard of again. Lilly Rattner Shirey tells of being detained in Ellis Island for 5 months during the year 1940 after escaping the Nazi occupation of Austria because her deaf family, who could not be shipped back to Austria due to wartime conditions, was financially unable to post the bond and was seen as a potential social burden (Baynton, 2006). Even as late as 1948, I myself as a 4-year-old deaf child with a British passport, having been born in England to hearing parents who were refugees from the Nazi Germany regime and therefore stateless, was briefly detained on Ellis Island as a potential "burden to the U.S. government." Fortunately, U.S. immigration policy no longer disqualifies deaf immigrants from entering the country based on their being deaf.

Branson and Miller (1998, 2002) report that Australian immigration policy incorporated prohibitions preventing deaf people from entering the country starting in the middle of the nineteenth century. Unfortunately, current prohibitions appear to continue in altered form. The 1993 amendments to the immigration policy are concerned both with individual requirements for significant care and/or treatment and the potential for being unable to work and becoming a significant charge on public funds. Branson and Miller (1998) note a trace of eugenics in one of the public interest criteria related to immigration policy, which indicates that if the applicant harbors a disease or condition that might affect future offspring, this could be grounds for rejecting the immigration application of a deaf person (p. 92). Such actions serve to reinforce the undesirability of deaf status in the eyes of a society often unwilling to accommodate diversity in hearing differences.

ENTERTAINMENT AND MEDIA

There is a tradition of film and literary portrayals of deaf people as isolated, ignorant, lonely, or the butt of jokes, reinforced by books such as Carson McCullers' *The Heart Is a Lonely Hunter.* Deaf characters were dumb, to be ridiculed. Or they were perfect speechreaders. Even in the silent film era, with rare exceptions deaf actors were not included, not even in deaf roles. The entry of sound did not change the stereotypical perception of the deaf person; it basically added the notion of the deaf person as a perfect speaker in the guise of hearing actors taking on deaf roles that included speaking.* Deaf people themselves decried how they were portrayed. They felt that these portrayals reinforced stereotypes of deaf persons as limited human beings (Schuchman, 1988).

* For details related to deaf people in entertainment, see Schuchman, J. (1988). Hollywood speaks. Urbana, IL: University of Illinois Press.

Schuchman credits the film *Johnny Belinda* (1948), in which hearing actress Jane Wyman delivered an Oscar-winning performance as a deaf nonspeaking woman, with finally portraying a nuanced deaf person who evolves from being perceived as a dummy to being perceived as a human being with natural thoughts and feelings. Subsequent breakthrough productions, such as the Broadway play *Miracle Worker* (1960) and its movie version (1962), which told the story of how Anne Sullivan worked to introduce deaf and blind Helen Keller to language, impressed the humanity of deaf persons on the public mind. These productions among others initiated the use of sign language and a more positive portrayal of deaf persons in entertainment media.

However, of concern was that the practice of engaging hearing actors to portray deaf characters insidiously belittled the capabilities of deaf actors. What hearing entertainment professionals did not know or accept was that deaf people themselves had a history of self-initiated acting traditions for theatrical and entertainment purposes (Baldwin, 1993). The NAD films of the early 1900s were produced to advance the cause of sign language, and there are sign language motion pictures for the deaf community dating back to 1902 (Schuchman, 1988, 2004).

As deaf actors continued to be excluded from prime mainstream entertainment roles, deaf people began to complain about inaccurate portrayals of themselves. Unbeknownst to the hearing public, these portrayals often projected an artificial image of how sign language was conveyed, which was quite obvious to deaf signers (Schuchman, 1988). However, deaf people themselves were for the most part grateful for the improved portrayal of nuanced signing deaf characters, although the lack of captioning precluded full access to sound film dialogue.

With the founding of the National Theater of the Deaf (NTD) in 1966, deaf actors were finally afforded a consistent opportunity for professional work. Joint deaf–hearing performances, in which hearing actors voiced what the deaf actors signed, were successful (Baldwin, 1993). The NTD was responsible for further introducing sign language and deaf people to a national hearing audience and improving awareness of Deaf lives.

Another entertainment breakthrough came in 1971 when Linda Bove, who was deaf, did her first *Sesame Street* stint on national television. By achieving a significant role in the 1978 cast of the highly successful Broadway musical *Runaways*, Bruce Hlibok showed that deaf actors had acting abilities equal to hearing actors. A deaf community protest against the exclusion of deaf actors began in 1979 when the film *Voices* cast a hearing actress in a deaf role (Schuchman, 1988). On Broadway, *Children of a Lesser God* (1980) engaged deaf actors for each deaf character, and deaf actress Phyllis Frelich won a Tony for her portrayal of Sarah, the main protagonist. The resounding success of this play culminated in a movie (1986) featuring deaf actress Marlee Matlin, whose Oscar-winning performance as Sarah reflected the strong influence deaf actors could have in entertainment media. Following that, the Emmy for best drama was awarded to the 1986 production of *Love Is Never Silent*, which focused on the lives of a Deaf couple struggling to raise hearing children.

All of these performances helped to reinforce the construct of deaf in the public eye, and they provided a positive valence of a signing Deaf identity. More productions followed: films such as *Four Weddings and a Funeral* and *Mr. Holland's Opus*; television productions such as *The West Wing, Star Trek,* and *Reasonable Doubts*; and theater showings such as Deaf West Theater's successful national production of *Big River* (starting in 2001) under the auspices of Deaf artistic director/producer Ed Waterstreet, which was the first deaf musical to have a Broadway run. Waterstreet included both Deaf and hearing actors, with the former using American Sign Language (ASL) in conjunction with speaking actors.

While these changes presaged greater acceptance of deaf people as individuals with full lives, the message that they are part of a vibrant community of Deaf people has rarely been emphasized. Although *Children of a Lesser God* and *Mr. Holland's Opus* briefly acknowledge this aspect, the only notable exception is the 1998 German film *Beyond Silence*, featuring Howie Seago of the United States and Emmanuelle Laborit of France as the deaf parents of a hearing child (Smith, 1998). Of particular significance is a segment portraying a large contingent of deaf worshipers signing the liturgy during a church service.

Despite this renaissance, which has introduced Deaf lives to the larger hearing community, mainstream journalism continues to de-affirm deaf identities. By marginalizing and medicalizing what deafness represents, the media generally reinforces the perception of a regretful adversity to be overcome or corrected, a negative state of affairs, a disability (Baynton, 1996). This message continues even in conjunction with the paradoxical idealizing of Deaf culture and the positive representation of the Deaf President Now (DPN) movement (Haller, 1993; see next section for a brief discussion of DPN), the proliferation of ASL classes, and the increasing number of Deaf Studies programs in colleges and high schools throughout the United States, which the news media reports with a touch of fascination. Articles such as *Signing and Dancing to Showcase a "Different World"* (M. Robinson, 2006, p. 5) focus on the novelty of using movement to introduce "Language of Deaf to the Hearing" high school students, a concept Deaf people have used for ages.

Media dissemination of well-known deaf persons and how they communicate has the power to influence public perceptions of deaf identities. Even though Marlee Matlin is an experienced signer and had signed her entire way through the film *Children of a Lesser God*, she was vilified by Deaf writers who saw her speaking on television when she presented at the Academy Awards (Loohauis, 1999). This action implied endorsement of speech over sign and denigration of a Deaf cultural identity, even though Matlin perceives both speech and sign as expressions of herself. Heather Whitestone McCallum, the 1995 winner of the Miss America pageant, which is televised annually, and the first deaf Miss America, became an inspiration to many deaf children and their parents. Since she relies on speaking in preference to sign language, she was not embraced by the Deaf community even though she knows sign language. Both women clearly have proudly striven to achieve fulfilling lives as deaf women in the public eye, portraying different facets of deaf identities and remaining true to themselves.

THE 1988 DEAF PRESIDENT NOW MOVEMENT

Much has been written about the role of Gallaudet University's 1988 Deaf President Now movement and its repercussions in the lives of deaf people (e.g., Christiansen & Barnartt, 1995; Gannon, 1989; Jankowski, 1997; Shapiro, 1993). Briefly, the university campus erupted after the Board of Trustees selected a hearing candidate for the presidency over two deaf finalists. Since its establishment in 1864, there had never been a deaf president, an irony for a higher institution setting dedicated to the educational advancement of its deaf students. The message was that deaf people could not assume leadership positions in a complex society. The weeklong movement, publicized worldwide through television and newsprint, rejected the stance of the Board of Trustees vote and pressed forward until the hearing candidate resigned and I. King Jordan, an adventitiously deafened individual, was elevated to the presidency. He rose to the challenge and subsequently become a national and international icon.

This historical movement, which essentially reflected the effort of a marginalized group to celebrate their uniqueness and overthrow the status quo, in this case hearing dominance, has created strong symbolic visibility. It had its antecedents in earlier social protests focusing on, for example, TV captioning access, inadequate access to higher education within the mainstream, and increased administrative influence in organizations for d/Deaf people going all the way back to the 1800s (Barnartt & Scotch, 2001; Humphries, 2004; Jankowski, 1997; Shapiro, 1993). The resulting expansion of, for example, civil rights legislation mandating communication access in higher education and on the job, the creation of formal sign language interpreting services, and advances in telecommunications facilitated the expression of a positive Deaf identity that found its voice in the Deaf President Now protest, which generated pride in being part of a Deaf social movement

(Maxwell-McCaw, 2001). There was validation that "Deaf" could reflect empowerment, solidarity, pride in the use of ASL, and the mastery of political action to achieve goals. In psychotherapy, it became easier to encourage deaf clients previously too embarrassed to sign in public to take pride in using ASL in public areas and overtly identify themselves as deaf (Leigh & Lewis, 1999).

At its very essence, the history of deaf people and the Deaf President Now protest serve to reflect how the socially framed undercurrent of deaf as defect and deficiency played to societal notions of hearing superiority in all domains of life, a superiority that could not subjugate the desire of a people for positive frames of their deaf identities. The next chapter provides an opportunity to further analyze how deaf and hard-of-hearing individuals are treated by society and their ability to cope with all too common experiences of discrimination and oppression.

6

Stigma, Oppression, Resilience, and Deaf Identities

Don't laugh at me
Don't call me names.
        Shanna Sorrells (2006, B21)

To Deaf People:
The most misunderstood among the sons of men,
But the gamest of all.
        Harry Best (1943, p. v) (with apologies for gender)

Despite the significant achievements of deaf individuals over the years and the popularization of studies focusing on d/Deaf people, life continues to be tough at times because the mainstream perceives deaf people as "different." To be different in ways that do not fit society's expectations of acceptability, to be part of a minority group, to communicate in a unique way, often generates negative reactions. Those experiences will shape how individuals feel about being deaf and how they determine their deaf or hard-of-hearing identities.

When I was a child, hearing people stared at me as I gestured with deaf friends on public buses. An experienced high school teacher of the deaf told me that I, as a 13-year-old high school entrant, could not handle the academically challenging classes my elementary school principal had recommended for me merely because I was deaf. The admissions director at the university I wanted to attend was forceful in telling me that I, as a deaf student, did not deserve admission even though my qualifications were superior to those of peers in my high school who had been accepted. I never saw a deaf teacher while growing up and did not encounter an inspirational adult deaf role model until my college years. On a job interview long after I had completed my doctorate, the interviewer explicitly questioned my proficiency in written English based on his expectation of inadequate English for deaf persons.

In addition to having grown up in proximity to deaf peers, these stereotypical reactions, which have remained in my psyche as experiential scars, fostered my connection to "us deaf people." Considering social identity theory and identification with minority groups (see Chapter 2), I asserted my proud minority deaf identity as a means of dealing with discrimination and threats to my integrity (also see Phinney, 2002 for a brief review). Others have shared similar experiences, such as Shanna Sorrells (2006), a deaf eighth grader, who was ridiculed and taunted by her classmates. Yet Shanna ultimately triumphed by writing the winning entry in a high school student essay contest related to human rights.

WHY THE STRUGGLE?

Even though we do have enlightened individuals among us, such as my elementary school principal, who not only affirmed notions of true equality between deaf people and their hearing peers but also backed up these notions with actions, narratives about d/Deaf lives too often reverberate with themes of isolation, tension, and struggle. These themes more often than not owe their existence to those who construct deafness as a tragedy, harbor stereotypical and limited expectations of adults with hearing differences, and attempt to integrate children with hearing differences into the mainstream without appropriate social skills or social support. They are blind to their inequitable treatment of such individuals despite overt support of equality for all (Branson & Miller, 2002). Their actions represent a conflict of values, perspective, and identity between them and the group they are stigmatizing (Gill, 2001). This creates internal conflict for those caught in the journey toward internalizing what it means to have a hearing difference or be d/Deaf.

Branson and Miller (2002) focus on the concept of normality as the culprit responsible for the pathologizing of deaf and hard-of-hearing individuals. The framing of deaf and hard of hearing as a disability, innocuous and obvious as it may appear to be for the general population, has had the unfortunate consequence of stigmatizing and marginalizing deaf children and adults, reinforcing the concept of difference as deviance instead of as a part of diversity in the human condition (Marschark, Lang, & Albertini 2002). Attitudinal barriers exist not only in the guise of lackadaisical or oppositional responses to the feasibility of alleviating environmental barriers but also, and more damaging, in the guise of limited academic and occupational achievement expectations for deaf students. These negative attitudes are based in large part on communication and safety issues as well as the lack of understanding about hearing difference issues (Baynton, 1996; Punch, Hyde, & Creed, 2004; Punch, Hyde, & Power, 2007).

The perception of disability is a long-standing one. Even during the age of the famous Paris Banquets run by prominent Deaf persons, deaf people were often seen as "incomplete" (Mottez, 1993). In the 1800s, while deaf teachers were hired, they were not accorded the status of their hearing white male peers and suffered inequities in pay and promotion (Baynton, 1996; Branson & Miller, 2002; Moores, 2001; Van Cleve & Crouch, 1989). In fact, they were sometimes seen as "good enough" for poor students who could not afford better (Branson & Miller, 2002). Few obtained positions of authority, and none sat on school governing boards (Baynton, 1996). Lennard Davis (2000) reports that his deaf parents "knew" they had to prove they were equal to hearing peers in various spheres of their lives. Social workers have shown a hearing, ethnocentric bias in selecting hearing parents over Deaf parents when considering fitness to adopt a deaf child, primarily because of concerns about the child's spoken language development, notwithstanding the fact that Deaf parents often are experts in teaching deaf children how to navigate the world of communication (White, 2001).

When I was growing up, the thought that deaf people could become medical doctors was as far-fetched as sending someone to Mars. But unbeknownst to me, there were individuals like Donald Ballantyne, Ph.D. (Lang & Meath-Lang, 1995), who was determined to challenge that perception. He attempted to gain entry to medical school in the 1940s based on impeccable premedical credentials but gave up after repeated rejections solely because he was deaf. After obtaining a Ph.D. in animal biology, he eventually became a renowned professor of experimental surgery at New York University Medical Center with expertise in skin and organ transplants. In fact, he trained surgeons in microsurgical techniques for plastic surgery.

In short, deaf and hard-of-hearing people like Dr. Ballantyne and others who fought for equal opportunities have achieved despite almost insurmountable obstacles. Why do people create such obstacles, which can lead to stigmatization and marginalization? And from where does the desire to overcome these obstacles originate in deaf people?

These obstacles are based on ignorance and the inability to recognize strengths in view of communication and linguistic mismatches. The irony of hearing difference is that it is a condition whose invisibility becomes visible when communication takes place and adjustments are necessary, or when a breakdown in communication occurs. Differences in speech quality, variability in receptive communication skills for spoken language, and attempts to communicate with hearing peers via writing or typing on technical devices can cause hearing people to feel uncomfortable. Also, the typical limitations hearing persons have in adjusting to the language and communication needs of their deaf counterparts, including noisy environments, lack of sign language skills, and inattentive listening among others all create potential distancing between deaf and hearing counterparts. This distancing occurs despite the versatility of deaf individuals in attempting to enhance communication. M. J. Bienvenu (2001) is forthright about this: "I don't know many deaf people who would define themselves as 'communication disordered,' yet that is the term many social service agencies and schools use to describe the deaf population with whom they work" (p. 320). Even the U.S. government reinforces this stereotype with its National Institute on Deafness and Other Communication Disorders. Depending on the situation, the repercussions related to perceptions that hearing difference automatically equates communication disorders or implied "can't do" perspectives when that is not necessarily the case can have far-reaching consequences for the saliency of deaf or hard-of-hearing identities.

Back in the 1960s, Leo Jacobs (1974), a prominent Deaf community member, stated that minority group status rather than the hearing loss itself was creating more problems due to the demand of conformity to hearing expectations while ignoring the unique issues of deaf persons. If the minority group is provided with restrictive opportunities generated by limited access to information, which in turn stunts their ability to achieve parity with the majority group, this perpetuates the dominant hearing group's proclivity to reinforce perceptions of the minority group's inferiority.

According to Lennard Davis (2001), the end goal of many identity groups has been that of minimizing disenfranchisement. However, to identify such groups in terms of politics or to focus on outrages perpetuated by the dominant society can be delimiting, since groups are more than just their disenfranchised status. Minority groups have endeavored to place positive emphasis on their minority group status to mobilize members and promote social changes to counteract negative constructs, such as stereotyping, stigma, discrimination, and oppression. At the risk of oversimplifying incredibly complex human dimensions of behavior, in this chapter I will explore these constructs and their influence on deaf identity formation as well as the resilience deaf people exhibit in confronting these negative forces in their lives.

STEREOTYPING, STIGMA, AND DISCRIMINATION

Stereotyping

When deaf people are perceived as "communication disordered," even though they may in fact have mastery of either or both signed and spoken languages, this reflects a stereotyping effect based on ethnocentrism. Stereotyping refers to judgments of individual members of a group that collectively represent agreements or a belief system about that group (Biernat, 2003; Biernat, Eidelman, & Fuegen, 2003; Corrigan, 2004). A contributing factor is that people tend to accentuate the differences between categories and minimize within-category differences (Turner & Onorato, 1999), thereby leading to a "spread" effect within specific categories. Even though some deaf individuals may actually have a communication disorder, the spread effect is so ubiquitous that all deaf people are assumed to have a communication disorder, thereby eliminating the within-category variability.

As belief systems go, stereotypes are not absolute; they shift depending on the situation and the interpretation of the person doing the stereotyping. Journalists very often portray deaf people as lonely and unhappy in their isolation, at least until they observe the excitement and vitality of a Deaf community gathering. An employer may be willing to consider a deaf job applicant. However, if writing is a requirement of the job, the employer may internally assume that the applicant is not sufficiently competent in writing requirements compared to hearing applicants despite clear evidence of grammatically correct spoken English (see my example above). Considering the standard expectation that deaf persons have to go the extra mile to demonstrate equivalency or superiority to hearing peers, all too often deaf people have to contend with a stricter inference standard in demonstrating their abilities.

Self-stereotyping is the process whereby individuals categorize themselves. While it is closely related to identification, it is a relatively stronger causal factor for in-group preference or bias (Schneider, 2004; Turner & Onorato, 1999). As part of this process, when people acknowledge a shared social category affiliation, such as hard of hearing or deaf, they are essentially focusing on similarities with the group as well as contrasts with the out-group, meaning those who hear. People want positive identities, and having the sense that their group affiliation is superior to those in the out-group supports their identification (Schneider, 2004). This often represents more of a preference rather than hostile perceptions of the out-group, although hostile perceptions can be a factor.

There are different levels of self-stereotyping, and different levels of acceptance of that self-stereotyping. When the group is negatively perceived by the individual confronting the group, self-stereotyping may be less likely, but when the devalued attributes of the group are perceived by outsiders as illegitimate or unreasonable, the endorsement of group membership gains positive overtures for identity as the person works to achieve positive self-perception (Schneider, 2004). For example, a person with sudden hearing loss will realize that deaf is now an identifying label, but acceptance of that will be low due to discomfort with the notion of identifying with what they perceive to be an alien group. If that person becomes involved with a group of similar adults who are late deafened and experiences the unfairness of viewing such individuals as less than capable, self-stereotyping moves to a different level and in a positive direction.

Prejudice

Prejudice emerges when, for example, an employer negatively evaluates a deaf applicant based on stereotypical perceptions of writing skills and subsequently discriminates by denying the position to the applicant. In this context, prejudice is a negative evaluation of individuals who are stereotypically mismatched with the requirements of a role in contrast to individuals who appear to be matched (Eagly, 2004), in this case hearing/speaking individuals. A specific group membership can trigger a lower evaluation, thereby contributing to role incongruity prejudice.

More broadly speaking, prejudice consists of affective reactions toward individuals related to their category memberships. These reactions can include pity, envy, contempt, hatred, etc. We are all prejudiced in how we respond to various categories. When prejudice becomes an unjustified use of category information to make judgments about other people, the potential for discrimination heightens (Schneider, 2004). For instance, during the Great Depression years the U.S. government placed deaf people in the unemployable category despite strong evidence of their work safety record (Burch, 2002). As deaf people increasingly aim for upward career mobility tracks, they may be stymied by stereotypical perceptions applying to the collective, not the individual, even in the face of disconfirmatory evidence. These stereotypical perceptions represent barriers to upward mobility against which deaf people go that proverbial extra mile to overcome. Additional categories also are prey to experiences of prejudice, including ethnicity, religion, and sexual orientation among others.

Discrimination

Discrimination represents behavioral responses in the guise of negative action against the out-group or positive action directed at the in-group (Corrigan, 2004; Schneider, 2004). Schneider (2004) mentions disability status as a gray area for discrimination. This is particularly true in reference to job accommodation requirements that may subtly encourage employers to hire those who do not overtly need such accommodations when the disability category masks strengths in specific skill areas.

Phinney (2002) points to visibility and identifiability as salient factors in discrimination as opposed to more subtle identifiers. Additionally, discrimination is reinforced by internalized subtle biases such as, for example, the presence of what we might call "hearing superiority." Ongoing reluctance to hire members of specific categories or provide challenging assignments in the workplace for members of minority groups can be viewed as evidence of subtle or passive-aggressive discrimination (Keener, 2005). In an adolescent identity study, Cole and Edelman (1991) identified being teased by hearing people as one persistent example of stigmatization expressed by their deaf adolescent participants. Such ongoing examples of discrimination focused on "inferiorities" can serve to reinforce group solidarity in terms of shared experiences and shared desires for solutions, though some do disavow such identification in the interest of merging into the larger hearing society. Confirming this inclination to coalesce, Schein (1989) lists five defining factors for Deaf community membership: demography, affiliation, education, milieu, and with relevance to this chapter, alienation in the direction of pulling deaf people away from hearing environments and toward each other.

Stigma

Stigma refers to a discredited attribute or cue that elicits a devalued stereotype (Corrigan, 2004; Dovido, Major, & Crocker, 2000; Goffman, 1963; Schneider, 2004). This can metamorphose into a discredited identity based on society's stereotypical response to what they perceive as one's inadequate attribute. Perceived inadequacies represent a threat to generalized perceptions of normalcy, a threat to be avoided by adhering to what the majority or dominant group defines as acceptable homogeneity.

Issues related to concealibility and the potential for interaction problems are relevant for stigmatized identity (Schneider, 2004). Efforts to conceal the hearing difference reinforce the notion that it is a stigmatizing element (Kent, Furlonger, & Goodrick, 2001). When communication breaks down, for example, in noisy situations, it is the deaf or hard-of-hearing person instead of the hearing person who is perceived as the inadequate one. The hearing person in fact may be just as or more inadequate in helping to overcome the communication conundrum, but he or she is not stigmatized by virtue of belonging to the idealized group. Such situations tend to create awkward feelings on the part of both hearing and deaf/hard-of-hearing communicators, which then may reinforce perceptions of stigma and stereotypical notions about limited deaf and hard-of-hearing communication, hearing communicator limitations notwithstanding. While the interaction may be tinged with compassion for the individual seen to be causing the interaction problem, the preference not to be in that situation reinforces the stigma.

Defining a stigmatized condition depends in large part on the social situation and the values related to that social situation. From a hearing perspective, to be deaf is often not psychologically or socially acceptable (Corker, 1996). As a result, having a clearly articulated positive deaf identity tends *not* to be reinforced when deaf children are isolated from others like them during their early formative years or when a hearing person acquires a hearing loss. It is not the hearing loss that is the stigma. Rather, it is when stigma surrounding the hearing loss is experienced that deaf or hard of hearing as a discredited identity may enter the individual's self-awareness and identity constellation. On this basis, if children are surrounded by similar others, any sense of stigmatization may fade away when they recognize their mutuality.

Discredited identity can be colored by what Corrigan (2004) describes as public stigma or self-stigma. Public stigma refers to societal endorsement of negative stereotyped group attributes, while self-stigma refers to the internalization of the public stigma, or, in other words, internalized oppression (see next section for further discussion). In the face of public stigma, the deaf or hard-of-hearing person can become the disability itself and is therefore derided or devalued by society (Hétu, 1996). If the deaf or hard-of-hearing person agrees, the stigma becomes a self-stigma infused with shame accompanied by self-esteem and self-efficacy problems. This detracts from the possibility of an internal sense of belonging to the larger social group, namely hearing society. The ultimate consequences can involve social rejection, self-isolation, and psychological pain for the person who is perceived as causing the problem.

With this in mind, it is not surprising that some individuals resort to maintaining secrecy about their hearing difference (Kent, Furlonger, & Goodrick, 2001), even though this may lead to heightened stress in the effort to follow discourse, stay on top of things, and appear hearing-oriented. The fear of social stigmatization, being the butt of jokes, and confronting restricted job opportunities and advancement contribute to this denial (Hétu, 1996). Sadly, denial and constant hiding may be viewed as a more acceptable alternative which in fact is harmful because it minimizes the possibility of advocating for oneself and improving communication access through united fronts with other hard-of-hearing or deaf individuals. Unfortunately, indirect forms of discrimination are an unremitting fact of life. Comments such as "Isn't it wonderful that she has a hearing roommate" (which implies the inferiority of having a deaf roommate) only serve to perpetuate this stigma. Consequently, decisions such as whether to inform potential employers of one's hearing status become a minefield of hit and miss in the desire to avoid stereotypical or prejudicial responses. Ultimately it is usually not possible to live a lie, and various situations create the need to decide when to pass and when it is safe to come out, whichever entails less risk.

In the Gregory, Bishop, and Sheldon study (1995; see Chapter 4), fewer parents mentioned that their young adult deaf children attended Deaf clubs compared to the young adults themselves. The authors consider the possibility of public stigma in that the parents who minimized the extent of Deaf club attendance might have preferred not to associate their child with the Deaf club, even though their children had resolved their identity issues through searching for others like themselves rather than internalizing their parents' prejudice. Hétu (1996) argues for the "normalization process" within the stigmatized identities, including hard of hearing as well as deaf, explaining it as the process of joining groups of people with hearing differences and thereby discrediting the stigmatized identity. This will enhance comfort in disclosing to outsiders once the internal sense of comfort with this identity is solidified.

Another fact of life is the existence of institutional discrimination, which occurs when institutions create policies that restrict qualified members of specific groups or favor one group over another, thereby perpetuating stigma (see Schneider, 2004). While restrictive policies may not necessarily be written down, the propensity to reject qualified candidates for consideration based on "potential need for accommodation" and the predicted cost to the institution, no matter how minimal or extensive the requested accommodations are, is a case in point (e.g., Hauser, Maxwell-McCaw, Leigh, & Gutman, 2000). The justificatory argument of threat to the institution's well-being overlooks the potential threat to the ideal of equality for all, thereby underscoring Branson and Miller's (2002) accusation of society as the culprit in reinforcing stigma.

Branson and Miller's (2002) accusation is supported by Nash (2000), who illustrates how social policies intended to counteract the stigma of hearing difference in society may actually result in exclusion depending on how the meaning of stigma is transformed in the interest of supporting the policies. As he explains it, the inadvertent consequence of social policies supporting mandated legislation to increase participation in the mainstream has been to shift stigma from the body, that is, the ears, to the autonomous social self. In other words, having a hearing difference per se is less stigmatized and made acceptable for intermingling within the mainstream. But the consequences of such intermingling can lead to stigmatizing as witness research evidence on the difficulties in hearing–deaf student interactions. Unquestionably, some students will thrive within the mainstream or inclusion setting with expanded opportunities for variations in social as well as academic experiences. Unfortunately, approximately half of the mainstreamed contingent gets tracked into specialized classes or programs (Gallaudet Research Institute, 2006), with severely limited opportunities, thereby being stigmatized not only by their hearing difference but also by being subjected to perceptions that they are unable to conform to hearing academic and cultural expectations and require a different set of restrictive expectations. If these students were in specialized or residential schools, stigma within these settings would recede in terms of hearing status.

Stigma affects not only the individual but the family as well, since the family may have to deal with the impact of the stigma. Preston (1994) remarks on how often hearing children of deaf parents had to explain away the stigmatizing questions and expressions proffered by strangers or suffered the stigmatizing ridicule of their peers because their deaf parents had a different take on language, communication, and behavior. If deafness was normalized such that there were large numbers of deaf people around, then such stigmatizing situations would recede in frequency, as exemplified by communities such as the one on Martha's Vineyard (see Chapter 5).

OPPRESSION

"Oppression" is based on the root of the word, specifically the element "press." "Something pressed is something caught between or among forces and barriers which are so related to each other that jointly they restrain, restrict or prevent the thing's motion or mobility. Mold. Immobilize. Reduce" (Frye, 1996, p. 163). In a nutshell, when options are systematically reduced to the point of deprivation and barriers are erected, oppression ensues. Oppressing others often takes place unconsciously, to the point that it shakes people up when they are told they oppress. The oppressed may acquiesce in order to show it is possible to do the bare minimum, rather than fight to maximize potential. The bind occurs when the individual being oppressed knows she or he can do better but cannot show it. The person with hearing difference is barred from showing potential or is limited in that process, while the hearing person is barred from seeing that potential, even as she or he creates that barrier by internalizing perceptions of inability.

External Oppression

Issues related to the oppression too often experienced by deaf and hard-of-hearing persons have been confronted directly by psychologists such as Michael Harvey (1993). Harvey wonders how he, as a hearing person, can *not* oppress, considering the ease with which hearing privilege is established. This type of condition is called external oppression. It reflects the use of power based on implicit value systems that people assume and follow, engendered by a sense of superior entitlement grounded in category-based inferences, such as White superiority or hearing superiority. This superior entitlement assumes, for example, the power to define what deaf means (Reagan, 2002), thereby taking this control away from deaf people themselves. Davidson (1996) explicitly defines power not only as a system of domination that eliminates resistance but rather a reflection of how practices and discourses that support normality function to control situations. Normality has power in that it involves control, adherence, and compliance with the expected and conventional and excludes the noncompliant (Branson & Miller, 2002). This type of power fails to acknowledge or empower less powerful groups, thereby leading to their social diminishing (Davidson, 1996; Prilleltensky & Gonick, 1994; Reagan, 2002; Schneider, 2004). Cerney (2007) goes as far as to say that the lack of power experienced by deaf students who sign extends beyond that of students from culturally diverse backgrounds or those with other disabilities. This is due to the fact that deaf students are limited to those individuals who can sign rather than interact freely at their school and are limited in terms of academic success by interpreter effectiveness, ability to interact with the curriculum, and the level of support services available.

Harvey (2003) attaches the appellation "ordinary evil" to the meaning of external oppression. Ordinary evil consists of repetitive acts of disrespect that can lead to self-hatred or rage at others if there is no appropriate outlet to work through these feelings and arrive at some rapprochement. It is an unfortunate fact that individual oppression or ordinary evil is an experience familiar to many, whether it is childhood rejection, damping of academic hopes, limited career mobility, etc. Harvey quotes a deaf adolescent as saying, "Ordinary evil happens to deaf people all the time. Sometimes I get used to it; and other times it boils up inside of me" (p. 204).

Oppression has clearly played a role in creating a vibrant, even somewhat contentious deaf community. Some perceive this process as a form of ghettoization (Ravaud & Stiker, 2001), meaning that this community may be seen to play no part in the dominant culture and is set apart as an enclosed entity. Ng (1996) questions the usefulness of such psychologically salient and self-enhancing identities when the parity of power with oppressive groups remains disparate and the minority group voice does not penetrate the power hierarchy. Of what use are deaf identities when, for example, educators of deaf children are largely hearing, deaf people struggle with insidious barriers to employment, and communication access during times of crisis is not provided. This happened during the anthrax crisis in the U.S. Postal Service when interpreters were not provided for deaf employees at emergency meetings (Suggs, 2001). Baynton (1996) drives home the point of powerlessness by outlining the historic marginality of deaf people in enforcing school policy, indicating that even in schools supporting sign language, the power resided in hearing authorities due to the ongoing presence of paternalism. He illustrates how these professionals saw deaf people as fundamentally flawed and decided on what necessary remediation to undertake. Deaf supporters of sign language were nonetheless able to engage in a form of resistance or rebellion by claiming their ownership of sign language whenever and wherever they congregated among themselves.

Ng (1996) refers to the power of language in reflecting the expectation of diminished capacities in the recipient through conversational discourse, such as managing turn allocation and topic as well as utilizing simplified language, which can be interpreted as patronizing. Language then becomes a means of social control, whether it is the actual terms themselves or the use of a language other than the dominant language in use to convey a feeling of solidarity (Reinharz, 1994). For example, planning for teleconferences involves setting up opportunities to speak with and hear each other. "Speak" and "hear" implicitly invalidate the equality of potential participants who do not hear equally or speak sufficiently clearly and in this manner create a power hierarchy. Substituting the concept of "setting up lines of communication" removes that layer of invalidation and intimidations of oppression.

Internalized Oppression

In addition to externalized oppression, we also have internalized oppression. There are individuals who manifest a sense of shame about themselves or dislike themselves because of, for example, specific racial/ethnic attributes or because of their hearing difference. This translates into internalized oppressive self-perceptions as incompetent, deficient, or lacking in attributes that will facilitate merging into the larger society (Corker, 1996; Prilleltensky & Gonick, 1994). Deaf persons have reported feeling that deaf is equivalent to stupidity and shame, reflecting the stereotypical messages conveyed by children who make fun of them when they respond incorrectly to shouted instructions, educational settings that imply lower expectations of their ability to achieve, and work settings where opportunities for advancement are constrained by attitudinal barriers (e.g., Ladd, 2003; Leigh & Lewis, 1999). There have been deaf psychotherapy clients who view hearing authority figures as more competent and knowledgeable by virtue of their hearing status and presumed superiority in knowledge compared to equally well-trained deaf professionals (Leigh & Lewis, 1999). The message within is that of being uncomfortable with deaf and hard-of-hearing identities and claiming that these identities create inferiority.

Liminality

Just as being white can marginalize or diminish people of color even when White individuals subscribe to the notion of equality, the general tendency for many is to marginalize and diminish or reject those whose ears do not function similarly as theirs. This can reinforce a sense of liminality, a concept based on the ambiguity of one's place in the surrounding society. As described by Robert Murphy, the feeling is that of being on the fringe, with minimal sense of belonging if they do not pass for "normal" in the dominant society (Goldin & Scheer, 1995; Scheer, 1994). Again, such oppressive experiences have caused deaf and hard-of-hearing people to create kinship with each other, thereby eschewing the aura of stigma and escaping the sense of liminality in creating their own societies.

Not all have done so. The meaning of being deaf or hard-of-hearing evolves in response to the unique life situations of the individual. Many hard-of-hearing as well as deaf people have struggled to create bridges to their hearing environments in order to find their own place and escape the sense of liminality. What is noteworthy is that the phrase "hard of hearing" does represent liminality for many because of inconsistent communication access within hearing environments. This perspective has encouraged some deaf people to go so far as to label their audiologically hard-of-hearing children as deaf in order to give them a sense of belongingness with a clearly identifiable group, the deaf community, and counteract the feelings of liminality and identity problems of hard-of-hearing persons who describe being caught between deaf and hearing worlds (Searls & Johnston, 1996).

Audism

The notion of "audism" has gained prominence ever since Tom Humphries coined this phrase in 1975 to mean implicit hearing superiority in the guise of auditory and speech competency and concomitant discrimination against those who lack hearing ability or who do not meet hearing standards, values, and behavior (Bauman, 2004). The concept of audism per se is nothing new, as it represents centuries-old hearing paternalism, however manifested. The most typical manifestation of audism is the assumption that speech makes people human and deafness chips away at that human condition because deaf people communicate differently (Bauman, 2004; Baynton, 1996; Brueggemann, 1999). Bauman (2004) argues that the ongoing efforts to discipline deaf people into following "the norm" of speech and phonetic writing, rather than enhancing the use of a language suited to vision instead of audition, reinforces the power of audism. The inclusion movement in education, which reflects the ideal of deviating as little as possible from a standard of "normalcy," is easily perceived as a social policy that is audist in nature. Audism is also invoked when communication becomes difficult, thereby reinforcing social distancing, and the blame is placed on the deaf person. The concept of audism has fueled debates about identity, particularly in reference to whether one is aligned with groups perceived to be oppressive.

Hearization

This is a term coined by Stephen Nover (1995) to reflect the institutional promotion and maintenance of spoken language and auditory values. The basic premise is that social and psychological reality is shaped by language. Using this as a guide, hearization appears when educational systems impose auditory-based languages on children ill-equipped to naturally acquire these, thereby delaying cognitive and social development. This can create a perception that hearing people are superior, a form of internalized oppression.

Justification

The issue of justification plays a role in ongoing stigmatization, audism, and oppression. Crandall (2000) defines justification ideology as a complex web of beliefs and assumptions that are untestable but which functions as a lens to view the world and enable individuals to feel their responses are natural and expectable, not consciously based on discrimination per se.

One kind of justification ideology is based on attributional approaches that place the responsibility for the stigma on the stigmatized individual. Based on this approach, deaf people who do not speak or easily respond to (hear) spoken language are blamed for their inability to communicate. Because they are not compensating sufficiently, they are responsible for causing their own problems. Therefore, their marginalization is to be expected. Deaf outsiders who try to access the Deaf community may encounter discriminatory responses from Deaf insiders, ranging from disinterest to outright social ostracization. These responses may be justified on the basis of some observable expression of discomfort in response to any manifestation of Deaf behavior/communication or expression of positive attitudes about mingling with hearing nonsigners. Such justifications serve to marginalize a group of people who are struggling to figure out their identity status.

The other kind of justification ideology is based on hierarchical approaches that rank individuals and attach value judgments to these ranks. Myths about the inferiority of certain groups are legitimatized, such as the belief that "deaf can't," thereby providing justification for discriminatory behavior. Both approaches can be blended, as witness the case of eugenics in the United States and Germany, which resulted in legal stigmatization of those in lower social hierarchies because of their disabilities (see Chapter 5).

Voice

The expression of voice is a means of affirming identity, whether personal or group, and in turn empowerment (Prilleltensky & Gonick, 1994; Reinharz, 1994). Reinharz (1994) identifies voice as a mega-metaphor for freedom, presence, participation, protest, and power in contemporary society. Historically, the silencing of voice reflects the usurpation of power in that the vanquished could no longer talk or influence events. As such, it presages oppression in terms of silencing a people. Silent people cannot be understood. As groups gain the courage to protest, they fight to be "seen" through verbalizing their own experiences, controlling their names and identity, and the language of the "other."

Researchers can facilitate this process. For example, as part of a longitudinal research project with six Deaf families, videotaped interviews of the parents were analyzed to elucidate perspectives about the education of Deaf children (Thumann-Prezioso, 2005). Based on this analysis, these Deaf parents viewed themselves as educated experts but felt that schools for the Deaf did not take advantage of their expertise and knowledge, and could not be depended on to provide the best education possible. Clearly, this group condemned the silencing of their voice and appreciated the opportunity to express themselves.

Silence

Baynton (1996) explores the use of "silence" as a metaphor to describe the experience and identity of deaf people, going back to the time when hearing people saw them as primitive, in need of enlightenment and religious salvation to rescue them from darkness and silence. From a hearing paradigm, the most basic meaning of "silence" is the absence of sound, and even more, the absence of voice (Davis, 1995), made "real" when hearing people plug their ears to capture that sensation. This reinforces the imagery of silent worlds, worlds without sound, in which deaf people reside (Padden & Humphries, 1988). Media routinely use "silence" in phrases such as "prison of silence" and "living in silence" to describe deaf people and signify their isolation and disengagement from a vibrant hearing society.

In earlier decades, Deaf people used "silent" to describe themselves, most notably through periodicals such as the now defunct *Silent Worker* and *Silent News* (Baynton, 1996; Padden & Humphries, 1988). For deaf people, the historical use of the word "silent" to describe their world was based not on a lack of hearing, but implicitly more on the representation of social relationships based on not speaking. As such, "silent" represented a collective identity encompassing people who rely on the eyes and hands, not the ears or vocal chords, for communication. This term was positively phrased as a way of life, connected with whom and what deaf people were, rather than as a negative loss with profound harmful consequences for the person.

There is a paradox in the fact that few deaf people are "stone deaf." This became quite evident with the development of audiometric hearing tests, which could identify residual hearing and demonstrate how this hearing could be made useful when amplified by hearing aids. But even before that, silence per se was unreal for deaf people. In their book, *Deaf in America: Voices from a Culture*, Padden and Humphries (1988) devote considerable space to underscoring how deaf people know the meaning of sound, albeit in different sensory ways than hearing people do. They use examples such as feeling the pounding of walls and floors and visually enacting the roar of the wind.

Today, the use of "silent" to describe the collective identity of deaf people has fallen into disuse on the part of deaf people themselves, if not hearing people. "Silent" has increasingly come to represent powerlessness, voicelessness, and vulnerability, all terms that deaf people in search of empowerment increasingly resist.

RESILIENCE AND SELF-AFFIRMATION

In confronting the effects of stigmatization or oppressive experiences, it is necessary to acknowledge the strengths of deaf or hard-of-hearing identities, examine and let go of hurts at the hands of others, and confidently advocate for one's interactive needs in transcending societal barriers. Much depends on individual acts, family frameworks, and school settings that reflect the incredible possibilities of the human being to strive for different psychological ways of being (Brooks, 2006; Jenkins, 2005) through encouraging creative ways of counteracting what seems to be firmly structured negative social or physical characteristics that can create psychological despair. These creative ways suggest the concept of resilience as a construct that emerges out of positive self-perceptions, social support networks, and the use of self-affirmative rhetoric such as "can do" as empowering tools.

Resilience is defined as the possibility of achieving positive outcomes despite risk (Brooks, 2006). People who are resilient have protective factors such as self-confidence and determination that enable them to manage their lives in constructive ways despite higher levels of risk for daily difficulties in life compared to the average. According to Paul Jacobs (2007), a self-described "neither-nor" (neither Deaf nor hearing), his less-than-ideal introduction to the world, which involved frustrating communication experiences, first with hearing peers and later with Deaf peers, forged within him a tenacity that has exposed him to greater personal growth and richer experiences. He sees power as coming from within that helps not only to confront stigmatization but also to achieve goals in life.

This process reflects a positive psychology approach that incorporates the roles of biological, environmental, and cultural factors separately and interactively in facilitating necessary human strengths and psychological resources critical for coping with complex situations (e.g., Dunn & Dougherty, 2005; Hintermair, 2008; Seligman & Csikszentmihalyi, 2000). These strengths and resources include courage, resiliency, creativity, sense of coherence, self-efficacy, and perseverance in dealing with challenges and ascribing meaning to experiences. The specific strengths demonstrated by the deaf adolescents in Sheridan's 2008 study (described in Chapter 4) included positive relationships with families and peers, a sense of humor, adaptability, possessing autonomy in terms of decision making, creativity and assertiveness in transcending various barriers, ability to articulate feelings and solve problems, comfort in educating others about deaf people's communication aspects and Deaf culture, and comfort with their deaf identities. These adolescents saw their future selves as being independent, educated, socially active, working, contributing members of society. They did not deny existing limitations, either within themselves or in their environments. Corollary with that, research, policy, and program planning need to focus on strengths in general rather than pose obstacles. The presence of hearing differences does not have to detract from potential or actual assets when appropriate intervention or accommodations in line with individual potential and affirming self-perceptions are instituted.

The process of preserving one's integrity and blunting the effects of stigmatization can involve devaluing characteristics that lead to rejection (i.e., poor hearing or speech), validating contact with similar others, as deaf and hard-of-hearing people are wont to do if they are comfortable with minimizing concealability, "coming out," and comparing themselves not with hearing people but with people like themselves (see Schneider, 2004), and using the "can-do" type of rhetoric (de Clerck, 2007). While society at large views normalization as hearing oriented in terms of matching hearing ways of human interaction, such that orally educated deaf persons like Heather Whitestone, the 1995 Miss America, view themselves as living a "normal" life (Whitestone, 2008) in implied contrast to signing deaf people, that can be viewed as a form of resilience or self-affirmation. Additionally, as a means of self-affirmation, Deaf people themselves can and do understand that there are many ways to be "normal" as Deaf people as there are many ways to be deaf, or even to be hearing. As such, interacting with d/Deaf as well as hearing people can be viewed as normal, and therefore self-enhancing in terms of identity.

A creative and self-affirming approach that requires inner strength includes that of projecting responsibility for effective communication on the hearing party rather than on the deaf person, as is usually the case, or, more equitably, on both parties. If the hearing person does not know sign language or how to speak clearly without mumbling, the hard-of-hearing or deaf person should therefore not be solely blamed for the awkward communication interaction. For example, a deaf professional was informed that payment for the use of sign language interpreters during a professional conference went against policy because his communication difficulties were his problem. In turn, during his on-stage presentation, he silenced the sign language interpreter, removed the microphone, and started signing his presentation. The audience protested. He responded that he was communicating and if the audience knew sign language there would be no problem. The policy was subsequently rescinded (Alfred Sonnenstrahl, personal communication, June 17, 2007). Interestingly, Albert Ballin (1930/2001) advocated that hearing people should be expected to learn sign language for daily interaction with deaf people. Such perspectives demonstrate a strong sense of self-affirmation, and in turn confident deaf identities encapsulated in a positive framework. This can set the stage for opportunities to shape linguistic parameters of equality between both d/Deaf persons and their hearing peers in the process of framing social paradigms.

STEREOTYPE CHANGE

The most frequently used mechanism of stereotype change is that of bringing diverse groups together. This forms the basis for the contact hypothesis, which assumes that stereotypes will therefore be challenged and positive results can ensue through intergroup contact between groups with theoretically equal status. This is not always the case, depending on group experiences and individual perceptions (Biernat & Dovido, 2000; Schneider, 2004). The "typicality paradox" wherein typical representatives confirm stereotypes while atypical representatives are seen as exceptions to the rule can come into play in derailing potential change (Biernat & Dovido, 2000; Schneider, 2004). Deaf and hard-of-hearing high achievers who are seen as unique and unrepresentative of their categories are prime examples of the exceptions perspective, while deaf adults who struggle to speak will reinforce the inferiority stereotype. Exemplar-based models posit that ideal examples when added or strengthened will positively influence perceptions of marginalized groups (Biernat & Dovido, 2000). In this vein, greater ongoing exposure to the capabilities of competent deaf and hard-of-hearing individuals should theoretically lessen negative perceptions and facilitate stereotype change.

Another example of stereotype change has to do with stigmatized people seizing opportunities for self-determination through creating their own voices, their own images that counteract notions of tragedy, deviance from the norm, and repudiation of hearing perceptions of disability as well as oppression. Deaf and hard-of-hearing people present with a diversity of voices that reflect their diverse identities. These diverse groups must create a context where they can be heard in order to get the dominant group to listen and confront the need for stereotype change. Harlan Lane (1997) strongly advocates that Deaf people not only drum up internal support for pertinent issues but also bring their message to hearing society with the goal of teaching them that Deaf people know what works for them. His focus is that of teaching people about an affirmative Deaf way of life based on American Sign Language (ASL) and community connections, but his advice applies equally well to oral deaf and hard-of-hearing people who are confronted with the need to advocate for themselves and dismantle broad stereotypes.

Deaf and hard-of-hearing individuals can use strategies to challenge stigmatized identities, such as appropriate on-the-spot responses that confront the prejudice inherent in stigmatizing statements (i.e., "Isn't it wonderful that she has a hearing roommate?"). There are also ways to gain entry to conference presentations, where their viewpoints, professional experience, or data can be presented, and to engage supportive hearing peers in presenting a collective voice that illustrates equal deaf–hearing participation, leadership, or experience sharing (Benedict & Sass-Lehrer, 2007; Higgins, 1990). To break out of the stereotypical confines placed on them, they can express their individual skills or strengths so that they are seen as complex individuals. Capitalizing on deaf and hard-of-hearing role models, particularly staff, is also an affirmative strategy, although unfortunately such role models tend to be in short supply depending on location.

The use of mediators to present the voice of oppressed groups presents another solution in the effort to change stereotypical images. The mediator can speak in the language of the dominant group and serve as a bridge, particularly in situations where the stigmatized have been deprived of their voice for various reasons. For example, medical audiences have been reluctant to hear the voices of Deaf people regarding their concerns about cochlear implantation (Lane, 1997). I recall that at one conference medical doctors sat through presentations done by those who advocate for this technology and left before I presented data on parent and Deaf community perceptions. Medically respected mediators would perhaps have solved this communication impasse. There are hearing mediators who have sought to mitigate discriminatory stances and modify stereotypes. However, these mediators run the risk of implicitly subjugating those for whom they speak by taking over the group's voice when they are not truly a part of that group.

Because of societal changes based on advances in technology as well as legal and educational support, the opportunities for deaf and hard-of-hearing children have increased exponentially, thereby counteracting the typically ubiquitous stigmatizing effect of their hearing difference. Sheridan (2001) highlights the critical aspects of "goodness of fit" between the individual and the various systems involving the individual, including families, schools, workplace, and broader sociocultural and political organizations. Because this goodness of fit varies according to individual, time, place, and appropriate support that is not always forthcoming (Cerney, 2007; Nash, 2000), work continues to be needed in renegotiating this goodness of fit and maintaining the expansion of opportunities for deaf and hard-of-hearing children.

Changing stereotypes additionally requires more far-reaching efforts on an institutional level through efforts such as public advocacy and political action. This is exemplified by historical deaf political activism and the Deaf President Now movement (see Chapter 5), with the latter forcefully awakening the world to the potential of deaf people and reinforcing the notion of egalitarianism through wide media dissemination. Corollary with that was the manifestation of control over personal identity through alternate conceptualizations and portrayals of how individuals live their lives and affirm themselves as deaf and hard-of-hearing persons. More specifically, these lives were portrayed not as lessened, restricted, or helpless, as often suggested by medical and media professionals, but rather as lived differently and equally fulfilling.

Academic efforts represent another institutional venue for stereotype change in terms of incorporating the often ignored disability classification within the spectrum of diversity. Disability-related identities can and do shift in terms of individual parameters and changes in societal paradigms or salience depending on environment. Considering this, the potential for the Deaf Studies discipline to study and publicize these shifts and reshape the normal-abnormal paradigm as one that takes into account variation is becoming a reality with the publication of books such as *Open Your Eyes: Deaf Studies Talking* (Bauman, 2008). This process might enable society to modify its language to incorporate a systemic change in framing what it means to be d/Deaf or hard of hearing.

STILL MORE COMPLEXITY

The empowering aspects reinforced by internal resiliency have led to the achievement of deaf people despite their significant vulnerability to society's oppressive attitudes and limited expectations. Such achievements make it possible for them to view themselves with pride, but the reality is that not everyone achieves this kind of resolution, for multiple reasons. We turn to a consideration of the effect of additional identities interacting with deaf identities, as discussed in the next chapter. This can set the stage for multiple and complex confrontations with discrimination and complicate the search for clarity in identity.

7

Not Just Deaf or Hard of Hearing

...there are 35 million African Americans; there are 35 million ways to be black.
    Henry Louis Gates, Jr. (2006)*

While the commonality of being d/Deaf or hard of hearing often serves as a connecting catalyst, it is a myth that this commonality automatically overrides or erases the influence of diverse group membership. There are many deaf and hard-of-hearing individuals who absorb the discriminatory values of their hearing societies in addition to those who absorb the embracing of diversity and difference. In this chapter we focus specifically on minority ethnic/racial, sexual orientation, and disability identities that can occur in conjunction with deaf identities. These identity constellations have significant salience in terms of strengths, oppression, disadvantages, and the need to work at achieving some sort of internal congruence. There are occasional references to gender; this is not meant to discount its importance for one's identity. Studies of gender and deaf identities are rare (Brueggemann & Burch, 2006).

THE ETHNIC DIMENSION

Until relatively recently, the homogenous white face of the deaf community has predominated in the public eye, with the presence of diverse ethnic groups barely acknowledged or purposefully kept out of sight in the literature. However, current statistical trends indicate that white deaf and hard-of-hearing students are on the cusp of becoming a minority group (Gallaudet Research Institute, 2006). At the fiftieth anniversary of the Boston Deaf Club, Black, Hispanic, and Asian members were present as well as the usual Caucasian contingent (Lane, Hoffmeister, & Bahan, 1996). This reflects the reality that ethnic plurality is increasingly a fact of life.

It is critical that we understand not only the social contexts of these growing constellations of ethnic minority deaf groups but also how these social contexts reinforce inequity and complicate

---

* Original source: Crews, C. (2006, February 1). "Lives" makes a present of Black Americans' past. *Washington Post, C01.*

the internalization and integration of ethnic and deaf identities. In undertaking this endeavor, I start with an examination of what ethnic identities* are and how these might interface with deaf identities.

Ethnic Identity

This construct has defied easy definition because of its malleable nature (Trimble, 2005). Typically, ethnic identity is considered to be an affiliative construct indicating membership within a particular ethnic or cultural group (Trimble, 2005). According to Phinney (2002, p. 63), ethnic identity is defined as "a dynamic, multidimensional construct that refers to one's identity or sense of self as a member of an ethnic group." She posits that shared elements of ethnic groups include one or more of the following: culture, phenotype, religion, language, kinship, or place of origin. Subjective aspects include (1) the ethnic self-label used by individuals; (2) the subjective sense of belonging to an ethnic group and their feelings about that belonging in terms of strength and valence; and (3) their level of ethnic identity development in terms of conscious self-exploration in the process of moving toward a fully internalized ethnic identity. How ethnic identity is expressed or perceived varies over the life span, depending on the individual, the circumstances surrounding that individual, and the status and cohesiveness of the particular ethnic community. The more cohesive and acceptable this identity is, the easier it will be to internalize that identity within oneself (Phinney & Rosenthal, 1992).

Skin color alone does not determine ethnic group membership, though it can be a critical factor in the process of identifying with certain groups. Responses to skin color, as well as other interactive experiences that include identifying physical differences in others and recognizing their implications in terms of differential treatment, contribute to identity formation and feelings of membership (Franklin, Carter, & Grace, 1993).

Language is often held up as an ethnic marker based on its role in interweaving one's personal identity with the related ethnic identity (Liebkind, 1999). But not every person who claims specific ethnic identities connects with these through specific languages, as witness third-generation immigrant children, for example, whose first language will likely be English and who are rarely bilingual. Acculturation to the dominant language can detract from the importance of the ethnic identity with its associated language. A move toward the bilingual affords

---

* The terms *ethnic identity* and *racial identity* are often used interchangeably, but they are difficult to differentiate (Tatum, 1997). I have chosen to use the term *ethnic identity* because the use of the term *race* has served to perpetuate the perception of biological differences in people, despite the fact that the concept of such differences has been disproven (Mio, Trimble, Arredondo, Cheatham, & Sue, 1999, p. 219; Smedley & Smedley, 2005).

the possibility of the two languages being equally valued as reflectors of one's multiple identities.

Implications

When the surrounding mainstream society reflects values and beliefs that differ from one's culture of origin, the task of internalizing a positively valued ethnic identity can be complicated by the presence of social inequalities and power group dominance, including but not limited to prejudice, discrimination, unconscious white privilege, and the limited possibility of full assimilation (Liebkind, 2006; Phinney & Rosenthal, 1992). It is often difficult to acknowledge the vaunted "white skin privilege" with its accompanying expectation of presumed advantage that protects white persons in the United States (Greene, 2003, p. 9). This privilege, which lies beneath the surface as diverse ethnic groups intermingle, serves to drive home the salient and often detrimental effect of not being White.

The d/Deaf community has not been immune to these repercussions (Ahmad, Atkin, & Jones, 2002; Anderson & Bowe, 1972/2001; Ladd, 2003; Lane, Hoffmeister, & Bahan, 1996; Padden & Humphries, 2005). African American Deaf people recount stories of being excluded from extracurricular functions despite the fact everyone was deaf (e.g., Anderson & Bowe, 1972/2001; Burch, 2002; Jankowski, 1997). Just as schools for hearing children were once separated by race, so were schools for deaf children. Subsequent to desegregation, the interaction of minority and lower socioeconomic status apparently results in inadequate service provision (Moores, Jatho, & Dunn, 2001). In 1982 the National Black Deaf Advocates organization was formed in part as a response to perceived insufficient attention to Black Deaf issues on the part of the National Association of the Deaf (NAD), an organization that claims to speak for all deaf and hard-of-hearing people in the United States (Merriweather, 2008).

Ethnic Identity Development

How ethnic identity emerges depends on the internal narrative of the individual. This narrative is shaped by interactions with family, peers, institutions, and the overarching social culture and consequently involves contextual and situational forces that reinforce the ethnic connection (Trimble, 2005). There are two basic models for conceptualizing ethnic identity development. One model presents racial/ethnic identity development stages, while the other focuses on acculturation as a basis for ethnic identity awareness.

Racial/Ethnic Identity Development Models

Racial/ethnic identity development models focus on how members of oppressed racial or ethnic groups develop a positive sense of self in difficult circumstances. Janet Helms (1994) views racial-group membership as forming a core aspect of identity. For these groups of color, identity development themes highlight the effort required to overcome typically negative evaluations of their specific group and develop an identity rooted in the group's culture and sociopolitical experiences.

Racial identity development was originally conceptualized by African American social scientists and educators as a linear series of stages comprising the process of internalizing a racial identity, with each stage involving specific response types of racial identities based on ego* perceptions (e.g., Cross, 1971; Helms, 1997).

This model presumes that these individuals move from a passive-acceptance, pre-encounter or conformity phase, during which they internalize the dominant White culture's oppressive views of their racial group, toward an immersion stage in which the White culture is rejected in favor of their racial group. Lastly, there is an integration phase where individuals freely select particular cultural behaviors that seem most appropriate for specific situations. This suggests that an integrative or bicultural stance ultimately leads to enhanced psychological health encompassing the possibility of finding values in both cultures. It also implies that individuals in this phase can adjust their cultural behavior to fit various situations without experiencing undue conflict.

Since Asian American and Latino/Hispanic social scientists also developed similar identity development models incorporating the issue of cultural oppression, Sue and Sue (2008) integrated the various models into an overarching Racial/Cultural Identity Development (R/CID) model based on stages and the interaction of these stages with related attitudes and beliefs. This model is outlined in Table 7.1.

Sue and Sue (2008) warn that progression from pre-encounter to integration is not necessarily linear. Culturally different persons may exhibit conformity characteristics in some situations and immersion type behavior in others, depending on environmental context. For example, an African American person might conform to the dominant White group at work and reflect resistance-immersion attitudes during a march for African American solidarity.

The racial/ethnic identity categories serve a useful function in providing diagnostic frameworks for mental health clinicians who can then deliver services with greater appreciation of client identities and how these relate to social dilemmas. These categories also serve to highlight sociopolitical influences that reinforce internalization of specific identity statuses, involving as these do perceptions of dominant and minority group influences. It is easy to recognize the implications

---

* Ego refers to the self as an evolving, meaning-constructing entity that makes sense of oneself and the world (Hy & Loevinger, 1996; Kegan, 1994).

Table 7.1 The Racial/Cultural Identity Development Model

Stages of Minority Development Model	Attitude toward Self	Attitude toward Others of the Same Minority	Attitude toward Others of a Different Minority	Attitude toward Dominant Group
Stage 1: Conformity	Self-depreciating or neutral due to low race salience	Group-depreciating or neutral due to low race salience	Discriminatory or neutral	Group-appreciating
Stage 2: Dissonance and appreciating	Conflict between self-depreciating and group-appreciating	Conflict between group-depreciating views of minority hierarchy and feelings of shared experience	Conflict between dominant-held and group-depreciating	Conflict between group-appreciating
Stage 3: Resistance and immersion	Self-appreciating	Group-appreciating experiences and feelings of culturocentrism	Conflict between feelings of empathy for other minority	Group-depreciating
Stage 4: Introspection	Concern with basis of self-appreciation	Concern with nature of unequivocal appreciation	Concern with ethnocentric basis for judging others	Concern with the basis of group-depreciation
Stage 5: Integrative awareness	Self-appreciating	Group-appreciating	Group-appreciating	Selective appreciation

Source: From *Counseling American Minorities: A Cross Cultural Perspective*, 5th ed., by D. R. Atkinson, G. Morten, & D. W. Sue, 1998, Dubuque, IA: Wm. C. Brown Publishers. Copyright 1998. All rights reserved. Reproduced with permission of McGraw-Hill.

suggested by the parallel Deaf Identity Development categories and their relationships to sociopolitical influences.

Acculturation Models

Acculturation models evolved from the immigration experience, specifically how immigrants related to their culture of origin as they were accommodating to the new cultures they entered (Birman, 1994). Recent work has incorporated an ecocultural framework that encapsulates the process of adaptation to ecological context, including contacts with other cultures, to explain how different cultural groups intersect with each other and change as they coexist (Berry, 2002; Berry & Sam, 1997; Rudmin, 2003; Sam & Berry, 2006). To understand the process of acculturation requires scrutiny not only of the different cultures relevant to the individual but also how the individual relates to both cultures. Two basic concepts are involved: acculturation per se (referring to broader cultural changes resulting from cultural encounters that lead to changes in cultural behavior and competence depending on the culture being acculturated to) and psychological acculturation (referring to the psychological changes accompanying acculturation experiences, such as those affecting the sense of well-being relative to the culture being adapted to). Both concepts serve to explain how individuals can be at varying points in terms of self-identity or various deaf acculturation categorizations (see Chapter 2) depending on their environments, where they are in the life cycle, and their cultural backgrounds.

To assess whether and how one is acculturating to another group, it helps to focus on the person's orientations toward both groups and how these are changing according to the situation. Four different acculturation strategies based on attitudes have been presented to explain this process: (1) The assimilation strategy refers to individual efforts to interact with another culture and in the process shed the original cultural identity; (2) when individuals want to hold on to one culture and avoid interacting with members of the other culture, they are relying on the separation strategy; (3) in the case of integration, there is an effort to maintain one's cultural identity while interacting with the other culture, and finally (4) marginalization indicates little possibility or interest in cultural maintenance and having cultural relationships with others (see Berry, 2002 for a brief review). These categories parallel the previously described racial identity development categories of conformity, resistance/immersion, introspection/integrative awareness, and dissonance/appreciating stages, respectively. Again, these categories ebb and flow depending on the level of psychological (or internalized) identification with each of the involved cultures, the degree of behavioral involvement in the cultures, and the level of cultural competence in these cultures.

Accompanying all of the above is the ecocultural context, including the presence of discrimination and oppression depending on individual cultural membership and whether the culture is dominant. Relative to psychological adjustment, marginalization is the most stressful and the most vulnerable to dysfunctional behaviors, while the pursuit of integration is least stressful, at least if the dominant society is accommodating. The assimilation and separation strategies fall in between, depending on the extent to which acculturative stress is present (Berry, 2002). It is helpful to keep in mind that those who are more marginalized or encounter visible discrimination will deal with their ethnic identity in ways that differ from those who are more easily accepted by the dominant society.

Before we proceed to further examine the integration of ethnic identities and deaf identities using the above models as a lens, it may help to be reminded that the concept of deaf as ethnicity previously introduced in Chapter 1 continues to be a debatable issue. How this concept can be interposed with other ethnic identities has yet to be fully explored in the literature.

Juxtaposition of Ethnic Identity and Deaf Identity

Visualize, if you can, how one's d/Deaf identity and ethnic identity evolve, based on identity development or acculturation models*. Both identities do not necessarily evolve in tandem. There is no set way in which these stages and experiences are sequenced and integrated to create internal ethnic and d/Deaf identities. Much depends on individual development trajectories and how they veer based on the ecoculture.

Ethnic identity tends to be recognized as a core identity that generally precedes other identities (Corker, 1996; Helms, 1994). That identity is more salient in the hearing family of origin, with d/Deaf identity gradually emerging as a response to recognition of differences from hearing family members in the auditory communication arena. The degree to which both identities are internalized depends on circumstance, family communication, environmental influence, and positive/negative associations with the hearing difference and the reactions of others. If the child is exposed to others who are deaf or hard of hearing, the positive or negative nature of that exposure will influence the evolution of that child's deaf identity. If the parents are d/Deaf as well as members of an ethnic minority, both identities may be identified and reinforced more simultaneously than might have happened otherwise.

Many explorations will be needed before the deaf person with ethnic minority status can find a comfortable identity niche, considering that the juxtaposition of the two identities will most typically create a "minority within a minority" status with reference to being both deaf and of ethnic minority (Anderson & Grace, 1991, p. 73). What this means is that d/Deaf and hard-of-hearing individuals may be experiencing their ethnic identity as well as their marginalization very differently from their hearing ethnic minority counterparts, depending on how they place themselves within or outside of that ethnic minority group because of that additional d/Deaf/hard-of-hearing identity. To complicate matters, deaf members of an ethnic minority group confront even more multiple identity issues emanating not only out of interactions

* Refer to Chapter 2 for a review of the Deaf Identity Development and Deaf Acculturation models.

with their hearing ethnic group members and their d/Deaf ethnic group contingent but also White hearing and d/Deaf groups, each of which has different salience for the individual and as such pulls for various manifestations of identity (Anderson & Grace, 1991; Andrews, Martin, & Velásquez, 2007; Corbett, 1999; Eldredge, 1999). Each membership requires dealing with different sets of norms and values, tensions and countertensions, all of which can compound issues of stigmatization and oppression. The specter of double oppression hovers over those who may feel excluded from both their dominant hearing society and from their ethnic group, thereby complicating the process of identity internalization (Corker, 1996; Ladd, 2003). Those who migrate to other countries have that much more to deal with in confronting a new language as well as the new country's perception toward both their ethnic identity and their being deaf or hard of hearing. How all these aspects play out for the d/Deaf or hard-of-hearing individual, whether an immigrant or born with ethnic minority status, can deeply influence identity development and acculturation. The examples below illuminate the complexity that ensues with the juxtaposition of both ethnic and d/Deaf identities.

In an interview study of nine, mostly Puerto Rican parents of deaf children in the United States, the nuclear family's love for the deaf child collided with ongoing overt stigmatization by extended families and communities in the guise of expressed rejection of or pity for that deaf child (Steinberg, Davila, Collazo, Loew, & Fischgrund, 1997). Although not addressed in this study, the influence of such stigmatization is likely to influence their children's perceptions of their Puerto Rican and deaf identities. Hernández (1999) describes the struggle of Latino deaf adolescent immigrants to the United States during their immigration experience with its attendant sense of isolation as they confronted a strange language and strange ways of being. The members of a support group she organized to deal with their adjustment to the United States needed assistance in maintaining a sense of self and cultural identity as they acculturated to their new environment and confronted an overpoweringly dominant American d/Deaf culture. Corbett (2003) portrays minority Deaf women as potentially caught between their competing minority and Deaf identities, particularly when their hearing communities see them as more allied with the Deaf community and the latter pulls for Deaf identity.

Ralph Sedano (2001/1997), a Hispanic Deaf adult, elaborates on this phenomenon. He identifies a significant linguistic and cultural gap between Deaf Hispanics and American Deaf culture due to the latter's reliance on the values of the dominant English/Protestant culture, which negates the Hispanic identity and minimizes the role of Spanish origin contributors to American Deaf culture. Sedano describes how the power of what he terms the Iberio-American tradition overpowered his Hispanic heritage and identity. The hearing Hispanic students and graduates of his Deaf-focused interpreter training program generally did not subscribe to the hegemonic notion of "deaf first, Hispanic second" despite the pervasiveness of that message, instead preferring to maintain the primacy of their Hispanic heritage, perhaps because of a threat to cultural integrity (p. 127).

Based on interviews with five deaf Native Americans as well as interactions with other representatives of this group, Dively (2001) concluded that it was difficult for them to maintain their ethnic identity within the greater deaf community due to lack of support and cultural reinforcement. They also confronted barriers to inclusion within their Native American hearing communities, since Indian Health Services are not well versed in issues regarding lifelong hearing difference beyond identification. Despite this, they took pride in their ethnic Native heritage and attempted to maintain their culture even in the face of inadequate services on reservations and the need to move to residential schools, where instruction on the home tribal culture was largely absent (Collins, Devine, & Paris, 2005).

After asking a sample of 60 Black Deaf individuals which they identified with first: their Black culture or their Deaf culture, Aramburo (1994) found that a larger percentage identified as Black first, based in part on the salience of their skin color. Those who identified as Deaf first tended to have been relatively more immersed in the Deaf community and therefore saw their Deaf identity as more prominent.

To reconcile the two identities in an integrative framework rather than continue the dichotomy, some identify as Black Deaf. As one person said, "I'm Black deaf. My community is the Black deaf community" (Anderson & Grace, 1991, p. 73). The forced educational and social segregation of this group of people through the 1970s (Padden & Humphries, 2005) most likely had a reinforcing aspect on this perception of identity. For other individuals, the process of transitioning to this interface is expressed by a young Asian male: "I always knew I was deaf, but I didn't realize how Asian I am!" (Wu & Grant, 1999, p. 205). Deaf people who are Mexican travel frequently across the Mexican-California border, comfortably juxtaposing their Deaf and Mexican identities (Padden & Humphries, 2005).

Māori deaf individuals in New Zealand appear to be overrepresented within the deaf community in comparison to hearing *Māoris* within the dominant society (Smiler & McKee, 2007). In view of the combined influences of the re-emerging *Māori* language and culture together with the increased awareness of Deaf culture, these deaf individuals currently are examining themselves. In doing they, they are transitioning from the institutionalized monocultural atmosphere of residential schools and the disenfranchisement of *Māori* culture toward a more concerted effort to incorporate their *Māori* culture into their identity constellation rather than remain subject to oppression of their native culture. In an effort to further explore this phenomenon, the authors examined interview responses from eight *Māori* Deaf participants and concluded that when families were aware of sensitive approaches to their deaf children, the more opportunities they provided for exposure to *Māori* culture. Families were also aware of the need for their deaf children to accommodate to the majority culture in the schools; therefore, they had to be sensitively aware of different ways of behaving within Deaf and within *Māori* cultural contexts. Interestingly, those deaf *Māori* students who were orally educated within the mainstream and exposed to hearing *Māori* peers were closer to their ethnic identity than those educated in specialized schools. One of them got tired of "passing for hearing" and transitioned from the conformity phase toward immersion in Deaf culture. This ultimately was unsatisfactory due to the importance of his *Māori* identity. He now shifts between the two depending on circumstances with the goal of integrating both *Māori* and Deaf identities into his self.

The message from these examples reinforces the importance of juxtaposing the two minority identities in ways that maintain the salience of both identities rather than acceding to the subtle message regarding the dominance of Deaf cultural ways of being. Again, how these identities manifest themselves depends on multiple types of contexts as indicated by Foster and Kinuthia (2003).

Foster and Kinuthia (2003) conducted in-depth interviews of ethnic minority deaf college students to explore how they conceptualized their identities. The 11 Asian Americans, 11 Hispanic Americans, and 11 African Americans were either immigrants, second-generation Americans, or born in the United States. They often described their specific ethnic heritage, for example, African Black as opposed to African American Black. Additionally, they would also label themselves as oral deaf, culturally Deaf, or hard of hearing as components of their identity, changing labels depending on social context. These deaf or hard-of-hearing labels would be regarded as relatively more prominent in juxtaposition with ethnic identities when individuals found themselves in situations colored with communication stress.

Foster and Kinuthia (2003) viewed their results as reflecting a contextual and interactive model of identity consisting of four contributory factors that evolve through time: individual characteristics, situational conditions, social conditions, and societal conditions. The individual characteristics, which include physical, mental, and spiritual attributes, such as gender, racial or ethnic heritage, language, age, and hearing level, are internal and reflect core elements of identity. The other three factors reflect interactions between the individual and the environment that are interpreted by the individual to further construct identity. Situational conditions include geographic, educational program, and functional (home, school, work, etc.) locations. Social conditions are described as, for example, feeling accepted, comfortable, rejected, or set apart. Societal conditions represent broad societal trends and patterns, such as racism, socioeconomic status, or popular culture, such as the civil rights movement. Taken together, these four factors can create congruent or dissonant sense of identities depending on context and individual perceptions.

Some of the respondents with multiple identities (ethnic hearing, ethnic deaf, and dominant Deaf) told of their struggles to find a niche within their larger cultural environment where none really existed to incorporate their multiple identities. While alienation can be a factor in shaping identity, the discovery of connections with critical others, such as deaf peers or similar ethnic peers, was an equally powerful factor. Some perceived themselves as more into Deaf culture but were aware their ethnic identity might be more salient for their peers. However, for the most part, the specific identity of the moment depended on the nature of the four factors. For example, the interviewees wished to connect with their ethnically similar peers but gravitated toward identifying with deaf counterparts because of communication ease, particularly when a critical mass of their ethnic deaf peers was lacking. Those with more positive internalized ethnic identity reported more positive reinforcement or ability to positively internalize that identity despite discriminatory experiences. The more discrimination was salient, the more the ethnicity pervaded one's identity. Gender identities were also salient, with cultural perceptions of gender interweaving with ethnic and deaf identities in ways that are difficult to disentangle.

Based on their findings, Foster and Kinuthia (2003) argue against a stringent reliance on Glickman's (1996a) stages of deaf identity (see Chapter 2), considering that development is not necessarily unidirectional and that every stage, including the marginal stage conceptualized by Glickman, can have healthy components depending on the four factors mentioned in the previous paragraph. They point out that marginality does not necessarily represent lack of group membership; it can also reflect the experience of being an outsider with opportunities to obtain unique perspectives about identity and awareness of differences as well as strategies for handling different cultural expectations. Above all, they emphasize that the fluid nature of how d/Deaf and ethnic identity conceptualizations are juxtaposed depends on the individual, the day, and the place.

The exercise that Ahmad, Atkin, and Jones (2002) conducted with 56 mostly Pakistani Muslim deaf young people in Britain involved selection of "identity cards" covering major identities. Each of these cards had one identity category on it (e.g., Deaf). The majority indicated a preference for Deaf identity, with about a third choosing "partially deaf" and eight identifying as "hearing." During interviews, the respondents generally endorsed the importance of participating in deaf networks to build up a stronger internal sense of self, mitigate isolation, and withstand implications of stupidity and cruelty. In terms of ethnic identity, the majority chose Pakistani identity. The endorsement of British identity by a number of participants represented a more deaf-friendly environment with more opportunities for these individuals in contrast to their countries of origin. Not only that, access to the home language was often limited due to communication constraints and parents not learning how to better communicate with their children or resort to signs as needed. However, complicating this choice was the implication of a White and British Christian–based Deaf identity in view of the apparent lack of a Pakistani Muslim–based Deaf identity. In support of Foster and Kinuthia (2003), some had begun to gravitate toward better integration of their ethnic and religious identity with their Deaf identity. Again, the authors conclude that the identities chosen by the participants are likely to be situation and context related. This is also reflected by the tendency to switch languages depending on context: different forms of spoken language in different situations and similarly differences in signing depending on ethnic group (Ahmad, Atkin, & Jones, 2002).

Similar points are highlighted in Skelton and Valentine's (2003) interview with a British Pakistani Muslim who endorsed being Muslim and Deaf and struggled in interactions with both communities due to difficulties in finding a Muslim Deaf community. Such incidences argue for the phenomenon of hybridity in contrast to the focus on cultural essentialism, particularly in view of globalization and immigration forces. In contrast, some discredit the notion of "in-between" or integrated identities on the basis that identities are more exclusive than inclusive (Ladd, 2003). For instance, some ethnic minority Deaf persons might not have an easy time acknowledging a "Hearing White" component to their identity, thereby discrediting in some form the ideal of multiculturalism or specific potential identities as valid internalized identities. The possible numerous variations reinforce the importance of one's narrative in juxtaposing identities that can either coexist or conflict, as the case may be.

Literature regarding the interface of ethnic and hard-of-hearing or oral deaf identities is scant. In Kent's (2003) study of identity issues with hard-of-hearing students in New Zealand, a very high percentage were *Māori*. While he did not examine correlations between willingness to acknowledge a hard-of-hearing identity and ethnicity, his results revealed that those who preferred not to acknowledge being hard of hearing were less lonely or alienated.

David James (2002), a mathematics professor at Howard University, writes that he is not really interested in deafness. Deafness does not define him, but he does recall the racial tension during the 1960s when he struggled in high school as 1 of 6 Blacks in a class of 240. Joe, a Black deaf adolescent, gravitated from a self-label as hard of hearing to deaf after connecting with a deaf social group of White adolescents who sign, not having yet had the opportunity to engage with a group of Black deaf peers (Sheridan, 2008). While he appreciated the part of himself that connects with his hearing family and peers, being isolated by spoken conversations in group situations made it hard for him to hold on to his hard-of-hearing identity. Additionally, he could not escape experiences of audism, communication barriers, and racism* at his predominantly white, hearing public school. His multiple cultures necessitated a process of shifting to accommodate to different situations and dealing with the intersections of African American, European American, hearing, and Deaf cultures.

In conclusion, it is becoming apparent that individuals dealing with both deaf/hard-of-hearing and ethnic identities are faced with the need to select what they project about themselves depending on their environment and status (Foster & Kinuthia, 2003; Mitchell, 2006; Parasnis & Fischer, 2005). Dymaneke Mitchell (2006), a Black deaf female, uses the metaphor of flashcards to illustrate how the visibility of one identity engenders the visibility or nonvisibility of her other identities. Since her gender, ethnic, and deaf identities could conflict at times, this metaphor served the function of helping her negotiate and mediate these identities depending on environmental context.

The effect of shifting identity is illustrated by the results of a survey of 333 African American women and an analysis of 71 interviews (Jones & Shorter-Gooden, 2004). To maintain internal balance, these African American women were constantly shifting** their frame of reference in the face of ongoing racism and gender stereotyping by presenting themselves in different ways depending on the expectations for them in various settings. This was done to minimize being demeaned because of stereotypical group membership expectations in, for example, the White-majority workplace or in a store serviced by White employees versus being with family, but emotional stress was a constant. They relied on their resiliency to affirm a positive ethnic identity perspective and avoid internalizing negative perceptions of themselves. How this shifting happens depends in part on how ethnic identity development takes place and is internalized within

* *Racism* is defined as a politically based phenomenon that combines prejudice and discriminatory exclusion based on real or perceived biological distinctions among groups of people (Mio et al., 1999, pp. 220–221); it essentially creates a system of advantage for the dominant group and disadvantage for nondominant groups.

** The authors define *shifting* as a form of subterfuge to ensure survival in a racist society through accommodation to differences in class and ethnicity.

each individual. The parallels to the deaf and hard-of-hearing experiences are self-evident. Those who have managed to overcome cultural stereotypes, maximize educational opportunities, and demonstrate significant achievement likely rely on resilience, persistence in the face of discrimination, and a positive self-identity, the result of parental support and reinforcement of cultural/ethnic pride (Anderson & Miller, 2005; Williamson, 2007).

Institutional Issues

Because of the significant changes in school demographics, the educational setting is now the focal point for dealing with cultural plurality, accepting diversity, confronting the need to counteract low expectations (Lane, Hoffmeister, & Bahan, 1996; Redding, 2000), and exploring means for creating a sense of belongingness for everyone. The low expectations tend to be reinforced by the ongoing underachievement typically demonstrated by deaf African American, Hispanic/ Latino, Native American, and to some extent Asian American students (Karchmer & Mitchell, 2003).

Increasingly, educational programs have come to recognize that positive valences assigned to ethnic diversity reinforce the development of an atmosphere that encourages overall learning. However, these atmospheres exist in conflict with societal ambivalence about ethnic identities (Davidson, 1996) as well as white privilege, thus constraining respect for diversity. During the years of educational segregation in the United States, schools for African American deaf students provided opportunities for enculturation into Black Deaf culture. As these schools were desegregated during the 1960s, "Black deaf children for the most part became cultural nonentities" (Hairston & Smith, 1983/2001, p. 198). The perpetual problem of minimally available ethnic minority role models in deaf educational settings and elsewhere has a potentially insidious effect on minority achievement motivation (Anderson & Grace, 1991; Andrews & Covell, 2007; Andrews, Martin, & Velásquez, 2007; LaSasso & Wilson, 2000). In a study focusing on self-esteem in 78 deaf college students at California State University, Northridge (CSUN) conducted by Jambor and Elliott (2005), the ethnic minority students (who constituted more than half the sample) demonstrated overall lower self-esteem than their Caucasian counterparts. The authors speculate that the positive self-esteem generally associated with hearing minority group membership may not extend to those who are deaf, perhaps because the combination of both may provide special challenges.

Compounding efforts to equalize the playing field, a survey of students at the National Technical Institute for the Deaf and Rochester Institute of Technology indicated positive attitudes toward diversity but differed in terms of perceptions related to racial conflict, friendship patterns, and campus comfort level among African American, Asian, Hispanic, and Caucasian students. This served to contraindicate efforts to deal with campus diversity issues by grouping all minority groups together (Parasnis, Samar, & Fischer, 2005). Interestingly, African American deaf students considering role models focused more on the importance of race and ethnicity rather than being deaf.

Formal Organizations

To consolidate the move away from monoculturalism and reinforce pride in deaf ethnic identity, several organizations have been established. Each has had conferences where issues of identity and self-determination were confronted, explored, and dissected.

The mission of the National Black Deaf Advocates (NBDA), which was formed in 1982 to counteract inadequate representation in leadership and policy decision-making activities affecting the lives of Black deaf persons in the United States, is to promote leadership development, economic and educational opportunities, social equality, and to safeguard the general health and welfare of Black deaf and hard-of-hearing people (http://www.nbda.org/about.htm).

The Intertribal Deaf Council was established in 1994 (Collins, Devine, & Paris, 2005). Its mission is to bring together Native Deaf tribal members and collaborate with agencies to provide input on services provided to Native Deaf persons. In 1997, the National Asian Deaf Congress was established to provide opportunities for cultural and ethnic identity exploration that can help to break down the walls of silence surrounding being Asian and deaf or hard of hearing (http://www.icdri.org/dhhi/nadc.htm). The National Council of Hispano Deaf and Hard of Hearing is the most recent organization in this category to emerge, having been established in 2006 (http://www.nchdhh.org). Its mission is to ensure equal access in social, recreational, cultural, educational, and vocational welfare. The mission of the Texas Latino Council of the Deaf and Hard of Hearing includes the promotion of cultural appreciation among its members (http://www.tlcdhh.org).

In its endeavor to address long-standing issues related to the implementation of ethnic plurality, the National Association of the Deaf (NAD) held a workshop on racism and the NAD at its 2006 Conference, with panel representatives from each of the ethnic deaf groups presented above. As Nancy Bloch (2006) reports, "sensitive issues and hard truths were exposed" (p. 7). As the first National Coalition of Deaf People of Color Conference indicated, the focus was on the concerns and challenges related to bias, stereotypes, prejudices, and myths faced by Deaf people of color, all of whom have been traditionally underrepresented and often invisible (Moore, 2007).

SEXUAL ORIENTATION

To claim an identity that is gay, lesbian, bisexual, or transgendered (GLBT) is to undergo a process of affirming a minority identity that supersedes identifying with the dominant heterosexual group (Brown, 1995; Gonsiorek, 1995). Interfacing sexual orientation identity with d/Deaf identity can be a daunting process, incorporating as it does the need to deal with multiple-minority status, depending on the influence of family, peers, ethnic background, cultural perspectives about sexual expression, and socioeconomic factors that can influence acceptance or rejection. When an individual can no longer suppress the desire to affirm identifying as gay, lesbian, bisexual, or transgendered, the need to confront social taboos about homosexuality and transgender changes in areas that hold heterosexuality to be the only permissible norm very often requires delicate and complex identity management.

There is no straightforward process for internalizing an identity that encompasses being an individual who identifies within the GLBT continuum. Unlike gender and ethnic identities, which are acknowledged earlier in life, sexual orientation typically does not get integrated into the core identity until later due to life situations and the need to accept this particular identity in the face of social stigma (Corker, 1996).

The coming-out experiences of many individuals who reveal their GLBT identities illustrate the impossibility of creating simple linear explanations of sexual orientation identity development. This process typically encompasses multiple changes in sexual behavior over time and place (Diamond & Savin-Williams, 2000; Fox, 1995; Rust, 1996). It is much more common to acknowledge fluid sexual identities, since various aspects of sexual identity are expressed at different times. Additionally, the coming-out process can happen at multiple ages during the life span. How this process evolves, with its multiple potential transitions and vacillations in adopting a social minority sexual identity, depends greatly on the nature of interactions between individuals and the social context.

The coming-out process has been framed as one that requires coming out as "different" and integrating a sense of that particular difference into one's self-perception in a positive way despite awareness of the difference's stigma (Corker, 1996). To accomplish this requires increased attention to the private self versus the public self and evaluating the safety of revealing one's sexual orientation. A solid sense of self-acceptance will facilitate the development of a comfort zone in managing such identities. This is not always easy to achieve, particularly when the end result can lead to alienation, disconnection, and internal dissonance because of nonaccepting environments. These environments discriminate against the individual if support from sympathetic peers, siblings, or significant others is not forthcoming or there is lack of opportunity for self-exploration (DeAngelis, 2002; Gutman, 1999). Positive resolution is likely to happen with support and affirmation that leads to commitment, reinforced by the presence of supportive role models that can fortify one in the face of anticipated rejection.

What about deaf and hard-of-hearing individuals who identify as GLBT? Breivik (2005) quotes a deaf colleague: "Exchange the label gay/lesbian with deaf, and you'll have a fairly good description of our situation" (p. 188). Going beyond this and juxtaposing the two together, keeping in mind the various developmental trajectories that may be occurring for both identities either simultaneously or at discontinuous times, a very complex picture of minority identity dynamics can emerge. To tease out the components of this complex picture for identity development and syntheses can be particularly daunting.

To bring this complex picture to life, it will be helpful to consider an example. Imagine a woman who has understandable speech but finds herself on the margin at parties organized by hearing friends. Her Deaf peers question whether she is Deaf or hard of hearing, which in turn engenders an internal struggle to figure out where she is on the continuum, or whether she can be both depending on context. At the same time, she may be considering whether it is the correct time for her to come out as a lesbian and whether her hearing family will still warmly keep her within their fold if she does so. Despite her strong bond with her d/Deaf community, they may be uncomfortable with this facet of her identity. She may also be searching for access to a d/Deaf community of lesbians, but if she is not in a major urban area, integrating her deaf sense of self with her lesbian identity could very well be more problematic. If she grew up in a Latino family, she could be juxtaposing her ethnic identity as well, and wondering whether, if she comes out, her Latina identity will be submerged into her lesbian identity and whether she will be threatened with family disapproval. Or she might be sufficiently light-skinned to ignore her Latina identity, allowing it to disappear as part of her identity if she does not maintain connections with her ethnic community. She uses American Sign Language, but is she also familiar with some variant of Spanish-based signed language? Will there be a deaf Latina lesbian community for her? And how much is each identity visible? Will she have to explain herself time and time again? Will she enjoy acceptance overall, or will one identity be the object of pejorative responses in contrast to the other two? And so the self-questioning goes on in the search for a zone of comfort about oneself in view of cultural, linguistic, geographic, socioeconomic, religious, and other factors that may influence the process.

The typically close-knit nature of small deaf communities may mitigate tendencies to reject one who has come out, particularly when members have known each other for years (Langholtz & Rendon, 1991–1992).

Raymond Luczak, editor of *Eyes of Desire 2: A Deaf GLBT Reader* (2007) claims that at least in Western countries if nowhere else, coming out continues to be a big deal, but not necessarily a "make-or-break proposition" (p. 2). The possibility of reconciling such multiple identities in a positive way is exemplified by one of the authors in the Luczak (2007) book. Lanetra "Rain" Williams (2007) is a Black Deaf lesbian with light brown skin who has confronted conservative elements in the African American community and gay homophobia in the deaf community. She focuses on her internal positive comfort level and separates herself from how others may view or label her. Others in the book describe the coming-out process as a struggle to recognize their sexual identity in deaf surroundings as well as family surroundings, sometimes being accepted and at other times having to surmount expressions of revulsion. Above all, they focus on how they shift identities depending on their surroundings, whether it is their d/D/hard-of-hearing part, their GLBT part, both together, or all their other identities (work, gender, ethnic, religious, etc.).

Based on a preliminary survey of deaf lesbians by Hecht and Gutman (1997), it appears that those reporting the most positive internalized images of deaf people also reported the highest self-esteem, more so than experiences within the lesbian community. Interestingly, Paddy Ladd (2007) suggests that the most inclusive Deaf–hearing social relationships are to be found in relationships between Deaf communities and gay and lesbian hearing communities. This perspective is endorsed by Neil Glickman (1996b), who, having suffered through blatant discrimination as a hearing gay man, could empathize with the oppression experienced by many Deaf persons. Thomas Kane (1994) provides examples of Deaf gay men's culture, including the observation that Deaf gay men tend to interact with hearing gay men in greater numbers than noted for heterosexual Deaf people, who tend to focus on relationships with other Deaf persons. This may have something to do with shared experiences of discrimination and oppression that enhances sensitivity and understanding between the two groups (Glickman, 1996b).

However, the situation can be different for hard-of-hearing individuals who may have less access to sexual orientation information and less connection with peers (Luczak, 2007; Swartz, 1995 as cited in Gutman, 1999). This is a group who has received little attention in the research literature. Again, the GLBT stories in Luczak's (2007) book reveal sufficient evidence to suggest the theoretical possibility that identity conflict and confusion could be more pronounced for this group. Not being really hearing or really d/Deaf as well as coming to terms with one's sexual orientation is bound to complicate the search for a positive sense of self-identity that incorporates all aspects of oneself.

The pull for identity synthesis is a strong one. Typically, we want to be clear about who and what we are, which often means comfortably juxtaposing our different identities within ourselves. And we want to be accepted, which pulls for the need to frame our identities in a way that connects us to communities. The Rainbow Alliance of the Deaf (http://www.rad.org), which was founded in 1977, is a national organization that attempts to create a safe haven where Deaf GLBT can follow a path to identity synthesis.

Halbertal and Koren (2006) question the possibility of identity synthesis in situations where the conflicting pull toward same-sex attraction collides with value systems that relate to ethnic or religious cultures of origin, particularly when these values appear to be incompatible. If Deaf settings do not welcome those who may endorse significantly different religious or cultural lifestyles, including sexual orientation, tensions between conflicting identities can have profound social implications despite the common Deaf bond (Skelton & Valentine, 2003). Based on their research with Orthodox Jewish gays and lesbians struggling with the official Orthodox Jewish prohibition against their sexual orientation, Halbertal and Koren (2006) report that what emerged was a picture of mutually exclusive selves that ultimately learned to coexist in uniquely shaped ways. They coined the term "identity coherence" to reflect this process. This requires being able to shift compartmentalized identities as needed, with the divergent aspects coalescing when within communities of others like them. To be true to oneself in such situations often requires a delicate balancing act, one with which many d/Deaf GLBT individuals are likely familiar.

DEAF AND DISABILITY COEXISTENCE

Before concluding, it is important to briefly acknowledge the interface between deaf and disability when there is an actual ancillary condition. For example, we have deaf-blind, deaf with cerebral palsy, deaf wheelchair users, deaf with learning disabilities, deaf and autistic, and so on. As Nielsen (2006) points out, each one has different bodily experiences based on race, class, sexual orientation, and ideology. This naturally complicates efforts to define what deaf and "disability" mean in terms of identity. These individuals have historically received minimal social support from d/Deaf groups as well as from society at large, based largely on their physical or functional differences.

These unique situations have led to the relatively recent formation of special interest groups, such as the American Association of the Deaf-Blind (AADP) and the Cerebral Palsy and Deaf Organization (CPADO). Because of the low-incidence nature of the deaf population and the typically less than optimal attention to the larger hard-of-hearing constellation, little is known about how interfaces with additional disabilities influence one's identity, particularly once these individuals leave educational settings. On the CPADO website (http://www.cpado.org), there is a statement that suggests that being deaf with cerebral palsy is experientially different than being only deaf or only having cerebral palsy. How that influences identity, however, requires further exploration.

The deaf-blind group consists of members who were born deaf-blind and those who developed both or blindness later in life. Usher syndrome, which most typically involves early-onset hearing loss and deteriorating vision as a result of retinitis pigmentosa, compromises more than half of deaf-blind adults (Miner, 1999). If these adults start off as culturally Deaf or culturally hearing, they eventually may feel estranged from their respective community as their vision worsens. This may occur because of intensifying communication limitations or frustrations, both on their part and the part of their seeing peers. But it may also arise from the discomfort the seeing peers may feel when confronted with fears about losing their own vision, causing them to distance themselves accordingly. As isolation, decreasing mobility, and decreasing self-sufficiency progress, the increasingly marginalized sense of self together with emotional turmoil in response to progressive losses can reverberate as individuals struggle with internalizing a deaf-blind identity. However, there are deaf-blind individuals who reject the pity of society, are comfortable with their difference, and attest to their normalcy as part of the diversity spectrum (Clark, 2006). They do not necessarily emphasize one over the other, as Helen Keller was pushed to do in selecting the saliency of her blindness over being deaf in her role as a public figure of awe (Nielsen, 2006). Möller and Danermark (2007) report on various Scandinavian studies that highlight the importance of self-determination and participation level for deaf-blind students as well as their relief when they are with peers like themselves. In their survey of students with Usher syndrome, what emerged was the importance of considerateness, meaning that these students felt validated as deaf-blind individuals when others were considerate of them and accepted them. There have been suggestions about an emerging Deaf-blind culture, but this evolution depends in large part on the extent to which deaf-blind people can interact with one another (Clark, 2006; MacDonald, 1994).

CONCLUSION

This chapter serves to reinforce the complexities of dealing with multiple-minority status and achieving self-actualization in the form of identity. Internalizing marginalized identities as congruent aspects of the self will enhance self-assurance in facing the challenges posed by a less-than-accepting society. Results from the studies presented in this chapter confirm the move from dichotomous types of categorizations to a more hybrid type of self-labeling depending on family, context, communication, comfort, support network, and a host of other potential environmental influences in addition to individual propensities. Ethnic identities have their roots within families of origin, and more typically reflect one's core identity, whereas sexual orientation is an identity that develops as the individual becomes aware of the sexual part of him/herself and environmental messages about sexuality. The deaf identity component interweaves with these other identities, as well as disability aspects, in evolving levels of awareness throughout development. Those who are able to come to terms with their double- or triple-minority status and find communities of acceptance have a greater chance of ascribing pride to the diverse identities they integrate into themselves.

8

The Influence of Technology

Now the computer will go inside *my body, literally woven into my flesh, in my* head.
Michael Chorost (2005, p. 21)

How does technology relate to identity, and how does it influence the ways in which deaf and hard-of-hearing people view themselves and relate to each other? Today's technology has generated multiple forms of communication that have changed the lifestyles of deaf and hard-of-hearing people. In this chapter, we will explore how these technologies have encouraged exploration and affiliation with specific deaf identities.

A powerful example of the interface between technology and identity surfaces in Michael Chorost's (2005) book *Rebuilt: How Becoming Part Computer Made Me More Human.* In this book, he describes becoming deaf, a state of being and an identity that he had difficulty internalizing. He subsequently obtained a cochlear implant, in the process becoming a self-described cyborg* able to reclaim his former hard-of-hearing identity.

In the eyes of people who affirm their disability, technology can sometimes be perceived as an intrusive fix when people have learned to live with what they have (Hintermair & Albertini, 2005). Take the case of a blind man whose eyesight was partially restored by surgery based on improved technology. He had great difficulty orienting himself to a sighted world after nearly an entire life of being blind. It was a relief to him when he could resume his blind status and maneuver without the distraction of confusing visual signals (Sacks, 1993). Some d/Deaf individuals have preferred the deaf status rather than use hearing aids or cochlear implants, which have been perceived as too noisy, causing headaches, or inadequate for sound discrimination, all of which detracted from their perceived quality of life (e.g., Christiansen & Leigh, 2002/2005). Yet others have embraced technology to overcome their sense of exclusion from mainstream society in the face of their hearing disability, as Chorost (2005) did. This

---

* Cyborg refers to the extension of human abilities by mechanical components inserted in the body.

conflict illustrates how technology can be both oppressive and emancipatory (Sheldon, 2004).

THE CONNECTION POSSIBILITIES OF TECHNOLOGY

Access to technology has profoundly influenced how deaf and hard-of-hearing people interact with their environments and with each other. The communication and geographical boundaries reinforcing distance between hearing and d/Deaf/hard-of-hearing people have been breached by electronic mail, text and video phones, the Internet, wireless text pagers, FM systems, Communication Access Real-Time Translation (CART), captioned television and film, cochlear implants, digital hearing aids, ad infinitum. Television and the Internet make news events appear more frequent and close to home. Students who are deaf or hard of hearing and scattered in mainstream educational programs can connect with Internet groups involving either deaf, hard-of-hearing, or hearing peers to counteract isolation. Hot issues generate high-tech discussion, often through the Internet, instant messaging, and pagers (Kinzie, 2006a). The Internet offers Deaf chat rooms, Deaf blogs, and Deaf listservs, to name just a few. The interactive Deaf eye gaze in face-to-face communication is giving way to the eye gaze of the bent head over the pager with fingers hitting the keys, or the eye gaze onto the computer monitor.

Sign language has also entered cyberspace, with broadband and video technologies capable of transmitting clear videos (Bernstein, 2006). The use of Deaf vlogs (essentially blogs in video format) has exploded. Video relay services provide easy communication between hearing and deaf parties; the deaf person views a sign language interpreter interpreting spoken dialogue to the deaf person via a monitor and voicing the signed language to the hearing person via voice phone. The deaf person can choose to speak using voice carry-over technology while viewing the sign language interpreter on screen interpreting for the hearing caller.* Using signed languages via cell phone cameras with real-time video is becoming popular.

The increased visibility of deaf people and sign language in popular culture has been buttressed by the use of filmmaking, television, and DVD technology. Films ranging from *Johnny Belinda* in 1948 to the more recent *Mr. Holland's Opus* and most recently Hallmark Hall of Fame's *Sweet Nothing in My Ear* (see further discussion in Chapter 5 regarding films) have entered the public consciousness in ways undreamed of decades earlier. In turn, Deaf people have increasingly

---

* Voice carry over is also available on caption telephones, which allow spoken language users to speak with the other party and receive text transmission displayed on a screen connected to the user's phone (Bernstein, 2006).

taken advantage of improved video technology to examine their lives (Bauman, 2008a,c; Brueggemann, 2007) and make their productions available in the public domain for all to view via the Internet or other technical venues.

At this point in time, technology in general has already significantly encroached upon traditional ways of human interaction and deaf face-to-face connections through the creation of virtual sites where communication can take place (Bernstein, 2006; Murray, 2008). This evolving transformation in ways of interacting with others reinforces the continual reshaping of Deaf cultures and communities as participants make arrangements to meet or set up dialogues via Internet communication or other technical devices, such as text pagers (Murray, 2008; Padden & Humphries, 2005). The question then becomes, How does this technology affect social identity relative to human connections, not only between deaf people but also between deaf and hearing people? To answer this, we first need to know more about the actual usage of communication technology.

National Organization on Disability survey results indicated that among adults with disabilities, those most likely to use the Internet at home were persons with hearing or vision disabilities (Hendershot, 2001). According to National Association of the Deaf (NAD) (2002) survey results, 75% of 884 responses indicated daily use of Instant Messaging (IM) because of the interactivity component. Virtually every respondent used E-mail, keeping in mind those not using E-mail were unlikely to take part in this Internet survey. The NAD concluded that IM technology facilitates meaningful communication between deaf, hard-of-hearing, and hearing individuals. In a Michigan survey related to medical information, 63% of 227 respondents relied on computers (Zazove et al., 2004). Computer use was associated with younger age, increased education, better English, and higher income (Power, Power, & Horstmanshof, 2007; Zazove et al., 2004).

In British, Australian, and German studies of how deaf people use communication technology, results indicated regular use of short-message service, TTYs, voice/TTY relay services, fax, and E-mail (Pilling & Barrett, 2008; Power, Power, & Horstmanshof, 2007; Power, Power, & Rehling, 2007). A study of 48 deaf Canadian adolescents who used two-way text messaging confirmed the importance of this form of communication in increasing deaf adolescent independence and indirectly reinforcing a positive and more mature social identity through exposure to others (Akamatsu, Mayer, & Farrelly, 2006). While studies of videophone usage are on the cusp of appearing in the literature, this presages the transformation of telecommunications in ways that will increasingly facilitate the interconnectivity of Deaf cultures across national boundaries. This will also allow for a reconfiguration of the experience of biculturalism with the inclusion of hearing people having access to this technology (Breivik, 2005; Power, Power, & Horstmanshof, 2007). In this regard, the virtual nature of face-to-face contact is taking on increased salience in how people connect with each other.

The ability to increasingly enter mainstream technology suggests that such technology approximates "universal access," meaning that most everyone can use it without stigmatization and with minimal need for adaptation due to individual needs. Individual identities, whether real or assumed, can now travel through cyberspace and evolve based on technical or virtual, rather than in-person, connections. The ability to control which identity is revealed can be seen as liberating in terms of freely communicating with strangers. As one deaf woman said, "I've made more friends online than in the real world. In the real world I am different. In the online, I am me" (Oglethorpe, 2006, p. 357). For many, to be online is to exist, to have the ability to hide the deaf/hard-of-hearing condition, to be "hearing," to achieve a sense of equality via access to spontaneous communication with anyone, provided they have written language capabilities.

Does this mean that hearing status is becoming less salient as individuals reach out to others, whether for business or social purposes (Breivik, 2005; Power, Power, & Horstmanshof, 2007)? Quite so, but at the same time, recognizing oneself as Deaf, deaf, or hard of hearing creates opportunities for increased contacts with others of similar identity categories. For example, the speed of Internet information centering on Deaf culture, hard-of-hearing, late-deafened, oral deaf, and other specific constituent group issues is revitalizing and strengthening ways of connection between members of these groups with access to the Internet.

How instant communication devices really connect or disconnect members of d/Deaf communities and how these may radically change these communities as well as individual identity perceptions are increasingly topics for study (Brueggemann, 2008; Murray, 2008). Whatever these changes may portend, the underlying typical assumption is that one's identity and preferences will guide efforts to connect with others who share these identities or preferences. Technology clearly is facilitating these connections.

THE CASE OF HEARING AIDS

Since the time of ear trumpets, the goal has been to enhance hearing and connect deaf and hard-of-hearing users with the hearing world (Branson & Miller, 2002). Hearing aids, which were developed to amplify sound, began as awkward pieces of equipment with external wires joining ear molds to bulky units inserted within clothing. They are now small, digital, ear-level products with significant improvement in quality. This process has provided greater access to the nuances of sound and in turn to spoken language for those who cannot hear without auditory enhancement.

The overarching assumption is that hearing aids should be capable of conveying environmental sounds and speech, facilitating communication, and minimizing the world of silence. However, this assumption may be a fallacy due to differences in individual abilities to benefit from this technology and environmental contexts, such as noisy rooms (Arnold & MacKenzie, 1998). More relevant to this discussion, an ongoing undercurrent has been that of stigmatization related to awkwardness in communication, aging, and having a mechanical appellation on the body (e.g., Arnold & MacKenzie, 1998; Branson & Miller, 2002; Kent & Smith, 2006).

The reluctance of many older adults to wear hearing aids affirms the existence of a stigmatizing factor related to the "hearing aid effect" despite the potential for some alleviation of communication difficulties. This effect was demonstrated in a study of factory workers who preferred to fake hearing even if this meant being perceived as socially incompetent (Hétu, Riverin, Getty, Lalande, & St-Cyr, 1990). The authors theorized that denial might be an adaptive process to avoid association with a devalued social group, specifically deaf people. One-third of the 225 respondents to survey questions, which were sent out to parents of dependents under age 22 with various levels of hearing loss, indicated that stigma associated with hearing aids and concern about how their child might be perceived factored in to their decision not to obtain hearing aids for their children (Kochkin, Luxford, Northern, Mason, & Tharpe, 2007). Arnold and MacKenzie (1998) speculate that there are two ways of wearing a hearing aid: the passive way, which accepts disability, stigma, and devaluation, versus the active way, which accepts hearing aid benefits and rejects self-devaluation. In efforts to counteract the "hearing aid effect," hearing aids are now being marketed either as entirely hidden or as a cool "fashion statement" like wireless headsets (Eisenberg, 2007), rather than a reflection of defectiveness.

There are children, including those of deaf parents, who comfortably wear their hearing aids all day and identify as deaf (Searls & Johnston, 1996). In a qualitative, unstructured interview study of 22 bilaterally, moderately hard-of-hearing adolescents in mainstream education, participants who perceived their use of hearing aids as "normal" were generally comfortable with their hard-of-hearing identity (Kent & Smith, 2006). The fact that hearing aids are often not noticeable (witness the title of the article reporting this study: "They only see it when the sun shines in my ears") reinforces the individual's ability to control identity. These adolescents' social and subjective experiences played a critical role in their comfort level with deaf-related identities. For example, one adolescent stated her friends did not mind whether she wore hearing aids, thereby increasing her comfort level and her awareness that the focus was on her as a person and not necessarily on her hearing aid. Those who were not comfortable tended to hide their hearing aids and, in tandem, their hard-of-hearing identity. This discomfort typically was compounded by feedback from naïve bystanders that tended to include negative stereotypical responses involving ridicule.

There are those who view hearing aids as the antithesis of maintaining quality signed languages (Murray, 2006). When hearing aids appeared on the scene, Deaf people viewed the push for hearing aids as one that reinforced oralism and detracted from the quality of signing. The passage of time has not dispelled this perspective but has only muted it by demonstrating that hearing aid users can and do hold on to their signed languages if they so desire. But the emergence of cochlear implants has been accompanied by concerns about the future of signing communities and their identity.

THE CASE OF COCHLEAR IMPLANTS

The research literature increasingly affirms that with appropriate intervention, cochlear implants* have the potential not only to develop and enhance receptive and expressive spoken language (e.g., Bat-Chava, Martin, & Kosciw, 2005; Christiansen & Leigh, 2002/2005; Geers, 2006; Klop, Briaire, Stiggelbout, & Frijns, 2007; Spencer & Marschark, 2003), but also to reconnect people who have lost their hearing to their former identities through improved quality of life (e.g., Chorost, 2005; Cohen, Labadie, Dietrich, & Haynes, 2005; Mo, Lindbæk, & Harris, 2005).

In contrast to individuals who decry the cochlear implant as a marginalizing tool that deprives deaf children and adults of connections with others like them by focusing on integrating into hearing societies, the general conclusion derived from parent perceptions of their children with cochlear implants is that social well-being is positive (Percy-Smith et al., 2006). Socialization with hearing peers improves as communication improves, not only with cochlear implants but also with hearing aids, as demonstrated in a longitudinal study with 41 young deaf children (Bat-Chava, Martin, & Kosciw, 2005). However, studies of children with cochlear implants playing in groups or participating in classroom discussion confirm the presence of ongoing struggle and lack of consistent success in group interactions with hearing peers (e.g., Boyd, Knutson, & Dahlstrom, 2000; Knutson, Boyd, Reid, Mayne, & Fetrow, 1997; Preisler, Tvingstedt, & Ahlström, 2005). Therefore, it cannot be assumed that cochlear implants are a universal panacea for ameliorating social difficulties with hearing peers. This gives some credence to

* Cochlear implants incorporate external and surgically implanted internal parts that operate to replace the role of the cochlea in transmitting sound to the brain.

the ongoing debate regarding the effectiveness and appropriateness of cochlear implantation in general and pediatric cochlear implantation in particular, a debate based on technological innovation and social policy that goes back to the 1970s (Christiansen & Leigh, 2002/2005).

How advantageous technology is for human interaction depends on the technology, the specific populations being affected, and the social context. In her treatise on social policies related to technology, Katherine Seelman (2001) explores how these policies change as a result of conflicting interests. While interest groups endorse "normalizing" types of technical devices developed for particular populations with specific disabilities, these same policies are also attacked by some population representatives who may not see the value of the specific device in question.

In the case of the cochlear implant, its interface with identity has become a battlefield. Some view the cochlear implant as denying the Deaf community a normal way of life, whereas others espouse the cochlear implant as a means of overcoming exclusion, connecting with hearing counterparts, and potentially disaffirming disability status. It has even been stated that the cochlear implant issue has caused more turmoil than anything else since the Milan Conference of 1880, which finalized the dominance of oralism over sign language in the education of deaf children (Hamerdinger, 2002).

When cochlear implants appeared on the scene, proponents of Deaf culture were outraged by the medicalization of cultural deafness and felt that Deaf people were being assaulted by an audist establishment (e.g., Christiansen & Leigh, 2002/2005; Ladd, 2007; Lane, Hoffmeister, & Bahan, 1996; Sparrow, 2005; Tellings, 1996). Harlan Lane's statement, "The idea of operating on a healthy baby makes us all recoil" exemplifies the depth of feeling against pediatric cochlear implantation (Nowak, 2006, p. 16). These feelings are in reaction to ongoing manifestations of the message that deaf is defective, reflective of a "spoiled identity," and therefore undesirable, rather than a natural human variation. To get an implant was to affirm the need to get rid of the "spoiled identity" of the deaf person through repairing a so-called defect and restoring some semblance of hearing identity to achieve a more "normalized" state (Cherney, 1999; Crouch, 1997; Lane, Hoffmeister, & Bahan, 1996; Mitchell, 2006b; Montgomery, 1991; Tellings, 1996). Inserting technical objects into humans creates so-called cyborgs, who are therefore deemed better than their previous defective state, even if they are artificially dependent on a permanent piece of technology (Cherney, 1999; Montgomery, 1991). This demonstrates the power of a technology inserted within the person to affect the perceived value and identity of the person.

The ultimate result of this effort to create an "artificial" hearing identity for the deaf child is viewed as reinforcing "outsider" status for cochlear implantees. They ostensibly can never be fully immersed in hearing culture because cochlear implants do not replicate the way hearing people hear sounds and do not guarantee full access to the hearing world (Ladd, 2003, 2007). Additionally, the absence of a clear Deaf identity due to lack of or limited exposure to Deaf people, which compounds the inability to integrate within the Deaf community, serves to reinforce this outsider status.

In contrast, advocates for cochlear implantation referred to a multitude of studies in passionately arguing for the usefulness of cochlear implants in facilitating interaction with hearing peers and improved educational opportunities (e.g., Balkany, Hodges, & Goodman, 1996; Tucker, 1998b). They claimed that denying the importance of audition created roadblocks to actualizing full potential as adults, taking into account the educational deficiencies traditionally noted for deaf students. In particular, Tucker (1998b), who obtained a cochlear implant at the age of 52 to get her first exposure to sound (her profound hearing loss precluded any benefit from hearing aids), emphatically rejected many of the arguments against cochlear implantation. While empathizing with the frustration and anger of Deaf people who have been subjected to discrimination as she was, she opined that rejecting such technology merely served to perpetuate their problems, problems that could at least be somewhat ameliorated by taking advantage of cochlear implants. According to her, cochlear implants represented a means of taking advantage of technology to facilitate daily living rather than a rejection of deaf identities.

The role of the media, dominated as it is by hearing contributors, has played a significant role in emphasizing the so-called cochlear implant miracle with its proclaimed potential for abolishing deafness and its focus on "hearing" replicas of deaf persons (Komesaroff, 2007; Ladd, 2007; Power, 2005). In addition to reinforcing the deficiency perspective of Deaf identities and minimizing the presence of Deaf adults who are satisfactorily handling their lives, various media outlets have essentially reduced the identity of nonimplanted deaf people to a concept of "silence" and disconnection from life (Baynton, 1996). However, there are some exceptions, such as *The New York Times Magazine*'s article: "Defiantly Deaf" (Solomon, 1994). A "cochlear implant" database search of the Australian daily press revealed that results predominantly focused on the medical model, with statements relying on a "prison of silence" and magical technology (Power, 2005). In contrast, the "deaf children" search had a slight preponderance of articles leaning toward the sociocultural model, which emphasizes the full lives of Deaf people.

The airing of the CBS "60 Minutes" segment on *Caitlin's Story* (which documented a 7-year-old girl who received a cochlear implant as a toddler) proved to be such a great endorsement of the normalization perspective that viewers were blinded to the rich lives in the Deaf community (Levesque, 2001). Additionally, publications by individuals such as Kathleen Treni (2002) and Michael Chorost (2005) reinforced the perspective that cochlear implants break down the "walls of silence" and connect deaf people more broadly. Treni, currently director of deaf and hard-of-hearing programs in Bergen County, New Jersey, was raised to rely on spoken language using speechreading augmented by a big body hearing aid to counteract her profound (110 dB) hearing level. (see Appendix) As an adult, she recognized herself as a visual oral deaf person. In 1992, she decided to get a cochlear implant in order to hear her children and her husband's musical productions. She regards the implant as having made a wonderful difference in terms of access to conversation, the telephone, and music.

Michael Chorost (2005) grew up as hard of hearing, relied on his hearing aids to reinforce his connections to his hard-of-hearing identity, went deaf, and then returned via cochlear implant to his hard-of-hearing status. In response to each change occasioned by software upgrades, he recognized new positive emotions that reinforced his sense of humanity as opposed to the loss of connection that accompanied the unexpected disappearance of his residual hearing. His current community is peopled by hearing persons, though interestingly he also expresses subtle regret at not being part of a Deaf community with its own unique connections, a community he is open to exploring.

Supporting the preponderance toward reinforcing "hearing" identities, the informed consent documents used by cochlear implant centers primarily focus on medical, audiological, communication, and educationally based information. Of the 121 centers responding to a survey soliciting feedback on the types of information provided to parents, not quite half (45%) reported presenting information on Deaf culture, American Sign Language use, and identity issues (Berg, Ip, Hurst, & Herb, 2007). This suggests that such information is not viewed equal in importance to the other information items.

The Oscar-nominated film *Sound and Fury* (Aronson, 1999) illustrates how the deaf and hearing members of a family were torn apart by the cochlear implant controversy. The hearing grandparents of 6-year-old Heather, who is deaf, argued vehemently against the Deaf parents' decision not to have their deaf daughter implanted. The Deaf parents, Peter and Nita, were fearful of losing their connection with the Deaf community and diminishing the Deaf identity that characterized their nuclear family.

But 6 years later, as a filmed sequel shows, the Deaf parents allowed Heather to get the implant, due both to pressure from the grandparents and to increasing recognition that children with implants can slide easily between hearing and deaf venues (Aronson, 2006). Peter, formerly adamant against the implant, said in the sequel that he has recognized the implant's usefulness for accessing the hearing world. He took comfort from the fact that Heather is nonetheless maintaining her ties to her Deaf identity. Peter's hearing sister-in-law, who has a deaf son with a cochlear implant, describes her son as benefiting fully from the implant while still embracing his Deaf identity (Putz, 2005).

The increasing acceptability of pediatric implantation by Deaf people is interposed with persistent anecdotes of Deaf community members claiming that Deaf parents who decide on having their deaf children implanted are betraying their culture. These Deaf parents do value their Deaf culture, but, similarly to Peter, they want their children to develop bicultural and bilingual competence in a complex, rapidly changing world. Their numbers are slowly increasing, as implied by the existence of relevant Internet blogs.

Most telling, after earlier vehement opposition to pediatric cochlear implantation (National Association of the Deaf, 1991), the NAD greatly softened its stance in a reissued position paper (National Association of the Deaf, 2000). This change is due in part to the exponential increase in cochlear implantees and their support of the procedure. Approximately 100,000 people worldwide have implants, with the United States showing 22,000 adults and roughly 15,000 children (Food and Drug Administration, 2005). In industrialized countries, the implantation rate is between 50% and 80% of profoundly deaf children (Hyde & Power, 2006). Clearly, this reflects consistent growth in succeeding years (Gallaudet Research Institute, 2006). In Australia, cochlear implantation has practically become a "standard" procedure. For this reason, Trevor Johnston (2004) doubts that many of these Australian implanted children will be exposed to any form of sign language, though some are. Based on various statistical analyses, he predicts the shrinking of the Deaf community with fewer deaf entrants.

However, there are no documented efforts to track late signers, oral deaf adults, and hard-of-hearing individuals who do enter and perpetuate the Deaf community (Carty, 2006; Hyde, Power, & Lloyd, 2006). Several authors have expressed doubt about whether sign language will die out even within the corpus of implanted children. It is believed that educational scenarios requiring visual access to language for a number of cochlear implant users or later entries into the deaf community based on a shared sense of experience and a desire to congregate with similar others will ensure the use of sign language (Brueggemann, 2008; Carty, 2006; Hyde, Power, & Lloyd, 2006; Mitchell, 2006b; Moores, 2006).

After Phil Aiello (Aiello & Aiello, 2001), a stalwart Deaf community member, was implanted in 1998, he was accused of being a traitor, being "sick," wanting to be "Hearing" by NAD convention attendees. He and his wife argued for welcoming cochlear implantees into the Deaf community, as they will "always be Deaf" (p. 412). "Deaf" is the identity they ascribe to this cochlear-implanted community of people, not as people who "think hearing" or who are a threat to the Deaf community (p. 411). Furthermore, there are supporting arguments that efforts to protect Deaf culture through denigrating the cochlear implant or cochlear implantees themselves not only run the risk of diminishing the Deaf community but also perpetuate the Deaf community's marginality in hearing society (Woodcock, 1992/2001).

Interestingly, while Australian and Swedish government funding is provided for cochlear implantation, the governments have also recognized Australian Sign Language (Auslan) and Swedish Sign Language, respectively, as the language of the Deaf community (Branson & Miller, 2002; Preisler, Tvingstedt, & Ahlström, 2005). In Australia, this direction represents policies that encourage opposing directions, with cochlear implanted children being channeled into mainstream educational programs focusing on spoken language and identity development that do not necessarily encompass d/Deaf identities (Hyde, Ohna, & Hjulstadt, 2006). In Sweden, cochlear-implanted (and hard-of-hearing) children can be found in both specialized and mainstream settings, with the latter setting focusing predominantly on spoken language (Brunnberg, 2005; Preisler, Tvingstedt, & Ahlström, 2005). In the United States, some children with cochlear implants may be separated from hard-of-hearing children and viewed as "hearing" in the educational domain (Luterman, 2004). This separation is worrisome because children with cochlear implants tend to be more like hard-of-hearing children than hearing children. Thus, their educational and social needs may not be met if their access to information is based on incorrect perceptions of how well they receive auditory information (Luterman, 2004; Marschark, 2004). While increasing numbers of these implanted children and young adults may choose to remain "hearing" if their environments are supportive and accessible, difficulties in satisfying social needs and the desire for stronger identity connections may foster curiosity about the Deaf world in later years.

The tenacity of Deaf people to survive every technological innovation devised thus far to draw them into assimilating within the hearing world reinforces the potential for creating a fusion between the cochlear implant and d/Deaf identities (Brueggemann, 2008; Padden & Humphries, 2005). In fact, this possibility is gaining credence in view of the increasing numbers of deaf students with cochlear implants attending specialized college programs for deaf students (Brueggemann, 2008; Ladd, 2007). As Lisa Herbert (2008) writes, "I'm grateful for the opportunities my cochlear implant offers me and I see it as completely compatible with being a signing Deaf person" (p. 139). Woodcock (1992/2001) informally observes that those deaf adults who have chosen the implant and maintained a positive Deaf identity appear happiest. Such individuals can hear quite well, speak well, sign well, and enjoy music without sacrificing their Deaf identity (Carty, 2006). Clearly, the pervasive perception of the "either-or" paradigm—either cochlear implantee or Deaf—is gradually becoming moot with the changing acceptance within Deaf communities today despite pockets of resistance (Hintermair & Albertini, 2005).

Current research evidence suggests that the fusion approach has some credibility. The 29 cochlear-implanted young adolescent interviewees in the Wheeler, Archbold, Gregory, and Skipp (2007) study felt positive about their cochlear implants and the decision made by their parents. They tended to be flexible in terms of signing or speaking, and they were comfortable with shifting as needed. While the majority did not demonstrate a strong Deaf identity, they represented themselves as intrinsically deaf. The possibility of stronger Deaf identity in young adulthood cannot be discounted, depending on their life circumstances, but their cochlear implants did not appear to be an insurmountable barrier to this process.

In a study of 45 adolescents with and without cochlear implants, hearing identity as measured by Glickman's Deaf Identity Development Scale (DIDS; see Chapter 2) was more frequently endorsed by cochlear-implanted participants compared to participants who did not use cochlear implants, possibly because of associated auditory benefits and comfort in socializing with hearing peers (Wald & Knutsen, 2000). The two groups were more similar than different in the bicultural, immersion, and marginal categories, with the bicultural identity receiving the strongest endorsement.

Observations based on interviews with 14 adolescent and young adult cochlear implant users indicated that most see themselves as deaf, while one who was 1 year postimplant labeled herself as hard of hearing (Christiansen & Leigh, 2002/2005). Most had deaf friends and desired contact with both deaf and hearing peers.

Based on a small qualitative interview study in Sweden, some children with cochlear implants see the implant as a natural part of their lives (Preisler, Tvingstedt, & Ahlström, 2005). They report on advantages such as awareness of environmental sounds and understanding of simple communication. Ease in understanding spoken communication was not a given, and interactions with hearing peers were often less than ideal due to noisy backgrounds or inability to sufficiently hear spoken language for comprehension purposes. Sign language was resorted to when understanding faltered. The authors conclude that developing a bicultural identity where one interacts with both deaf and hearing environments in a fluid way would be ideal for their interviewees.

Identity and attitudes toward cochlear implantation on the part of 115 deaf and hard-of-hearing Israeli adolescents were studied using Glickman's DIDS (see Chapter 2) and an attitudes questionnaire (Most, Wiesel, & Blitzer, 2007). Ten of the participants had cochlear implants,

92 had hearing aids, and 13 reported no auditory aids. Eleven of the participants used sign language, 73 used both signed and spoken languages, and 31 used speech only. Most participants (89) were in special classes within regular schools, while 26 were mainstreamed with only hearing peers. Results indicated the presence of positive attitudes toward the cochlear implant. Overall, bicultural identity was strongest, and stronger bicultural identity was positively correlated with more positive attitudes, in contrast to those endorsing a Deaf identity, which was associated with less positive attitudes although not a pronounced strong correlation. Adolescents with cochlear implants expressed more positive attitudes than all other participants in family climate, self-esteem, and communication, but they did not significantly differ in terms of attitudes regarding social status, academic achievements, Deaf culture, or in terms of identity classification. The authors concluded that bicultural identity allows for the potential to benefit from technological advances without feeling threatened with the loss of the Deaf experience. They recommend ongoing exposure to both Deaf culture and the auditory advantages of the cochlear implant.

The aforementioned studies imply that implants are not necessarily creating a body of children stuck between the deaf and hearing worlds, lacking a clear identity. Rather, they appear to be assuming more of a bicultural stance or comfort in shifting identities. In addition, how their identity takes shape is probably also influenced by how much the focus is on the technology as opposed to the child. For example, if a child says, "My name is.... I have a cochlear implant," how prominent is the cochlear implant appendage itself for the child's identity? Does it reinforce the cyborg status and the dependency on the technology as integral identity aspects? Could the child with a cochlear implant be simply an amalgam of both human and technology, "a metaphor for assimilation?" (Cherney, 1999, p. 33). Does this represent a problematic body image, as often depicted in Deaf-related media?

Chorost (2005) writes about the technology of cochlear implants making him "more human" in the process of attaining cyborg status. In this vein, he frames the interaction between technology and identity as a positive process that enhances his sense of self. In his eyes, humans control how technology is used and framed. Humans can replace the stigma of using hearing aids or cochlear implants with the coolness of people wearing these as they wear i-pods, walkmans, and other head-related technological attachments, thereby attenuating the negative implications for identity as a shamed and spoiled one. Appended technology per se has become more mundane and less stigmatizing, illustrating the power of humans in reframing perceptions about the interface of technology and identity.

Another way to view the interface between the individual and technology is to speak of a state of hybridity, a blending of two diverse cultures or traditions (Merriam, 1980). The reality is that cultural dichotomies are giving way to the process of cultural interchanges, which result in new forms and practices reflecting components of both cultures (Hermans & Kempen, 1998). For instance, hybridization can be reflected in a person with a cochlear implant being part of Deaf culture. Even those who are able to alternate between being a so-called cyborg who speaks and a Deaf culture member will somehow find both aspects overlapping depending on the situation. This process suggests that biculturalism can evolve into some sort of hybridization that reflects the fluidity of specific identities.

From the parents' perspective, to refuse the cochlear implant may limit the extent to which the child will assimilate into the hearing world, and to accept it may limit the extent to which Deaf becomes part of the child's identity (Berg, Herb, & Hurst, 2005; Christiansen & Leigh, 2002/2005). Hearing parents often feel that giving the child a cochlear implant will open up all possibilities rather than precluding any one option, including that of entering the Deaf community, while denying a child the cochlear implant will preclude participation in the hearing culture of the parents.

In light of the premise that the cochlear implant incorporates all possibilities, the prevailing practice of using spoken languages in the home forces the question of how the child's Deaf identity can evolve in conjunction with a hearing or hard-of-hearing identity. A considerable number of parents do attempt to sign in the home to ensure ongoing access to language (Christiansen & Leigh, 2002/2005; Zaidman-Zait, 2008). A recent British study involving 142 parents who responded to a mailed questionnaire noted the presence of a tendency for children to lead the change to increased spoken language use postimplant even when the parents continued to use signed communication (Watson, Hardie, Archbold, & Wheeler, 2008). Parents still valued the use of signing in certain circumstances but also felt that the usefulness of spoken language was a critical factor in reinforcing the child's reliance on that language. This is a situation that defies an easy solution in the early years, but it is one that may be resolved in later years in the direction of either assimilation into the hearing society or gravitation toward contact with d/Deaf people and a bicultural or hearing/deaf identity.

Boundaries between cochlear implants and Deaf communities need not exist. These boundaries can be broached by deaf individuals with cochlear implants when they demonstrate openness toward their country's signed language and Deaf people, even as they keep on speaking (Lloyd & Uniacke, 2007; Woodcock, 2001). Attitude rather than cochlear implants per se are key, as the Aiellos eventually demonstrated (Aiello & Aiello, 2001). If individuals project an attitude reinforcing the superiority of speech over sign and find that they do not fit in with Deaf peers, they may then interpret their inability to fit in as a rejection of their cochlear implant instead of recognizing the effect of their attitude. In turn, the attitude of Deaf persons in welcoming implantees appears to be increasingly contingent upon the implantee demonstrating respect for Deaf culture.

While cochlear implants may typically be framed as a social good, this perspective must be tempered with caution related to the nature of expectations regarding language, communication, education, happiness, and identity. Again, much depends on individual variables and environmental opportunities. Some benefit amazingly, others receive no benefit, and many find themselves in-between. Recognizing the efficacy of the cochlear implant while simultaneously recognizing that it is not a panacea can hopefully lead to a reduction in oppositional terminology and minimization of the expectations that a hearing/normalized identity will be achieved (Hyde & Power, 2006). This may also provide common ground for recognizing the fluidity of identities that a person with a cochlear implant may demonstrate depending on life circumstances.

IMPLICATIONS OF GENETIC TECHNOLOGY FOR IDENTITY

Approximately 60% of hearing loss present at birth or occurring very early in life is genetic, and there are more than 400 different forms of hereditary deafness (Arnos, 2002; Dagan & Avraham, 2004). For two-thirds of hereditary cases, deafness is nonsyndromic, while the remaining one-third results in syndromic deafness, meaning that there are associated medical or physical features, such as white forelocks or heart defects (Arnos, 2002). In addition to the fact that only a few dozen of the estimated 400 genes for deafness have been characterized, the size and complexity of many of these genes currently preclude tests. Testing is now widely available for a few common forms of genetic deafness, the most prevalent of which is the gene *GJB2* (more commonly referred to by the name of the protein the gene produces, connexin 26).

The hearing status of children of a person deaf from connexin 26 depends upon the genetic status of their hearing or deaf partner. This is confirmed by a review of available data on deaf parents and their offspring as well as computer simulations illustrating how the tendency of deaf and hearing people who communicate using sign language (linguistic homogamy) to select each other as marriage partners results in a significant increase in the frequency of connexin deafness (Nance, 2004). In fact, Nance asserts that selective mating is integral in human evolution. However, based on the ways in which most genes for deafness are transmitted (an autosomal recessive pattern), there is no guarantee of generational deafness.

Genetic testing is often available for several different purposes. Examples include testing used to determine the genetic status of a deaf child or adult (called diagnostic testing), carrier testing in the hearing relatives of deaf persons to determine whether they carry genes for deafness, and prenatal testing to determine the genetic status of a fetus. Preimplantation genetic diagnosis (PGD) is a newer technique that combines genetic testing of embryos within days of egg fertilization with in vitro fertilization in a Petri dish to allow parents to select the desired genetic outcome (Johnston, 2005; Nance, 2003; Rolland & Williams, 2006).

Diagnostic testing in deaf infants or children may carry the benefit of early genetic identification related to preventing or preparing to deal with complex medical conditions associated with syndromic deafness. This may prevent progressive hearing loss, which can be devastating for those so affected, and allow for assistance to parents who are psychologically dealing with the identification of deafness and considering ways of integrating their deaf child into the home setting. Diagnostic genetic testing for common genes for deafness in infants and children newly identified with hearing loss is now considered a standard of care (Pandya & Arnos, 2006). It is natural for deaf adults to be curious about the cause of their deafness, and some seek diagnostic testing to understand this along with their chances of having deaf or hearing children. However, while they are curious about possible outcomes, many prefer to let nature follow its course and would not consider the use of prenatal diagnosis or PGD (Arnos, 2002). In this context, the distinction between the use of genetic testing to learn more about the cause of one's own deafness and reproductive possibilities, which can be empowering, and the choice not to use prenatal diagnosis or PGD to change reproductive outcomes is quite important.

To date, findings from several studies have attempted to answer the question of how the possibilities of having genetically deaf or hearing babies are perceived. In a study of participants with equal involvement in both deaf and hearing communities, disinterest in selecting a partner to ensure children with specific hearing status was typical (Taneja, Pandya, Foley, Nicely, & Arnos, 2004). The results of a survey of 87 Deaf adults who strongly identified with Deaf cultural issues indicated the presence of a predominately negative attitude toward genetics and concern about its potentially adverse impact on Deaf people, with a majority thinking genetic testing would do more harm than good (Middleton, Hewison, & Mueller, 1998). Only 16% were supportive of prenatal diagnoses for deafness. A follow-up study by Middleton, Hewison, and Mueller (2001) indicated that half of the hearing participants would consider prenatal diagnosis for genetic deafness compared to 21% of deaf and 39% of hard-of-hearing and deafened participants. Preference for deaf children was expressed by 8% of the deaf participants who endorsed prenatal genetic testing for deafness. Whether they would actually follow through with "genetic selection" is open to debate, considering that self-report may not necessarily reflect internal opinions. Of note is that most participants in this study who endorsed genetic testing for deafness did so ostensibly to prepare to support the child as needed.

Other attitudinal studies support the Middleton et al. (2001) findings indicating that hearing participants express higher percentages of interest in prenatal diagnosis for genetic deafness compared to deaf participants (Brugner et al., 2000; Martinez, Linden, Schimmenti, & Palmer, 2003). This suggests the presence of ongoing negative perceptions of deafness on the part of hearing participants, while culturally Deaf people may be more inclined to value the continuance of the Deaf community through having deaf children. This perspective is endorsed in a study including deaf participants from Gallaudet University and the National Association of the Deaf and hard-of-hearing participants who were members of Self Help for the Hard of Hearing (Stern et al., 2002), as well as results from focus groups eliciting attitudes toward genetic testing (Burton, Withrow, Arnos, Kalfoglou, & Pandya, 2006). Additionally, results from a questionnaire distributed to 106 Gallaudet University students asking about hearing status preferences for future children resulted in 74% indicating no preference, while the rest overwhelmingly indicated a preference for deaf children (one preferred to have a hearing child) (Miller, Moores, & Sicoli, 1999). Those who preferred deaf children most likely view having a deaf child as affirming the possibility of a clear Deaf identity and full participation in their culture from birth onward, parallel to what hearing parents anticipate for their hearing children in terms of home culture affiliation. There is a caveat, however, in that Johnston (2005, 2006) makes the argument that the actual preference for having a deaf child may be far less common than indicated by the aforementioned studies. This may be primarily because these individuals do not want their child to experience the difficulties associated with the deaf experience but may not feel comfortable overtly acknowledging this. For these individuals, the contradictory message of normal variation and deficiency coexists, making it a struggle to determine genetic priorities.

Clearly, there are profound social and psychological implications related to the increasing "power of knowledge" regarding genetic inheritance and choices about human characteristics. Confronting these is unavoidable as advances in genetic technology evolve into ever-increasing possibilities for selecting certain genes or genetic mutations, including those that can create deaf or hearing characteristics in babies. While genetic-related decisions will be profoundly influenced by cultural beliefs and experiences within particular social communities, awareness of the possibilities related to genetic manipulation will force individuals to acknowledge perceptions about themselves relative to their identities and their level of comfort in choosing to go with nature as opposed to making specific reproduction choices. This knowledge, however, raises the specter of social control related to passing judgment on the value of certain kinds of human lives. The process of prenatal testing has been framed as a social decision, reflecting covert societal views about the unacceptability of disabilities as a variation of the human race and as a different way of being, with unique forms of identity.* As such, accepting prenatal testing in actuality challenges the oft-endorsed proclamations of societies that persons with disabilities, including deaf persons and those affiliated with Deaf communities, are entitled to respect and equal treatment with those not in the disability category (Asch, 2001; Burke, 2006; Sandel, 2007). When reproductive choices are made that counteract prevailing views of "normalcy," repercussions are sure to follow.

To increase the chances of having a deaf baby, a Deaf lesbian couple visited a sperm bank and were informed that potential donors were eliminated if congenital deafness was a possibility (Mundy, 2002). Subsequently, a deaf friend agreed to be the donor. The baby turned out to be deaf. Public reactions ranged from support to vitriolic opposition. In Australia, a couple was allowed to discard embryos carrying the connexin 26 gene mutation because the state viewed the embryos as defective prior to implantation (Henderson, 2002; Johnston, 2004). The Infertility Treatment Authority in Australia has sanctioned the use of PGD to support the possibility of hearing children, but not deaf children (Middleton, 2004). In Great Britain, new fertility legislation was proposed that stipulated the following: (1) restriction of the use of embryos produced through in vitro fertilization procedures that contain genetic abnormalities when embryos without such genetic makeup are available, and (2) the same restriction for those who may serve as an embryo donor. This legislation proceeded with support (House of Lords, 2007). The stipulation is that embryo selection must be based on the grounds of avoiding disease. From the perspective of legislators supporting this effort, genes such as the connexin 26 mutation can easily fall into the disease category. Those deaf individuals who opposed the bill saw themselves as leading perfectly normal lives; they were comfortable with their d/Deaf identities and resented being pathologized (e.g., Bova, 2008).

The emergence of such legislative efforts and the reproductive decisions reported so far reflect society's devaluation of deaf lives. In a world focused on auditory channels of communication, these actions evoke intense emotions from Deaf individuals who are concerned about the

---

* The implications of managing life-threatening medical issues through the use of genetic technology is also a critical area of consideration, one that is beyond the scope of this chapter.

future of their culture and the potential of genetic technology to enable unethical reproductive choices.

Walter Nance (2003), a researcher on genetic deafness, questions whether future critics will view the potential diminishing of the deaf community as a medical triumph or as an "egregious" example of cultural genocide. In turn, Arnos (2002) alerts us to the importance of recognizing the distinction between eugenics as practiced by the Nazis who promulgated a "lives not worth living philosophy" that resulted in the extermination of millions of lives (see Chapter 5) and modern human genetics. This is critical in order to avoid falling prey to ideologies directed at restricting reproductive freedom at the cost of sacrificing our humanity and sensitivity to differences. These ideologies can take the shape of efforts to ensure that deaf persons deal with the ramifications of choosing to be deaf rather than burden society, identity issues notwithstanding, even while society has obligations to accommodate those who are deaf (Tucker, 1998b). The ethical complexities are beyond the scope of this chapter, but underlying all this is the comfort level of both hearing and deaf societies related to affirming the possibility of deaf identities when children with different hearing status are born. Genetic researchers such as Nance (2003) are sensitive to this aspect and the need for empowering deaf parents to the same degree hearing parents are empowered in terms of genetic choices.

The increasing prevalence and acceptability of genetic testing, together with the real possibility of institutional eradication of genes for deafness based on political decisions as genetic technology evolves, is extremely suggestive of the devaluation of deaf identities. Consequently, the number of children born deaf may very well contract. However, from an economic perspective, the current cost of genetic testing and the fact that many families may not be aware of familial inheritance possibilities may limit the scope of this contraction. Additionally, the limited availability of technology in evolving countries where signing Deaf communities have been found to exist presages the ongoing existence of individuals who claim a Deaf identity (Christiansen & Leigh, 2002/2005).

CONCLUSION

The interactive technology of today is capable of providing deaf and hard-of-hearing individuals with new ways of relating through avenues of communication that permit not only the coalescing of various communities but also the potential for clashes of perspectives between communities based on identity affiliations. Far greater attention has been devoted to medically related technology (specifically cochlear implantation and genetic engineering) directed at the amelioration of hearing difference and the enhancement of normalized "lives worth living" (Hintermair & Albertini, 2005). This has had the consequence of polarizing communities into "either-or" paradigms: either for being Deaf or for speaking and "hearing." However, as suggested in this chapter, evolving technology does not have to lead to such "either-or" dichotomies that constrain the development of various identities related to hearing status. In today's complex society, the fluidity of identities takes on greater meaning as people are exposed to and learn different ways of being, whether in auditory or signing communities. Additionally, even with cochlear implantation and genetic technology, there is no realistic way to eradicate worldwide populations of deaf people. Providing opportunities for interacting with various d/Deaf and hearing communities through ever-improving interactive technology will allow deaf or hard-of-hearing children and adults to discover identities that fit their particular needs.

9

Perspectives

...the identity story is characterized by the moments at which boundaries are drawn, redrawn and transgressed.
    Kath Woodward (2002, p. 167)

Deaf and hard-of-hearing people *are* diverse. They reflect the diversity of the world we all live in. They do not learn how to be deaf or hard of hearing in isolation. They learn through their perceptions of the messages conveyed to them by others at different stages of their lives (Mottez, 1990). They assert their identities through their acceptance or rejection of these messages and their reframing of themselves as time passes. How they manifest their identities differs from era to era and from individual to individual. The intersections of their individuality, including their personalities, ethnicity, religion, skills and limitations, gender, socioeconomic status, sexual orientation, etc., and their deaf or hard-of-hearing identities will metamorphose as they proceed throughout time from one environmental context to another.

It is increasingly apparent that specific deaf identity categories run the danger of oversimplifying the meanings of being deaf, Deaf, hard of hearing, or hearing. Because of this limitation, which essentially denies the complexities of integrating into diverse environments, reliance on a single and primary unifying identity is giving way to the plurality of identities/self-labels (Mishler, 2004), some of which can conflict with each other. The apparent incompatibility of Deaf with its associated relative disinterest in speech and reliance on visual cues with the "hearing and speaking" auditory component that may manifest within the bicultural label is a case in point. This incompatibility has, for example, created incongruous situations for hearing children of Deaf parents, who all too often find themselves on the margin between the culture of hearing that they have full access to and the culture of Deaf that they grew up within.

As portrayed throughout the book, the roles of families and peers, of culture, language, communication, education systems, technology, self-perceptions, and environmental messages play critical and variable roles in how identities related to being d/Deaf, hard of hearing, and hearing are conceptualized, played out, and integrated into the self. As

Lindsey Rentmeester, currently pursuing a clinical doctorate in audiology, looks back on her educational history, during which she started in the mainstream, transitioned to a specialized school at age 11, and then returned to the mainstream for high school, she states:

> My Clarke* experience gave me an opportunity to really accept my hearing loss as part of who I am. It may provide additional challenges in my life, but it does not and will not limit me. By accepting that part of me, I developed a stronger self-identity. (Rentmeester, 2006/2007)

As various groups of deaf and hard-of-hearing people continue to live their increasingly diverse and multifaceted existences, contacts with different and new groups (e.g., cochlear implantees, international d/Deaf groups with different perspectives) become almost inevitable. This can lead either to consolidating a specific identity category or exploring new dimensions of identity to see whether these can be slipped on like new gloves.

However, if the plurality of identities as exemplified in the fluid identity construct is taken to be more reflective of reality, the questions, "Who am I?" and "Who is 'the real me'?" become increasingly salient. If I experiment with different facets of my deaf or hard-of-hearing identity and show these in different settings, which one is my real "deaf identity"? With auditory aids, I could be "hearing." When my auditory aids are turned off or if I am hearing and turn to relying on my eyes, I become part of the People of the Eye (Deaf). And if I use both auditory and visual avenues to communication, I could be deaf or bicultural, as the case may be. Clearly, representations of deaf identity can no longer be static and dichotomous in the sense of "either-or." Rather, these are evolving, based on different facets of the inner "real" me that are influenced by where I am and who I am with, either by choice or necessity. There often may be tension and ambiguity on the borders of different deaf identity constellations, throwing us into uncertainty as to who we are, as we struggle during various phases of our lives to determine our inner core. This constitutes the dynamic nature of this inner core construct. Underlying all this, it is critical to acknowledge that comfort with oneself as a person who hears differently or who is attuned to the world of the eye is a sine qua non for positive emotional health and quality of life.

Are people always aware of their deaf or hard-of-hearing identities? These identities were historically centered within the body,

* The Clarke School for the Deaf is also a Center for Oral Education located in Northampton, Massachusetts, with satellite centers in various locations. Its goal is to prepare students for mainstream education.

specifically in the guise of malfunctioning ears. But with technology, various cultural/linguistic influences, the emergence of Deaf Studies as a scholarly discipline, and the situation of hearing children of Deaf parents, the locus of the deaf or hard-of-hearing identity within the body is giving way to social constructions depending on setting. How we are as deaf, hard of hearing, or hearing, how we use language to communicate, and the quality of that communication, whether spoken, signed, or a mixture of both, serve to subtly shape how our identity becomes manifested to ourselves and to others. The extent of this awareness can shift from consciousness to unconsciousness and back again. People can be aware of themselves and who/what they are without having to constantly conceptualize their selves as related to deaf, hard of hearing, or hearing. Mottez (1990) does us a service by reminding us to move away from over-intellectualizing components of ourselves.

Do these d/Deaf or hard-of-hearing identities encompass who people are? Again, these identities are one of many identities inherent within each individual. But when these identities are used in isolation, they become monoliths that stereotypically color the entire person and in turn an entire category of people. When we discuss schools for the deaf, jobs for the so-called "hearing impaired," organizations for the hard of hearing, and so on, the meaning inherent in these phrases is that of a homogeneity that masks the diverse peoplehood encompassed by each term, a diversity that has been emphasized throughout this book. As Ellen Rhoades, an auditory verbal therapist who is deaf and works with children who are deaf, exclaims:

> ...I dislike it when we people with hearing disabilities are objectified, such as when we are referred to as "the hearing impaired" or "the deaf." Many schools, organizations, and programs continue in this vein; I wish they would at least refer to us as people. How much more difficult would it be to refer to us as "people (or children) with hearing impairments" or "people who are deaf"? Regardless of how profound, a hearing impairment is one of many descriptors or characteristics. Whether the deafness is or is not *the* most important characteristic should be left up to the individual or parent. Because I perceive this objectification pejoratively, I feel diminished whenever I hear my colleagues refer to themselves as "teachers of the deaf." (E. Rhoades, personal communication, November 23, 2007)

Should deaf and hard-of-hearing people formally learn about Deaf culture and history? Storbeck and Magongwa (2006) argue about the importance of doing so as a way of enhancing self-understanding and identity development through connections to a rich Deaf heritage. They also acknowledge the importance of recognizing the interconnectivity of Deaf identity and identity connections with the larger (hearing and diverse) communities. This emphasizes the development of multicultural and multilingual components of identity in addition to the Deaf component and reinforces awareness of the complexities of these rich historical traditions.

However, this is easier said than done because of the oft-noted separations between perceptions of Deaf and non-Deaf identity constellations. These separations are highlighted by (1) potential prejudices that upon contact lead to tensions, interpersonal stereotyping, and intergroup biases; and (2) the undermining of communication, cooperation, and focused effort/productivity. When identities confront each other stubbornly, organizational and psychological conflict can escalate.

To deal with these problems, Jones, Lynch, Tenglund, and Gaertner (2000) emphasize the need to better understand and manage diversity in order to reduce tensions. Based on an extensive review of the literature, they recommend that the contact hypothesis be augumented by the diversity hypothesis to counteract prejudice. The contact hypothesis affirms the principle that the more the contact with others of equal status or in pursuit of a common goal, the less the prejudice. The diversity hypothesis argues that four conditions are required: (1) full participation occurs across all levels of society for members of diverse groups; (2) the degree of participation approximates population demographics for these groups; (3) there is a common purpose between the groups; and (4) cultural identity is valued. When the perspective of the minority group is positively acknowledged, the positive effects of contact are enhanced for majority group members and other minority group members as well. The possibility of interpersonal, decategorizing processes concomitant with group recategorizing processes may influence how the diverse groups can move toward coalescing into a "we" affirmation and mutual respect while at some level still maintaining their uniqueness.

Within the context of this book, maintaining one's deaf identity type label while recognizing membership in the larger and cohesive group of people who are deaf and hard of hearing is an important goal. And in striving for it, deaf individuals will continue to reduce tension and enhance collaboration on common causes related to communication accessibility and quality educational access, whether visual, auditory, or both. Additional sequelae could also include increasing comfort with alternate possibilities of "being" that will permit identity permutations depending on context and time. In essence, this endorses a model whereby deaf identities can alternate as needed without sacrificing one's primary deaf identity choice.

The contact hypothesis is gaining credence as the boundaries between deaf and hearing increasingly show fissures. This is not only because of technology but also because of educational trends. Within inclusion settings, there are more opportunities for hearing–deaf interactions, although too often (but not always) the quality of deaf–hearing interactions can be far less than ideal. The Maryland School for the Deaf (MSD) in Frederick, Maryland, has begun to explore the possibility of providing potential opportunities for hearing–deaf interactions by admitting hearing students; this may also attract students with cochlear implants (Hernandez, 2007). MSD students have suggested that this is one way for groups to learn from each other, with the qualification that American Sign Language (ASL) remain at the core to avoid marginalization of Deaf students. In other words, hearing students and students with cochlear implants must be competent in ASL to survive in this particular environment, in which written English is also valued. As one student observed, such a move will serve to break down the typical separation of Deaf children within Deaf families from the hearing community. There are reports of increasing deaf and hearing collaboration within school programs, organization boards, administration entities, and universities (e.g., Andrews, Leigh, & Weiner, 2004; Benedict & Sass-Lehrer, 2007), among the most noteworthy being the increased component of d/Deaf members of the Gallaudet University Board of Trustees relative to hearing board members.

DIASPORA

It might not be far-fetched to state that deaf people are increasingly in a state of diaspora, at least in the United States and Australia, among other countries. This is engendered not only by technology but also by the education movement toward inclusion and the shrinking population in schools for the deaf that formerly produced a strong sense of community and identity (Johnston, 2004). In short, the history of Deaf community as a central place…deaf schools, deaf clubs, deaf sports, is metamorphosing into the present deaf community with more fragile interconnections through distance and greater interactions with the surrounding hearing community. While diaspora populations may expect to or dream of returning "home," this is not necessarily the case with deaf dispersed communities (Murray, 2008). Their "home" may be temporary public spaces where deaf people gather at one time or another.

Paul Gilroy (2004) refers to the notion of diaspora as having an effect on identity. Diaspora relates to a relational network that emerges out of forced dispersal, relocation, and transition. Gilroy (2004) compares his perception of diaspora to seeds of the same species taking root in different places, with the resulting, still-related plants manifesting different results depending on environmental variables. He considers the results to reflect a transcultural mixture, "a hybrid, recombinant form, that is indebted to its 'parent' cultures" (p. 323). In part because of this diaspora, an essentialist, absolute Deaf identity becomes less viable even while owing its ongoing solidarity to the Deaf ways of the past, including historical signed language, historical events such as the Deaf President Now protest, and various Deaf culture events. Even though Deaf people are more visible than ever, more of them are distant from each other and at the mercy of chance encounters or internal needs to seek out others like themselves. Interconnections with hearing culture are increasingly feasible due to technological advances. Ongoing popular media portrayals of deaf persons are most often in an interactive mode with hearing contemporaries, for example, the deaf actor on one of the *Star Trek* series, Marlee Matlin in *The West Wing*, deaf characters in *Four Weddings and a Funeral*, the deaf child in *Mr. Holland's Opus*, and other films. In this way they portray the identity of the body and deaf ways of being, but at the same time they are part of the mainstream and not so often set apart as lonely, isolated, individuals who are limited in their communication. As part of the mainstream, exposure to mainstream ways of relating and living are sure to influence how deaf individuals feel about themselves and the ways in which they behave and feel as d/Deaf.

Considering that most public schools do not have programs or courses of study involving Deaf studies or the history of deaf people, the emergence of diaspora means that deaf and hard-of-hearing identities increasingly involve indirect and convoluted, often tension-filled journeys toward exploration. These may include various possibilities of being as a person who hears differently or with sign skills before settling on some congenial deaf identity constellation. Whether these journeys involve exposure to deaf gatherings, Internet information, interactive technology that improves access to both deaf and hearing peers, public policies affecting communication access for persons with hearing differences, sign language classes, etc., they will differently influence the journey toward internalizing specific identities.

THE 2006 GALLAUDET UNIVERSITY PROTEST

The appointment of Jane K. Fernandes as the new president-designate of Gallaudet University sparked a controversy that led to the May and October 2006 Gallaudet University protest, a protest that was widely publicized in the media. The rationales for this protest were often obfuscated by the diverse reasons reported to the press (e.g., Bauman, 2008b; Brick, 2006; Davis, 2007; Kinzie, 2006b; Schemo, 2006), which naturally created confusion for many observers as to exactly what the protesters were fighting for.

Due to the recent nature of this protest, only now has there been an initial effort to produce in-depth analyses of the issues that gave rise to and played out in the protest. According to Dirksen Bauman (2008b), the 2006 Gallaudet University protest was an anomaly. Typically, there is a lack of on-campus protests at other universities against, for example, administrative excesses, including inappropriate benefits for administrators, and decisions not always in the best interest of the higher education setting in question. The passion generated by this protest, which fueled threats against those who were not part of the protest and who were seen as traitors to the cause (e.g., Allen, 2007; Cohen, 2006), led students to defy administrative edicts and submit to arrests by local police. This supports the premise that the protest was in part a protest about identity, particularly what Deaf today means.

Some background will help to provide context. In large part, the protest was not only a response to perceived problematic aspects of Fernandes' administrative style as observed during her stewardship of the Clerc Center at Gallaudet University and her tenure as Gallaudet University Provost but also to questions about the legitimacy of the process used to elevate her to the presidency. Simmering beneath the surface was frustration about the following: where Gallaudet was going as an institution in the face of technology focused on the use of audition and educational trends supporting mainstreaming and inclusion (shades of the diaspora, both of which are significantly influencing the nature of future students coming to Gallaudet University); claims of audism (see Chapter 6) on a campus ostensibly devoted to the elevation of Deaf people through education and work; and the perceived exclusion of the campus community occasioned by what was labeled as a lack of transparency during a presidential search process perceived as vital to the future of the University. Due to the elimination of an African American Deaf applicant prior to the final round in the application process, allegations of racism also surfaced.

During the protest, among the many points of discussion was that of Jane Fernandes' deaf identity. The issue exploded when Fernandes was asked about her perceptions of the reasons for the protest and suggested that her not being Deaf enough was a bone of contention (Davis, 2007). This angered protestors who saw otherwise. Fernandes herself grew up using spoken language and learned ASL in early adulthood, a process that replicated that of a good number of faculty and students who actively opposed her selection based on her leadership style and denied the "not Deaf enough" as a factor. Many of them reflected the diversity of identity and communication described throughout the book, including hearing, hard-of-hearing, and deaf late signers; hearing, hard-of-hearing, and Deaf ASL native users; late-deafened adults; and those claiming diverse ethnic heritages. However, Davis (2007) asserts that the issue of identity could not so easily be ignored, since the "not Deaf enough" does highlight the tension caused by and inherent in deaf identity attributions. He focuses attention on its valence for the core of Gallaudet University's existence and asks about its importance within the context of deaf identities and the symbolism of Gallaudet University.

Bauman (2008c) considers that a key component contributing to the rationale for the protest, in addition to Fernandes' personal and professional credentials for the presidency, has to do with the previous administration. He argues that the previous administration, of which she was a part, did not take a concerted stand on the inclusion of bilingual education, meaning ASL as well as English, and pitted "inclusion against bilingualism" (p. 330). He essentially accuses the previous administration of yielding to the forces of diverse communication methodologies, which advocate for different forms of access to classroom discourse rather than creating a clear focus on ASL as an academic expectation for all students.

Even though Fernandes defended her positive valuation of ASL, a number of protesters nonetheless viewed her implied dilution of ASL as a deaffirmation of the value of Deaf culture. At some level, the protest was a rally for the ongoing existence of a Deaf community and the centrality of ASL within the context of a Deaf identity that permitted greater inclusion and interaction with others through appropriate and relevant educational approaches. Essentially, what evolved was a loud cry to the world that Deaf is a psychologically healthy way to be, ASL is linguistically deserving of respect on par with English, and the use of ASL will enhance deaf lives and interaction possibilities. This overpowered arguments against the narrow cultural absolutism criticism and accusations by the public at large that cultural segregation was implied by the increased focus on Deaf culture (Bauman, 2008c).

As a result of the protest, Gallaudet University's accreditation was called into question based not only on the fact that students shut down the university against accreditation regulations but also on the need to scrutinize Gallaudet's performance in meeting higher education standards. These standards included mission and implementation procedures. Gallaudet University subsequently redefined its mission statement to indicate an institutional commitment to embracing diversity within the deaf community by respecting and appreciating choices of communication while guiding students through their process of linguistic and cultural self-actualization. It is clear what this means from an identity perspective. The focus is to develop bilingual proficiency in ASL and English, thereby enhancing access to Deaf cultural ways as a self-actualizing process. Such a process ostensibly has the goal of confronting the diaspora and countering predictions by Johnston (2004) and other doomsayers regarding the potential demise of ASL and the Deaf community. Through embracing academically rigorous ways of teaching and guiding deaf students, the University endeavors to create a new generation of students intellectually capable of understanding the meanings of Deaf identity.

DEAF ENOUGH?

In the postprotest atmosphere at Gallaudet University, which continues to be accredited, there are new efforts directed at welcoming diverse students and overcoming the negative sequelae to the "not Deaf enough" slogan, which could easily frighten away potential students new to Deaf culture who are nonsigners. In the effort to project a less rigid attitude about who is sufficiently Deaf and develop inclusive strategies for new nonsigning students, various venues have been organized to discuss communication diversity and the role of ASL on campus. At one panel session focusing on cochlear implant issues that I witnessed during the Spring 2008 academic semester, two panelists with cochlear implants who already knew ASL prior to arriving on campus remarked on the ease with which they were accepted. In contrast, a senior, also with a cochlear implant, described the struggles she faced when she arrived on campus as a new signer. She had difficulties in acclimating to the campus at first, but her determination to remain despite the wariness expressed by peers who signed fluently was an experience similar to that reported by Dianne Brooks (1996; see Chapter 3). Even more telling, she reported that of all the new signers she met on campus, not one remained.

If one is "not Deaf enough," one runs the danger of not belonging. This has bearing on the question of authenticity and what Deaf really means. In his attempt to examine the "not Deaf enough" concept, Davis (2007) focuses on the inability to sign pure ASL as disqualifying one from being a bona fide representative of Deaf culture. His perspective is that the essentialist perspective of Deaf culture marginalizes the "other" who would like to fit in but does not meet essentialist background or interaction criteria. This holds even in the face of claims about the heterogeneity and contested boundaries of "Deaf" (Krentz, 2007). Bastions of Deaf culture are going to have to deal with the shifting boundaries between essentialism and nonessentialism if the Deaf community and Gallaudet University are going to remain viable and welcoming to new entrants. This is an issue that Gallaudet University is vigorously working to resolve.

CONCLUSION

As this book demonstrates, there is no objective reality regarding identity. Identity emerges out of narration and labeling efforts, with people revising who and what they are depending on occasion, audience, and reason for explaining (Mishler, 2004). As Jenkins (2005) puts it, psychology needs to move toward broader cultural perspectives related to the different psychological ways of being normal and human. Hermans and Dimaggio (2007) as well as Raggatt (2006) write of the movement toward a multivoiced dialogical self involved in internal and external interchanges (with others) that is evolving, without an ultimate final destination. Different cultures can come together or oppose each other in the self, resulting in multiple representations of identity.

We are now moving from binary notions of identity (deaf versus hearing, hard of hearing versus Deaf, or Deaf versus hearing) to a far more multifaceted notion of identity (Davis, 2008; Skelton & Valentine, 2003), though some will resist this evolution and revert to the safety of a clearly delineated identity and cultural home. Pollard (2004) emphasizes how permutations of what "deaf" means vary along dimensions of foreground or background issues and simultaneously negative versus positive perceptions depending on an individual's context. This leads to heterogeneity regarding self-perceptions or perceptions generated by "others." In today's globalized environment, where the technology that has created cyberspace can be a great equalizer, where "deaf" or Deaf or "hard of hearing" less often means communication interference when the playing field is equal, where manifested deaf identities are increasingly fluid depending on circumstances and desire, the possibilities of yet-to-be-defined new concepts of *deaf* are emerging. These are possibilities that incorporate flexibility in meeting new expectations going beyond biology, linguistics, historically adverse oppression, and fixed understandings of shared experiences (Davis, 2007). With a more equal playing field, the need to firmly assert any type of deaf identity could even recede, evidenced by the Martha's Vineyard situation and similar examples.

Deaf Studies has undertaken the huge task of examining what Deaf means and the heterogeneity along with the homogeneity manifested in those claiming Deaf identity. There is also a scholarly duty to more forcefully acknowledge and study the complexity of deaf and hard-of-hearing identities over and beyond Deaf. Specifically, more study is needed on deaf identities that reflect a very large group with diverse language and communication choices, albeit connected through their understandings of common parameters of experiences, an effort being led by Brueggemann (2008).

We are now in the midst of a renaissance during which we deaf people ourselves are exploring who we are apart from the "can't do" perspectives imposed on us by those who hear. In an attempt to define whom we are, to paraphrase Jenkins (2005), we can appreciate the plurality inherent in construing the meaning of deaf and can be open to imagining a range of different possibilities rather than being forced to choose. To be fully open to what it is to be a person who is deaf or hard of hearing is to recognize the many distinct contributions related to different ways of being. The bottom line is that of comfort with the d/Deaf or hard-of-hearing self, as the case may be.

We want to do "the right thing" but sometimes it is awfully difficult to figure out exactly what that right thing is related to our deaf identity perception. To be judgmental is a problem. It makes us scared to make a mistake about whom and what we are. Above all, our identity, however it is manifested, must feel comfortable, natural, emanating from positive reinforcement. When there is unease about deaf identity within oneself, that is a consequence of negative reinforcement, and it will detract from one's search for a comfortable inner self (Corker, 1994; Mitchell, 2006). Specifically, if one's inner self or an obvious aspect (i.e., hearing difference) is denigrated, ignored, or devalued, a self will emerge that is predicated on false premises reinforced by "others" to conform to their own perceptual beliefs (Gill, 1997; Harter, 1997). This "false self" represents attempts at connecting with others to obtain approval, but paradoxically this prevents authentic relationships and authentic comfort with the inner self. It is essentially up to the individual to determine the authenticity of whatever deaf or hard-of-hearing identity resides within. Once that authentic identity is recognized, the person will feel validated related to that sense of self.

This authenticity will help deaf and hard-of-hearing persons as they work to claim their places in the sun, particularly in relation to hearing societies. Deaf and hard-of-hearing people have all too often been denied substantive decision-making roles in situations that will directly or indirectly affect their lives or the lives of deaf and hard-of-hearing children (Andrews, Leigh, & Weiner, 2004; Benedict & Sass-Lehrer, 2007). The implication for identity is to minimize who they are and deny them their right to thrive, a further reinforcement of deaf identity denigration. The crumbling of divisive boundaries occasioned by improved communication pathways has facilitated the process of emerging mutual respect, although there is still a long way to go.

As we learn about ourselves in relation to others, and about the cultures we live in or interact with, our views of ourselves will change as we encounter different contexts (Cross & Gore, 2003). It is time for us to move to an authentic "deaf or hard of hearing in my own way" state of being, but not necessarily in terms of Ohna's (2004) classification, which suggests that people find their way to being deaf or hard of hearing when they acknowledge ambivalence in relating to hearing persons in an existential frame (see Chapter 2). Rather, let us strive to define ourselves in bold, individual terms: how *I* live my life as a d/Deaf or hard-of-hearing person, how *I* intermingle with d/Deaf, hard-of-hearing, or hearing others, how *I* communicate, and with whom *I* prefer to socialize. If you want to know me, know me through my story (McAdams, 1993). The abundance of unique stories reveals that, after all, there are many ways to be deaf, Deaf, or hard of hearing.

Appendix: Audiology 101 and Demographics

Who are the people we explore in this book? These individuals represent the spectrum of auditory diversity, ranging from those who hear to persons classified as having a hearing loss. "Hearing loss" reflects multiple hearing levels, ranging from the 16 decibel (dB)* cutoff for identifying a slight hearing loss to 26 dB for mild hearing loss, 41dB for moderate hearing loss, 71 dB for severe deafness, and 91dB and up for profound deafness (Clarke, 1981). Individuals who are profoundly deaf cannot hear without auditory amplification, but those who are moderately to severely deaf may be able to hear something, depending on the amount of hearing they have at each frequency within the speech range of 500 to 2000 Hz. Those with hearing levels between 26 dB and 70 dB are generally considered to be hard of hearing. They have the capability of developing or using linguistic skills primarily through auditory pathways with appropriate amplification, but they may also rely on vision as a backup (Ross, 2005).

Not every person with a hearing difference pays attention to hearing-level categories (Brueggemann, 1999; Woll & Ladd, 2003). Even though demographics tend to be based on audiological categorizations, individuals who respond to surveys may select categories or labels that do not necessarily match their hearing level (Mitchell, 2006a). For example, a severely hard-of-hearing person may select the "deaf" category based on unique life circumstances. Why this happens is what this book purports to explore.

The estimated number of persons with hearing loss ranging from mild to profound levels in the United States is approximately 34 million adults, most of whom have age-related hearing loss (Plies & Coles, 2002). The estimated prevalence of severe to profound hearing loss ranges from 464,000 and up to approximately a million when those who have difficulty hearing "normal conversation" even with auditory

* Decibel represents the unit of measurement of sound intensity (loudness).

assistance are included (Blanchfield, Feldman, Dunbar, & Gardner, 2001; Mitchell, 2006a). This constitutes the functionally deaf category. Within this category, those individuals who use ASL number approximately 500,000 based on a 1974 population study, with subsequent larger estimates extrapolated from population estimates of increasing numbers of persons with hearing loss (Mitchell, Young, Bachleda, & Karchmer, 2006). One fast-growing segment anticipated to expand the population of deaf people represents those within the anticipated 76 million baby boomers entering their 60s who become deaf as part of the aging process (Bowe, 2005).

Hard-of-hearing individuals are estimated at 10 million (Mitchell, 2006a). Obviously, in comparison to those who are functionally deaf, hard-of-hearing individuals constitute the great majority of individuals with significant hearing loss. The rest of the estimated 34 million categorized as having a hearing loss likely include the larger population for which hearing loss does not seriously hinder normal conversation.

Out of every 1,000 U.S. children, 83 have an educationally significant hearing loss (U.S. Public Health Service, 1990). Nonetheless, many are in the educational mainstream. Approximately 39,500 children and youth (representing an estimated 65%–75% of the total figure) have been reported by schools and programs serving deaf and hard-of-hearing children and youth (Gallaudet Research Institute, 2006).

References

Abrams, J. (1998). *Judaism and disability*. Washington, DC: Gallaudet University Press.

Ahmad, W., Atkin, K., & Jones, L. (2002). Being deaf and being other things: Young Asian people negotiating identities. *Social Science & Medicine, 55*, 1757–1769.

Aiello, A. P., & Aiello, M. (1999/2001). Cochlear implants and deaf identity. In L. Bragg (Ed.). *Deaf world* (pp. 406–412). New York: New York University Press.

Akamatsu, C. T., Mayer, C., & Farrelly, S. (2006). An investigation of two-way text messaging use with deaf students at the secondary level. *Journal of Deaf Studies and Deaf Education, 11*(1), 120–131.

Allen, C. (2007, April 2). Identity politics gone wild. *Weekly Standard, 12*(28). Retrieved March 26, 2007, from http://www.weeklystandard.content/Public/Articles/000/000/013/458tonjc.asp.

Anderson, G., & Bowe, F. (1972/2001). Racism within the deaf community. In L. Bragg (Ed.). *Deaf world* (pp. 305–308). New York: New York University Press.

Anderson, G., & Grace, C. (1991). Black deaf adolescents: A diverse and under-served population. *Volta Review, 93*(5), 73–86.

Anderson, G., & Miller, K. (2005). Appreciating diversity through stories about the lives of deaf people of color. *American Annals of the Deaf, 149*(5), 375–383.

Andersson, Y. (1994). Comment on Turner. *Sign Language Studies, 83*, 127–131.

Andrews, J., & Covell, J. (2006/2007). Preparing future teachers and doctoral-level leaders in deaf education: Meeting the challenge. *American Annals of the Deaf, 51*(5), 464–475.

Andrews, J., Leigh, I. W., & Weiner, M. (2004). *Deaf people: Evolving perspectives from psychology, education, and sociology*. Boston: Allyn & Bacon.

Andrews, J., Martin, T., & Velásquez, J. (2007, April 23). The need for additional Latino professionals in deaf education. *Hispanic Outlook*, 40–43.

Angelides, P., & Aravi, C. (2006/2007). A comparative perspective on the experiences of deaf and hard of hearing individuals as students at mainstream and special schools. *American Annals of the Deaf, 151*(5), 476–487.

Antia, S., & Kreimeyer, K. (2003). Peer interaction of deaf and hard-of-hearing children. In M. Marschark & P. Spencer (Eds.). *Oxford handbook of deaf studies, language, and education* (pp. 164–176). New York: Oxford University Press.

Aramburo, J. (1994). Sociolinguistic aspects of the Black Deaf community. In C. Erting, R. Johnson, D. Smith, & B. Snider (Eds.). *The Deaf way* (pp. 474–482). Washington, DC: Gallaudet University Press.

Arnett, J. (2002). The psychology of globalization. *American Psychologist, 57,* 774–783.

Arnold, P., & MacKenzie, I. (1998). Rejection of hearing aids: A critical review. *Journal of Audiological Medicine, 7,* 173–199.

Arnos, K. (2002). Genetics and deafness: Impacts on the deaf community. *Sign Language Studies, 2*(2), 150–168.

Aronson, J. (Producer & Director) (1999). *Sound and Fury* [Film]. (Available from Aronson Films & Public Policy Productions, 35 E. 20th St., New York, NY 10003).

Aronson, J. (Producer & Director) (2006). *Sound and Fury: Six Years Later* [Film]. (Available from Aronson Films & Public Policy Productions, 35 E. 20th St., New York, NY 10003).

Asch, A. (2001). Disability, bioethics, and human rights. In G. Albrecht, K. Seelman, & M. Bury (Eds.). *Handbook of disability studies* (pp. 297–326). Thousand Oaks, CA: Sage.

Association of Late-Deafened Adults, Inc. (2008). Retrieved November 17, 2008, from http://www.alda.org.

Backenroth, G. (1995). Deaf people's perception of social interaction in working life. *International Journal of Rehabilitation Research, 18,* 76–81.

Bagga-Gupta, S., & Domfors, L. (2003). Pedagogical issues in Swedish deaf education. In L. Monaghan, C. Schmaling, K. Nakamura, & G. Turner (Eds.). *Many ways to be Deaf* (pp. 67–88). Washington, DC: Gallaudet University Press.

Bahan, B., & Bauman, H-D. (2005, September 14). *Narrative, identity, and theory in Deaf Studies.* Presentation. Gallaudet University, Washington, DC.

Bain, L., Scott, S., & Steinberg, A. (2004). Socialization experiences and coping strategies of adults raised using spoken language. *Journal of Deaf Studies and Deaf Education, 9,* 120–128.

Baker, C. (1999). Sign language and the deaf community. In J. Fishman (Ed.). *Handbook of language and ethnic identity* (pp. 122–139). New York: Oxford University Press.

Baldwin, S. (1993). *Pictures in the air.* Washington, DC: Gallaudet University Press.

Balkany, T., Hodges, A., & Goodman, K. (1996). Ethics of cochlear implantation in young children. *Otolaryngology–Head and Neck Surgery, 114*(6), 748–755.

Ballin, A. (1930/2001). Coming to California. In L. Bragg (Ed.). *Deaf world* (pp. 27–32). New York: New York University Press.

Barnartt, S., & Scotch, R. (2001). *Disability protests.* Washington, DC: Gallaudet University Press.

Barnes, C., & Mercer, G. (2001). Disability culture: Assimilation or inclusion. In G. Albrecht, K. Seelman, & M. Bury (Eds.), *Handbook of disability studies* (pp. 515–534). Thousand Oaks, CA: Sage.

Bat-Chava, Y. (1993). Antecedents of self-esteem in deaf people: A meta-analytic review. *Rehabilitation Psychology, 38,* 221–234.

Bat-Chava, Y. (1994). Group identification and self-esteem of deaf adults. *Personality and Social Psychology Bulletin, 20,* 494–502.

Bat-Chava, Y. (2000). Diversity of deaf identities. *American Annals of the Deaf, 145,* 420–428.

Bat-Chava, Y., & Deignan, E. (2001). Peer relationships of children with cochlear implants. *Journal of Deaf Studies and Deaf Education, 6*(3), 186–199.

Bat-Chava, Y., & Martin, D. (2002). Sibling relationships of deaf children: The impact of child and family characteristics. *Rehabilitation Psychology, 47*(1), 73–91.

Bat-Chava, Y., Martin, D., & Kosciw, J. (2005). Longitudinal improvements in communication and socialization of deaf children with cochlear implants and hearing aids: Evidence from parental reports. *Journal of Child Psychology and Psychiatry, 46*(12), 1287.

Bauman, H-D. (1997). Towards a poetics of vision, space, and the body. In L. Davis (Ed.). *The disability studies reader* (pp. 315–331). New York: Routledge.

Bauman, H-D. (2004). Audism: Exploring the metaphysics of oppression. *Journal of Deaf Studies and Deaf Education, 9*(2), 239–246.

Bauman, H-D. (2005). Designing deaf babies and the question of disability. *Journal of Deaf Studies and Deaf Education, 10*(3), 311–315.

Bauman, H-D. (2008a). Introduction: Listening to Deaf Studies. In H-D. Bauman (Ed.). *Open your eyes: Deaf Studies talking* (pp. 1–32). Minneapolis, MN: University of Minnesota Press.

Bauman, H-D. (2008b). On the disconstruction of (sign) language in the Western tradition: A Deaf reading of Plato's *Cratylus*. In H-D. Bauman (Ed.) *Open your eyes: Deaf Studies talking* (pp. 127–145). Minneapolis, MN: University of Minnesota Press.

Bauman, H-D. (2008c). Postscript: Gallaudet protests of 2006 and the myths of exclusion. In H-D. Bauman (Ed.). *Open your eyes: Deaf Studies talking* (pp. 327–336). Minneapolis, MN: University of Minnesota Press.

Bauman, Z. (1996). From pilgrim to tourist—or a short history of identity. In S. Hall & P. duGay (Eds.). *Questions of cultural identity* (pp. 18–36). London: Sage.

Baumeister, R. (1997). The self and society: Changes, problems, and opportunities. In R. D. Ashmore & L. Jussim (Eds.). *Self and identity* (pp. 191–217). New York: Oxford University Press.

Baumeister, R., & Leary, M. (1995). The need to belong: Desire for interpersonal attachments as a fundamental human motivation. *Psychological Bulletin, 117,* 497–529.

Baumeister, R., Twenge, J., & Ciarocco, N. (2003). The inner world of rejection: Effects of social exclusion on emotion, cognition, and self-regulation. In J. Forgas & K. Williams (Eds.). *The social self: Cognitive, interpersonal, and intergroup processes* (pp. 161–174). New York: Psychology Press.

Baynton, D. (1993). "Savages and Deaf-Mutes": Evolutionary theory and the campaign against sign language in the nineteenth century. In J. Van Cleve (Ed.). *Deaf history unveiled* (pp. 92–112). Washington, DC: Gallaudet University Press.

Baynton, D. (1996). *Forbidden signs*. Chicago: University of Chicago Press.

Baynton, D. (1997). A silent exile on this earth. In L. Davis (Ed.). *The disability studies reader* (pp. 128–150). New York: Routledge.

Baynton, D. (2005). Defectives in the land: Disability and American immigration policy, 1882–1924. *Journal of American Ethnic History, 24,* 31–44.

Baynton, D. (2006). "The undesirability of admitting deaf mutes": U.S. immigration policy and deaf immigrants, 1882–1924. *Sign Language Studies, 6*(4), 391–415.

Baynton, D. (2008). Beyond culture: Deaf studies and the deaf body. In H-D. Bauman (Ed.). *Open your eyes: Deaf Studies talking* (pp. 293–313). Minneapolis, MN: University of Minnesota Press.

Benedict, B. S., & Sass-Lehrer, M. (2007). Deaf and hearing partnerships: Ethical and communication considerations. *American Annals of the Deaf, 152*(3), 275–282.

Berg, A., Herb, A., & Hurst, M. (2005). Cochlear implants in children: Ethics, informed consent, and parental decision-making. *The Journal of Clinical Ethics, 16*(3), 239–250.

Berg, A., Ip, S., Hurst, M., & Herb, A. (2007). Cochlear implants in young children: Informed consent as a process and current practices. *American Journal of Audiology, 16,* 13–28.

Bernstein, P. (2006, June 4). March of technology opens doors to deaf. Retrieved June 4, 2006, from http://www.baltimoresun.com/technology/bal-id.vision-04jun04,0.1476375.story?coll=bal-technology-headlines.

Berry, J. W. (2002). Conceptual approaches to acculturation. In K. Chun, P. B. Organista, & G. Marín (Eds.). *Acculturation* (pp. 17–37). Washington, DC: American Psychological Association.

Berry, J. W., & Sam, D. L. (1997). Acculturation and adaptation. In J. W. Berry, P. R. Dasen, & T. S. Saraswathi (Eds.). *Handbook of cross-cultural psychology, Volume 3: Basic processes and human development* (2nd ed.) (pp. 291–326). Needham Heights, MA: Allyn & Bacon.

Bertling, T. (1994). *A child sacrificed to the Deaf culture.* Wilsonville, OR: Kodiak Media Group.

Best, H. (1943). *Deafness and the deaf in the United States.* New York: Macmillan.

Bienvenu, M. J. (1991/2001). Can Deaf people survive "deafness?" In L. Bragg (Ed.). *Deaf World* (pp. 318–324). New York: New York University Press.

Biernat, M. (2003). Toward a broader view of social stereotyping. *American Psychologist, 58*(12), 1019–1027.

Biernat, M., & Dovido, J. (2000). Stigma and stereotypes. In T. Heatherton, R. Kleck, M. Hebl, & J. Hull (Eds.). *The social psychology of stigma* (pp. 88–125). New York: Guilford.

Biernat, M., Eidelman, S., & Fuegen, K. (2003). Judgment standards and the social self: A shifting standards perspective. In J. Forgas & K. Williams (Eds.). *The social self: Cognitive, interpersonal, and intergroup processes* (pp. 51–72). New York: Psychology Press.

Biesold, H. (1999). *Crying hands.* Washington, DC: Gallaudet University Press.

Birman, D. (1994). Acculturation and human diversity in a multicultural society. In E. Trickett, R. Watts, & D. Birman (Eds.). *Human diversity* (pp. 261–284). San Francisco, CA: Jossey Bass.

Bishop, M., & Hicks, S. (2005). Orange eyes: Bimodal bilingualism in hearing adults from Deaf families. *Sign Language Studies, 5,* 188–230.

Blanchfield, B., Feldman, J., Dunbar, J., & Gardner, E. (2001). The severely to profoundly hearing-impaired population in the United States: Prevalence estimates and demographics. *Journal of the American Academy of Audiology, 12,* 183–189.

Bloch, N. (2006, February/March). Executive View. *NADmag, 5(6),* 7.

Blotzer, M., & Ruth, R. (1995). *Sometimes you just want to feel like a human being.* Baltimore: Paul H. Brookes.

Bochner, S. (1982). The social psychology of cross-cultural relations. In S. Bochner (Ed.). *Cultures in contact: Studies in cross-cultural interaction* (pp. 5–44). Oxford, England: Pergamon Press.

Bova, M. (2008, March 17). Retrieved March 26, 2008, from http://abcnews. go.com/print?id=4464873

Bowe, F. (2005, September 27). Disability meets the boom. *Ragged Edge Magazine.* Retrieved November 17, 2008, from http://www.raggededgemagazine.com/ departments/closerlook/00106.

Boyd, R., Knutson, J., & Dahlstrom, A. (2000). Social interaction of pediatric cochlear implant recipients with age-matched peers. *Annals of Otology, Rhinology, and Laryngology, 109*(Suppl. 185), 105–109.

Boyd, R., & Van Cleve, J. (2007). Deaf autonomy and deaf dependence: The early years of the Pennsylvania Society for the Advancement of the Deaf. In J. Van Cleve (Ed.). *The deaf history reader* (pp. 153–173). Washington, DC: Gallaudet University Press.

Branson, J., & Miller, D. (1998). Achieving human rights. In A. Weisel (Ed.). *Issues unresolved* (pp. 88–100). Washington, DC: Gallaudet University Press.

Branson, J., & Miller, D. (2002). *Damned for their difference: The cultural construction of deaf people as disabled.* Washington, DC: Gallaudet University Press.

Branson, J., Miller, D., & Marsaja, I. (1996). Everyone here speaks sign language, too: A deaf village. In C. Lucas (Ed.). *Multicultural aspects of sociolinguistics in Deaf communities* (pp. 39–57). Washington, DC: Gallaudet University Press.

Breivik, J. (2005). *Deaf identities in the making.* Washington, DC: Gallaudet University Press.

Brewer, M., & Pickett, C. (2003). The social self and group identification: Inclusion and distinctiveness motives in interpersonal and collective identities. In J. Forgas & K. Williams (Eds.). *The social self: Cognitive, interpersonal, and intergroup processes* (pp. 255–271). New York: Psychology Press.

Brick, K. (2006, November 2). First step in Gallaudet Revolution? *The Baltimore Sun.* Retrieved November 14, 2006, from http://www.baltimoresun.com/ news/opinion/oped/ballop.gallaudet02nov02,0,1636443.story.

Bronfenbrenner, U. (2005). Ecological systems theory. In U. Bronfenbrenner (Ed.). *Making human beings human: Bioecological perspectives on human development* (pp. 106–173). Thousand Oaks, CA: Sage.

Brooks, D. (1996). Experiences of a deaf African-American. In I. Parasnis (Ed.). *Cultural and language diversity and the Deaf experience* (pp. 246–257). New York: Cambridge University Press.

Brooks, J. (2006). Strengthening resilience in children and youths: Maximizing opportunities through schools. *Children and Schools, 28*(2), 69–76.

Brown, L. (1995). Lesbian identities: Concepts and issues. In A. D'Augelli & C. Patterson (Eds.). *Lesbian, gay, and bisexual identities over the lifespan: Psychological perspectives* (pp. 3–23). New York: Oxford University Press.

Brueggemann, B. J. (1999). *Lend me your ear: Rhetorical constructions of deafness.* Washington, DC: Gallaudet University Press.

Brueggemann, B. J. (2007). Introduction: Deaf lives leading deaf lives. *Sign Language Studies, 7*(2), 111–134.

Brueggemann, B. J. (2008). Think-between: A Deaf Studies commonplace book. In H-D. Bauman (Ed.). *Open your eyes: Deaf Studies talking* (pp.177–188). Minneapolis, MN: University of Minnesota Press.

Brueggemann, B. J., & Burch, S. (Eds.). (2006). *Women and deafness: Double visions.* Washington, DC: Gallaudet University Press.

Brugner, J., Murray, G., O'Riordan, M., Mathews, A., Smith, R., & Robin, N. (2000). Parental attitudes toward genetic testing for pediatric deafness. *American Journal of Human Genetics, 67,* 1621–1625.

Brunnberg, E. (2005). The school playground as a meeting place for hard of hearing children. *Scandinavian Journal of Disability Research, 7*(2), 73–90.

Buchanan, R. (1999). *Illusions of equality.* Washington, DC: Gallaudet University Press.

Buehl, K. (2002). Kristin Buehl. In J. Reisler (ed.). *Voices of the oral deaf* (pp. 5–13). Jefferson, NC: McFarland and Company.

Bull, T. (1998). *On the edge of Deaf culture.* Alexandria, VA: Deaf Family Research Press.

Burch, S. (2002). *Signs of resistance: American Deaf cultural history, 1900 to 1942.* New York: New York University Press.

Burch, S., & Joyner, H. (2007). *Unspeakable.* Chapel Hill, NC: University of North Carolina Press.

Burke, T. B. (2006). Comments on "W(h)ither the Deaf Community." *Sign Language Studies 6*(2), 174–180.

Burton, S., Withrow, K., Arnos, K., Kalfoglou, A., & Pandya, A. (2006). A focus group study of consumer attitudes toward genetic testing and newborn screening for deafness. *Genetics in Medicine, 8*(12), 779–784.

Buss, D. M. (2004). *Evolutionary psychology: The new science of the mind* (2nd ed.). Boston: Allyn & Bacon.

Calderon, R., & Greenberg, M. (1999). Stress and coping in hearing mothers of children with hearing loss: Factors affecting mother and child adjustment. *American Annals of the Deaf, 144*(1), 7–18.

Calderon, R., & Greenberg, M. (2003). Social and emotional development of deaf children. In M. Marschark & P. Spencer (Eds.). *Oxford handbook of deaf studies, language, and education* (pp. 177–189). New York: Oxford University Press.

Cambra, C. (2002). Acceptance of deaf students by hearing students in regular classrooms. *American Annals of the Deaf, 147*(1), 38–45.

Camilleri, C., & Malewska-Peyre, H. (1997). Socialization and identity strategies. In J. W. Berry, P. R. Dasen, & T. S. Saraswathi (Eds.). *Handbook of cross-cultural psychology, Volume 2: Basic processes and human development* (2nd ed.) (pp. 41–67). Needham Heights, MA: Allyn & Bacon.

Cappelli, M., Daniels, D., Durieux-Smith, A., McGrath, P., & Neuss, D. (1995). Social development of children with hearing impairments. *The Volta Review, 97,* 197–208.

Carty, B. (1994). The development of Deaf identity. In C. Erting, R. C. Johnson, D. Smith, & B. Snider (Eds.). *The Deaf way* (pp. 40–43). Washington, DC: Gallaudet University Press.

Carty, B. (2006). Comments on "W(h)ither the Deaf Community." *Sign Language Studies, 6*(2), 181–189.

Centre for Deaf Studies (2006). Retrieved February 11, 2006, from http://www.bris.ac.uk/deaf/library/deafstudies_info

Cerney, J. (2007). *Deaf education in America*. Washington, DC: Gallaudet University Press.

Charlson, E., Strong, M., & Gold, R. (1992). How successful teenagers experience and cope with isolation. *American Annals of the Deaf, 137*(3), 261–270.

Cherney, J. L. (1999). Deaf culture and the cochlear implant debate: Cyborg politics and the identity of people with disabilities. *Argumentation and Advocacy, 36,* 22–34.

Chorost, M. (2005). *Rebuilt: How becoming part computer made me more human*. Boston: Houghton Mifflin.

Chovaz McKinnon, C., Moran, G., & Pederson, D. (2004). Attachment representations of deaf adults. *Journal of Deaf Studies and Deaf Education, 9*(4), 366–386.

Christensen, K. (Ed.). (2000). *Deaf plus: A multicultural perspective*. San Diego, CA: DawnSign Press.

Christiansen, J. B., & Barnartt, S. (1995). *Deaf president now!* Washington, DC: Gallaudet University Press.

Christiansen, J. B., & Leigh, I. W. (2002/2005). *Cochlear implants in children: Ethics and choices*. Washington, DC: Gallaudet University Press.

Clark, J. L. (2006, January). Being DeafBlind is normal. *Signews, 4*(1), 17.

Clarke, J. B. (1981). The uses and abuses of hearing loss classification. *ASHA, 23,* 493–500.

Cohen, L. H. (2006, October 31). Signs of revolution. *New York Times*. Retrieved October 31, 2006, from http://www.nytimes.com/2006/10/31/opinion/31cohen.html?

Cohen, S., Labadie, R., Dietrich, M., & Haynes, D. (2005). Quality of life in hearing-impaired Adults: The role of cochlear implants and hearing aids. *Otolaryngology–Head Neck Surgery, 131*(4), 413–422.

Cole, S., & Edelman, R. (1991). Identity patterns and self- and teacher-perceptions of problems for deaf adolescents: A research note. *Journal of Child Psychology and Psychiatry, 32,* 1159–1165.

Collins, R. (2005a). *Can't tell the players without a program—One of a series of articles on the awakening oral hearing loss community*. Retrieved March 28, 2006, from http://www.hearinglossweb.com/Issues/Identity/ohl/nat/nat.htm.

Collins, R. (2005b). *Few HOH people employed by "Deaf and HOH" agencies—One of a series of articles on the awakening oral hearing loss community*. Retrieved March 28, 2006, from http://www.hearinglossweb.com/Issues/Identity/ohl/nat/nat.htm.

Collins, S., Devine, D., & Paris, D. (2005, May). *Navigating the path to understanding: The Arizona Native American deaf and hard of hearing task force*. Lecture presented at ADARA Biennial Conference, Orlando, FL.

Connor, L. (1992). *The history of the Lexington School for the Deaf (1864–1985)*. New York: The Lexington School for the Deaf.

Corbett, C. (1999). Mental health issues for African American Deaf people. In I. W. Leigh (Ed.). *Psychotherapy with deaf clients from diverse groups* (pp. 151–176). Washington, DC: Gallaudet University Press.

Corbett, C. (2003). Special issues in psychotherapy with minority Deaf women. In M. Banks & E. Kaschak (Eds.). *Women with visible and invisible disabilities* (pp. 311–329). New York: The Haworth Press.

Corker, M. (1994). *Counselling—The deaf challenge*. London: Jessica Kingsley.

Corker, M. (1996). *Deaf transitions*. London: Jessica Kingsley.

Corker, M. (1998). *Deaf and disabled, or deafness disabled?* Buckingham, England: Open University Press.

Cornell, S., & Lyness, K. (2004). Therapeutic implications for adolescent deaf identity and self-concept. *Journal of Feminist Family Therapy, 16*, 31–49.

Corrigan, P. (2004). How stigma interferes with mental health care. *American Psychologist, 59*, 614–625.

Côté, J. (2006). Emerging adulthood as an institutionalized moratorium: Risks and benefits to identity formation. In J. J. Arnett & J. L. Tanner (Eds.). *Emerging adults in America* (pp. 85–116). Washington, DC: American Psychological Association.

Côté, J., & Levine, C. (2002). *Identity formation, agency, and culture: A social psychology synthesis*. Mahwah, NJ: Lawrence Erlbaum.

Côté, J., & Schwartz, S. (2002). Comparing psychological and sociological approaches to identity: Identity status, identity capital, and the individualization process. *Journal of Adolescence, 25*, 571–586.

Cowan, P., & Cowan, C. (2007). Attachment theory: Seven unresolved issues and questions for future research. *Research in Human Development, 4*(3–4), 181–201.

Coyner, L. (1993). Academic success, self-concept, social acceptance, and perceived social acceptance for hearing, hard of hearing, and deaf students in a mainstream setting. *Journal of the American Deafness and Rehabilitation Association, 27*, 13–20.

Crandall, C. (2000). Ideology and lay theories of stigma: The justification of stigmatization. In T. Heatherton, R. Kleck, M. Hebl, & J. Hull (Eds.). *The social psychology of stigma* (pp. 126–150). New York: Guilford.

Cross, S. E., & Gore, J. (2003). Cultural models of the self. In M. Leary & J. Tangney, (Eds.). *Handbook of self and identity* (pp. 536–564). New York: Guilford.

Cross, W. (1971). The Negro to black conversion experience. *Black World, 20*, 13–27.

Crouch, R. (1997). Letting the deaf be Deaf. *Hastings Center Report, 27*(4), 14–21.

Croucher, S. (2004). *Globalization and belonging: The politics of identity in a changing world*. Lanham, MD: Rowman & Littlefield.

Cuéllar, I., & Glazer, M. (1996). The impact of culture on the family. In M. Harway (Ed.). *Treating the changing family* (pp. 17–36). New York: Wiley.

Cushman, P. (1995). *Constructing the self, constructing America: A cultural history of psychotherapy*. Reading, MA: Addison-Wesley.

Dagan, O., & Avraham, K. (2004). The complexity of hearing loss from a genetics perspective. In J. Van Cleve (Ed.). *Genetics, disability, and deafness* (pp. 81–93). Washington, DC: Gallaudet University Press.

Davidson, A. (1996). *Making and molding identity in schools*. Albany, NY: State University of New York Press.

Davie, C. (Director). (1992). *Passport without a country* [videotape]. Queensland, Australia: Griffith University.

Davis, J., Elfenbein, J., Schum, R., & Bentler, R. (1986). Effects of mild and moderate hearing impairments on language, educational, and psychosocial behavior of deaf children. *Journal of Speech and Hearing Disorders, 51*, 53–62.

Davis, L. J. (1995). *Enforcing normality: Disability, deafness, and the body.* London: Verso.

Davis, L. J. (2000). *My sense of silence.* Urbana, IL: University of Illinois Press.

Davis, L. J. (2001). Identity politics, disability, and culture. In G. Albrecht, K. Seelman, & M. Bury (Eds.). *Handbook of disability studies* (pp. 535–545). Thousand Oaks, CA: Sage.

Davis, L. J. (2007, January 12). Deafness and the riddle of identity. *The Chronicle Review, 53*(19), B6.

Davis, L. J. (2008). Postdeafness. In H-D. Bauman (Ed.). *Open your eyes: Deaf Studies talking* (pp. 314–325). Minneapolis, MN: University of Minnesota Press.

De Clerck, G. (2007). Meeting global deaf peers, visiting ideal deaf places: Deaf ways of education leading to empowerment, an exploratory case study. *American Annals of the Deaf, 152*(1), 5–19.

de St. Aubin, E., Wandrei, M., Skerven, K., & Coppolillo, C. (2006). A narrative exploration of personal ideology and identity. In D. McAdams, R. Josselson, & A. Lieblich (Eds.). *Identity and story* (pp. 223–248). Washington, DC: American Psychological Association.

DeAngelis, T. (2002). A new generation of issues for LGBT clients. *Monitor on Psychology,33*(2), 42–44.

DePoy, E., & Gilson, S. (2004). *Rethinking disability.* Belmont, CA: Brooks/Cole.

Desselle, D. (1994). Self-esteem, family climate, and communication patterns in relation to deafness. *American Annals of the Deaf, 139,* 322–328.

Diamond, L., & Savin-Williams, R. (2000). Explaining diversity in the development of same-sex sexuality among young women. *Journal of Social Issues, 56,* 297–313.

Dively, V. (1999/2001). Contemporary Native Deaf experience: Overdue smoke rising. In L. Bragg (Ed.). *Deaf world* (pp. 390–405). New York: New York University Press.

Dixon, R. (2006). Managing bullying of students who are deaf or hearing-impaired. *Deafness and Education International, 8*(1), 11–32.

Dobie, R., & Van Hemel, S. (2005). *Hearing loss: Determining eligibility for Social Security benefits.* Washington, DC: The National Academies Press.

Dovido, J., Major, B., & Crocker, J. (2000). Stigma: Introduction and overview. In T. Heatherton, R. Kleck, M. Hebl, & J. Hull (Eds.). *The social psychology of stigma* (pp. 1–28). New York: Guilford.

Dunai, E. (2002). *Surviving in silence.* Washington, DC: Gallaudet University Press.

Dunbar, N., & Grotevant, H. (2004). Adoption narratives: The construction of adoptive identity during adolescence. In M. Pratt & B. Fiese (Eds.). *Family stories and the life course* (pp. 135–161). Mahwah, NJ: Lawrence Erlbaum.

Dunn, D., & Dougherty, S. (2005). Prospects for a positive psychology of rehabilitation. *Rehabilitation Psychology, 50*(3), 305–311.

Dye, M., Kyle, J., Allsop, L., Dury, A., & Richter, J. (2001). *Deaf people in the community: Health and disability.* Bristol, U.K.: Deaf Studies Trust.

Eagly, A. (2004). Prejudice: Toward a more inclusive understanding. In A. Eagly, R. Baron, & V. L. Hamilton (Eds.). *The social psychology of group identity and social conflict* (pp. 45–64). Washington, DC: American Psychological Association.

Eisenberg, A. (2007, September 24). The hearing aid as fashion statement. *The New York Times.* Retrieved January 14, 2007, from http://www.nytimes.com/2006/09/24/business/yourmoney/24novel.html?ei=5070&en=8c8.

Eldredge, N. (1999). Culturally responsive psychotherapy with American Indians who are Deaf. In I. W. Leigh (Ed.). *Psychotherapy with deaf clients from diverse groups* (pp. 177–201). Washington, DC: Gallaudet University Press.

Emerton, G. (1996). Marginality, biculturalism, and social identity of deaf people. In I. Parasnis (Ed.). *Cultural and language diversity and the deaf experience* (pp. 136–145). New York: Cambridge University Press.

Eriks-Brophy, A., Durieux-Smith, A., Olds, J., Fitzpatrick, E., Duquette, C., & Whittingham, J. (2006). Facilitators and barriers to the inclusion of orally educated children and youth with hearing loss in schools promoting partnerships to support inclusion. *The Volta Review, 106*(1), 53–88.

Erikson, E. (1968). *Identity: Youth and crisis.* New York: W.W. Norton.

Erikson, E. (1980). *Identity and the life cycle.* New York: W.W. Norton.

Eriksson, P. (1993). *The history of deaf people.* Örebro, Sweden: SIH Läromedel.

Evans, R. (1967). *Dialogue with Erik Erikson.* New York: Harper & Row.

Fellinger, J., Holzinger, D., Gerich, J., & Goldberg, D. (2007). Mental distress and quality of life in the hard of hearing. *Acta Psychiatrica Scandinavica, 115*(3), 243–245.

Fernandez, M. (2005, February 6). Turning the volume down: Hearing student at Gallaudet blossoms in Deaf culture. *The Washington Post,* pp. A1, A9.

Fidler, C. (2004). Bullying: A school responds. *Odyssey, 5*(2), 24–27.

Fischer, L. C., & McWhirter, J. J. (2001). The Deaf Identity Development Scale: A revision and validation. *Journal of Counseling Psychology, 48,* 355–358.

Fitzgerald, T. (1993). *Metaphors of identity.* Albany, NY: State University of New York Press.

Foddy, M., & Kashima, Y. (2002). Self and identity: What is the conception of the person assumed in the current literature? In Y. Kashima, M. Foddy, & M. Platow (Eds.). *Self and identity: Personal, social, and symbolic* (pp.3–25). Mahwah, NJ: Lawrence Erlbaum.

Food and Drug Administration (2005). Retrieved November 17, 2008, from http://www.nidcd.nih.gov/health/hearing/coch.htm.

Forgas, J., & Williams, K. (2003). The social self. In J. Forgas & K. Williams (Eds.). *The social self: Cognitive, interpersonal, and intergroup processes* (pp. 1–18). New York: Psychology Press.

Foster, S. (1996). Communication experiences of deaf people. In I. Parasnis (Ed.). *Cultural and language diversity and the Deaf experience* (pp. 117–135). New York: Cambridge University Press.

Foster, S., & Kinuthia, W. (2003). Deaf persons of Asian American, Hispanic American, and African American backgrounds: A study of intraindividual diversity and identity. *Journal of Deaf Studies and Deaf Education, 8*(3), 271–290.

Fougeyrollas, P., & Beauregard, L. (2001). An interactive person–environment social creation. In G. Albrecht, K. Seelman, & M. Bury (Eds.). *Handbook of disability studies* (pp. 171–194). Thousand Oaks, CA: Sage.

Fox, R. (1995). Bisexual identities. In A. D'Augelli & C. Patterson (Eds.). *Lesbian, gay, and bisexual identities over the lifespan: Psychological perspectives* (pp. 3–23). New York: Oxford University Press.

Franklin, A. J., Carter, R., & Grace, C. (1993). An integrative approach to psychotherapy with Black/African Americans. In G. Stricker & J. Gold (Eds.). *Comprehensive handbook of psychotherapy integration* (pp. 465–479). New York: Plenum.

Friedburg, I. (2000). *Reference group orientation and self-esteem of deaf and hard-of-hearing college students.* Unpublished doctoral dissertation, Gallaudet University.

Friedlander, H. (2002). Holocaust studies and the deaf community. In D. Ryan & J. Schuchman (Eds.). *Deaf people in Hitler's Europe* (pp. 15–31). Washington, DC: Gallaudet University Press.

Frye, M. (1996). Oppression. In K. Rosenblum & T. Travis (Eds.). *The meaning of difference* (pp. 163–167). New York: McGraw-Hill.

Gallaudet Research Institute (December 2006). *Regional and national summary report of data from the 2006–2007 annual survey of deaf and hard of hearing children and youth.* Washington, DC: GRI, Gallaudet University.

Gannon, J. (1981). *Deaf heritage.* Silver Spring, MD: National Association of the Deaf.

Gannon, J. (1989). *The week the world heard Gallaudet.* Washington, DC: Gallaudet University Press.

Geers, A. (2006). Spoken language in children with cochlear implants. In P. Spencer & M. Marschark (Eds.). *Advances in the spoken language development of deaf and hard-of-hearing children* (pp. 244–270). New York: Oxford University Press.

Geld, E. (2005, September 27). Deaf at the Dragon [Electronic version]. *The Cornell Daily Sun.*

Gesser, A. (2007). Learning about hearing people in the land of the deaf: An ethnographic account. *Sign Language Studies, 7*(3), 269–283.

Gill, C. (1997). Four types of integration in disability identity development. *Journal of Vocational Rehabilitation, 9,* 39–46.

Gill, C. (2001). The social experience of disability. In G. Albrecht, K. Seelman, & M. Bury (Eds.). *Handbook of disability studies* (pp. 351–372). Thousand Oaks, CA: Sage.

Gilroy, P. (2004). Diaspora and the detours of identity. In K. Woodward (Ed.). *Identity and difference* (pp. 299–343). Thousand Oaks, CA: Sage.

Glickman, N. (1986). Cultural identity, deafness, and mental health. *Journal of Rehabilitation of the Deaf, 20,* 1–10.

Glickman, N. (1996a). The development of culturally deaf identities. In N. Glickman & M. Harvey (Eds.). *Culturally affirmative psychotherapy with deaf persons* (pp. 115–153). Mahwah, NJ: Lawrence Erlbaum.

Glickman, N. (1996b). What is culturally affirmative psychotherapy? In N. Glickman & M. Harvey (Eds.). *Culturally affirmative psychotherapy with deaf persons* (pp. 1–55). Mahwah, NJ: Lawrence Erlbaum.

Glickman, N., & Carey, J. (1993). Measuring deaf cultural identities: A preliminary investigation. *Rehabilitation Psychology, 38,* 277–283.

Goffman, E. (1963). *Stigma.* Englewood Cliffs, NJ: Prentice-Hall.

Golan, L. (1995). *Reading between the lips.* Chicago: Bonus Books.

Goldin, C., & Scheer, J. (1995). Murphy's contributions to disability studies: An inquiry into ourselves. *Social Science and Medicine, 40,* 1443–1445.

Gonsiorek, J. (1995). Gay male identities: Concepts and issues. In A. D'Augelli & C. Patterson (Eds.). *Lesbian, gay, and bisexual identities over the lifespan: Psychological perspectives* (pp. 24–47). New York: Oxford University Press.

Goulder, T. (1997). *Journey through late deafness: Results of a focus group study.* San Diego, CA: California School of Professional Psychology Rehabilitation Research and Training Center on Mental Health for Persons Who are Hard of Hearing or Late Deafened.

Graham, B., & Sharp-Pucci, M. (1994). The special challenge of late-deafened adults: Another Deaf way. In C. Erting, R. C. Johnson, D. Smith, & B. Snider (Eds.). *The Deaf way* (pp. 504–511). Washington, DC: Gallaudet University Press.

Greene, B. (2003). What difference does a difference make? In J. Robinson & L. James (Eds.). *Diversity in human interactions* (pp. 3–20). New York: Oxford University Press.

Greenwald, B. (2004). The real "toll" of A. G. Bell. In J. Van Cleve (Ed.). *Genetics, disability, and deafness* (pp. 35–41). Washington, DC: Gallaudet University Press.

Gregory, S., Bishop, J., & Sheldon, L. (1995). *Deaf young people and their families.* New York: Cambridge University Press.

Groce, N. (1985). *Everyone here spoke sign language.* Cambridge, MA: Harvard University Press.

Groce, N. (2003). The cultural context of disability. In J. Van Cleve (Ed.). *Genetics, disability, and deafness* (pp. 23–33). Washington, DC: Gallaudet University Press.

Grosjean, F. (1996). Living with two languages and two cultures. In I. Parasnis (Ed.). *Cultural and language diversity and the deaf experience* (pp. 20–37). New York: Cambridge University Press.

Grotevant, H. D. (1992). Assigned and chosen identity components: A process perspective on their integration. In G. R. Adams, T. P. Gullota, & R. Montemayor (Eds.). *Adolescent identity formation* (pp. 73–90). Newbury Park, CA: Sage Publications.

Grushkin, D. (2003). The dilemma of the hard of hearing within the U.S. Deaf community. In L. Monaghan, C. Schmaling, K. Nakamura, & G. Turner (Eds.). *Many ways to be Deaf: International variation in Deaf communities* (pp. 114–140). Washington, DC: Gallaudet University Press.

Gutman, V. (1999). Therapy issues with deaf lesbians, gay men, and bisexual men and women. In I. W. Leigh (Ed.). *Psychotherapy with deaf clients from diverse groups* (pp. 97–120). Washington, DC: Gallaudet University Press.

Hadadian, A. (1995). Attitudes toward deafness and security of attachment relationships among young deaf children and their parents. *Early Education and Development, 6*, 181–191.

Hadjikakou, K., & Nikolaraizi, M. (2007). The impact of personal educational experiences and communication practices on the construction of deaf identity in Cyprus. *American Annals of the Deaf, 152*(4), 398–413.

Hahn, H. (1999). The political implications of disability definitions and data. In R. P. Marinelli & A. E. Dell Orto (Eds.). *The psychological and social impact of Disability* (4th ed.) (pp. 3–11). New York: Springer.

Hahn, H., & Belt, T. (2004). Disability identity and attitudes toward cure in a sample of disabled activists. *Journal of Health and Social Behavior, 45*, 453–464.

Hairston, E., & Smith, L. (1983/2001). Black deaf students. In L. Bragg (Ed.). *Deaf world* (pp. 193–198). New York: New York University Press.

Halbertal, T. H., & Koren, I. (2006). Between "being" and "doing": Conflict and coherence in the identity formation of gay and lesbian Orthodox Jews. In D. McAdams, R. Josselson, & A. Lieblich (Eds.). *Identity and story* (pp. 37–61). Washington, DC: American Psychological Association.

Haller, B. (1993). Paternalism and protest: Coverage of deaf persons, *The Washington Post* and *New York Times. Mass Communication Review, 20,* 3–4.

Hamerdinger, S. (2002). Book review: Cochlear implants in children: Ethics and choices. *JADARA, 35*(3), 47–48.

Harter, S. (1985). *The Self-perception profile for children.* Denver, CO: University of Denver.

Harter, S. (1988). *The self-perception profile for adolescents.* Denver, CO: University of Denver.

Harter, S. (1997). The personal self in social context. In R. D. Ashmore & L. Jussim (Eds.). *Self and identity* (pp. 81–105). New York: Oxford University Press.

Harter, S. (1999). *The construction of the self.* New York: Guilford.

Harvey, M. (1993). Cross cultural psychotherapy with deaf persons: A hearing, white, middle class, middle aged, non-gay, Jewish, male, therapist's perspective. *Journal of the American Deafness and Rehabilitation Association, 26,* 43–55.

Harvey, M. (2001). *Listen with the heart: Relationships and hearing loss.* San Diego, CA: DawnSign Press.

Harvey, M. (2003). *Psychotherapy with deaf and hard-of-hearing persons: A systemic model* (2nd ed.). Mahwah, NJ: Lawrence Erlbaum.

Haualand, H., & Hansen, I. (2007). A study of Norwegian deaf and hard of hearing children: Equality in communication inside and outside family life. In L. Komesaroff (Ed.). *Surgical consent: Bioethics and cochlear implantation* (pp. 151–164). Washington, DC: Gallaudet University Press.

Hauser, P., Maxwell-McCaw, D., Leigh, I. W., & Gutman, V. (2000). Internship accessibility issues for deaf and hard of hearing applicants: No cause for complacency. *Professional Psychology: Research and Practice, 31,* 569–574.

Hearing Loss Web (n.d.). Retrieved March 7, 2006, from http://www.hearing-lossweb.com/

Hecht, A., & Gutman, V. (1997, August). *Identity formation and self-esteem in D/deaf lesbians.* Paper presented at the annual meeting of the American Psychological Association, Chicago, IL.

Helms, J. (1994). The conceptualization of racial identity and other "racial" constructs. In E. Trickettt, R. Watts, & D. Birman (Eds.). *Human diversity* (pp. 285–311). San Francisco: Jossey Bass.

Hendershot, G. (2001). *Internet use by people with disabilities grows at twice the rate of non-disabled, yet still lags significantly behind.* Retrieved June 8, 2007, from http://www.nod.org/index.cfm?fuseaction=page.viewPage7pageID=1430&nodeID=1&Feat.

Henderson, S. (2002, September 25). Our right to be normal. *Herald Sun,* p. 19.

Heppner, C. (1992). *Seeds of disquiet.* Washington, DC: Gallaudet University Press.

Herbert, L. (2008). Deaf, signing and oral: My journey. In D. Napoli, I. W. Leigh, D. DeLuca, & K. Lindgren (Eds.). *Access* (pp. 122–139). Washington, DC: Gallaudet University Press.

Hermans, H., & Dimaggio, G. (2007). Self, identity, and globalization in times of uncertainty: A dialogical analysis. *Review of General Psychology, 11*(1), 31–61.

Hermans, H., & Kempen, H. (1998). Moving cultures. *American Psychologist, 53*(10), 1111–1120.

Hernández, M. (1999). The role of therapeutic groups in working with Latino deaf adolescent immigrants. In I. W. Leigh (Ed.). *Psychotherapy with deaf clients from diverse groups* (pp. 227–249). Washington, DC: Gallaudet University Press.

Hernandez, N. (2007, January 2). MSD seeks guidance on admitting hearing students. *Frederick News-Post*, 1.

Hétu, R. (1994). Mismatches between auditory demands and capacities in the industrial work environment. *Audiology, 33*, 1–14.

Hétu, R. (1996). The stigma attached to hearing impairment. *Scandinavian Journal of Audiology, 25*, 12–24.

Hétu, R., Riverin, L., Getty, L., Lalande, N., & St-Cyr, C. (1990). The reluctance to acknowledge hearing difficulties among hearing-impaired workers. *British Journal of Audiology, 28*, 313–325.

Higgins, P. C. (1980). *Outsiders in a hearing world: A sociology of deafness*. Beverly Hills, CA: Sage Publications.

Higgins, P. C. (1990). *The challenge of educating together deaf and hearing youth: Making mainstreaming work*. Springfield, IL: Charles C. Thomas.

Higgins, P. C., & Nash, J. E. (1996). *Understanding deafness socially: Continuities in research and theory*. Springfield, IL: Charles C. Thomas.

Hintermair, M. (2000). Hearing impairment, social networks, and coping: The need for families with hearing-impaired children to relate to other parents and to hearing-impaired adults. *American Annals of the Deaf, 145*, 41–53.

Hintermair, M. (2004). Sense of coherence: A relevant resource in the coping process of mothers of deaf and hard-of-hearing children? *Journal of Deaf Studies and Deaf Education, 9*(1), 15–26.

Hintermair, M. (2006). Parental resources, parental stress, and socioemotional development of deaf and hard of hearing children. *Journal of Deaf Studies and Deaf Education, 11*(4), 493–513.

Hintermair, M. (2008). Self-esteem and satisfaction with life of deaf and hard-of-hearing people—A resource-oriented approach to identity work. *Journal of Deaf Studies and Deaf Education, 13*(2), 278–300.

Hintermair, M., & Albertini, J. (2005). Ethics, deafness, and new medical technologies. *Journal of Deaf Studies and Deaf Education, 10*(2), 185–192.

Hoffman, K. (1996). *Concepts of identity: Historical and contemporary images and portraits of self and family*. New York: HarperCollins.

Hoffmeister, R. (2008). Border crossings by Hearing children of Deaf parents: The lost history of Codas. In H-D. Bauman (Ed.). *Open your eyes: Deaf Studies talking* (pp. 189–215). Minneapolis, MN: University of Minnesota Press.

Hoffmeister, R., & Harvey, M. (1996). Is there a psychology of the hearing? In N. Glickman & M. Harvey (Eds.). *Culturally affirmative psychotherapy with deaf persons* (pp. 73–97). Mahwah, NJ: Lawrence Erlbaum.

Hogg, M. (2003). Social identity. In M. Leary & J. Tangney (Eds.). *Handbook of self and identity* (pp. 462–479). New York: Guilford.

Holden-Pitt, L. (1997). A look at residential school placement patterns for students from deaf- and hearing-parented families: A ten year perspective. *American Annals of the Deaf, 142,* 108–114.

Holland, D., Lachicotte, W., Skinner, D., & Cain, C. (1998). *Identity and agency in cultural worlds.* Cambridge, MA: Harvard University Press.

House of Lords (2007). *Human fertilization and embryology bill.* Retrieved March 28, 2008, from http://www.publications.parliament.uk/pa/ld200708/ldbills/006/en/08006x--.htm.

Huebner, M. (2001). Hearing loss: A challenge, not a restriction. In J. Davis (Ed.). *Our forgotten children: Hard of hearing pupils in the schools* (3rd ed.) (pp. 131–136). Bethesda, MD: SHHH Publications.

Humphries, T. (1993). Deaf culture and cultures. In K. Christensen & G. Delgado (Eds.), *Multicultural issues in deafness* (pp. 3–15). White Plains, NY: Longman.

Humphries, T. (1996). Of deaf mutes, the strange, and the modern Deaf self. In N. Glickman & M. Harvey (Eds.). *Culturally affirmative psychotherapy with deaf persons* (pp. 99–114). Mahwah, NJ: Lawrence Erlbaum.

Humphries, T. (2004). The modern Deaf self: Indigenous practices and educational imperatives. In B. Brueggemann (Ed.). *Literacy and Deaf people* (pp. 29–46). Washington, DC: Gallaudet University Press.

Humphries, T. (2008). Talking culture and culture talking. In H-D. Bauman (Ed.). *Open your eyes: Deaf Studies talking* (pp. 35–41). Minneapolis, MN: University of Minnesota Press.

Hurwitz, B. (2004). Bernard R. Hurwitz, Esq. In J. Adams & P. Rohring. *Handbook to service the deaf and hard of hearing* (pp. 36–43). San Diego, CA: Elsevier Academic Press.

Hy, L., & Loevinger, J. (1996). *Measuring ego development* (2nd ed.). Mahwah, NJ: Lawrence Erlbaum.

Hyde, M., Ohna, E., & Hjulstadt, O. (2006). Education of the deaf in Australia and Norway: A comparative study of the interpretations and applications of inclusion. *American Annals of the Deaf, 150,* 415–426.

Hyde, M., & Power, D. (2006). Some ethical dimensions of cochlear implantation for deaf children and their families. *Journal of Deaf Studies and Deaf Education, 11*(1), 103–111.

Hyde, M., Power, D., & Lloyd, K. (2006). Comments on "W(h)ither the Deaf Community." *Sign Language Studies, 6*(2), 190–201.

Igoa, C. (1995). *The inner world of the immigrant child.* New York: St. Martin's Press.

Israelite, N., Ower, J., & Goldstein, G. (2002). Hard-of-hearing adolescents and identity construction: Influences of school experiences, peers, and teachers. *Journal of Deaf Studies and Deaf Education, 7*(2), 134–148.

Jackson, C. W., & Turnbull, A. (2004). Impact of deafness on family life: A review of the literature. *Topics in Early Childhood Education, 24,* 15–29.

Jacob, L. (1974). *A deaf adult speaks out.* Washington, DC: Gallaudet College Press.

Jacobs, P. (2007). *Neither-nor.* Washington, DC: Gallaudet University Press.

Jambor, E., & Elliott, M. (2005). Self-esteem and coping strategies among deaf students. *Journal of Deaf Studies and Deaf Education, 10*(1), 63–81.

James, D. (2002). David James. In J. Reisler (Ed.). *Voices of the oral deaf* (pp. 52–59). Jefferson, NC: McFarland & Company.

Janger, M. (2002). Michael Janger. In J. Reisler (Ed.). *Voices of the oral deaf* (pp. 60–68). Jefferson, NC: McFarland & Company.

Jankowski, K. (1997). *Deaf empowerment.* Washington, DC: Gallaudet University Press.

Jenkins, A. (2005). The incredible possibilities of being. *Journal of Constructivist Psychology, 18,* 331–343.

John Tracy Clinic (2003). John Tracy Clinic: 60 years later. Retrieved April 14, 2006, from http://www.healthyhearing.com/library/article_content. asp?article_id=193.

Johnson, R. C. (2000). *Gallaudet forum addresses cochlear implant issues. Research at Gallaudet, Spring 2000.* Washington, DC: Gallaudet University, Gallaudet Research Institute.

Johnston, T. (1994). Comment on Turner. *Sign Language Studies, 83,* 133–138.

Johnston, T. (2004). W(h)ither the Deaf community? Population, genetics, and the future of Australian Sign Language. *American Annals of the Deaf, 148*(5), 358–375.

Johnston, T. (2005). In one's own image: Ethics and the reproduction of deafness. *Journal of Deaf Studies and Deaf Education, 10*(4), 426–441.

Johnston, T. (2006). Response to comments. *Sign Language Studies, 6*(2), 225–243.

Jones, C., & Shorter-Gooden, K. (2004). *Shifting.* New York: Perennial (Harper Collins).

Jones, J., Lynch, P., Tenglund, A., & Gaertner, S. (2000). Toward a diversity hypothesis: Multidimensional effects of intergroup contact. *Applied and Preventive Psychology, 9*(1), 53–62.

Jonsen, A., Siegler, M., & Winslade, W. (1998). *Clinical ethics* (4th ed.). New York: McGraw-Hill.

Kane, T. (1994). Deaf gay men's culture. In C. Erting, R. C. Johnson, D. Smith, & B. Snider (Eds.). *The Deaf way* (pp. 483–485). Washington, DC: Gallaudet University Press.

Kannapell, B. (1994). Deaf identity: An American perspective. In C. Erting, R. C. Johnson, D. Smith, & B. Snider (Eds.). *The Deaf way* (pp. 44–48). Washington, DC: Gallaudet University Press.

Karchmer, M., & Mitchell, R. (2003). Demographic and achievement characteristics of deaf and hard-of-hearing students. In M. Marschark & P. Spencer (Eds.). *Oxford handbook of deaf studies, language, and education* (pp. 21–37). New York: Oxford University Press.

Keener, J. (2005, November 1). They still say "you can't." *Deaf Professional Network.* Retrieved November 1, 2005, from http://www.deafprofessional. net/index.php?option=com_content&task=view&id=133&Ite.

Kef, S., & Deković, M. (2004). The role of parental and peer support in adolescents well-being: A comparison of adolescents with and without a visual impairment. *Journal of Adolescence, 27,* 453–466.

Kegan, R. (1982). *The evolving self.* Cambridge, MA: Harvard University Press. Kegan, R. (1994). *In over our heads: The mental demands of modern life.* Cambridge, MA: Harvard University Press.

Kent, B. (2003). Identity issues for hard-of-hearing adolescents aged 11, 13, and 15 in mainstream settings. *Journal of Deaf Studies and Deaf Education, 8,* 315–324.

Kent, B., Furlonger, B., & Goodrick, D. (2001, December). Toward an understanding of acquired hearing loss in a family: Narrative play format as a new voice in qualitative methodology. *The Qualitative Report, 6*(4). Retrieved February 16, 2008, from http://www.nova.edu/ssss/QR/QR6-4/furlonger.html.

Kent, B., & Smith, S. (2006). "They only see it when the sun shines in my ears": Exploring perceptions of adolescent hearing aid users. *Journal of Deaf Studies and Deaf Education, 11*(4), 461–476.

Kinzie, S. (2006a, June 3). Deaf students express dissent along a high-tech grapevine. *The Washington Post,* p. B3.

Kinzie, S. (2006b, October 23). Source of Gallaudet turmoil is up for debate. *The Washington Post,* p. B1, B4.

Kirby, K. (2002). Karen Kirby. In J. Reisler (Ed.). *Voices of the oral deaf* (pp. 69–80). Jefferson, NC: McFarland & Company.

Kirchner, C. (2004). Co-enrollment: An effective answer to the mainstream debacle. In D. Power & G. Leigh (Eds.), *Educating deaf students* (pp. 161–173). Washington, DC: Gallaudet University Press.

Kisch, S. (2003). Negotiating (genetic) deafness in a Bedouin community. In J. Van Cleve (Ed.). *Genetics, disability, and deafness* (pp. 148–173). Washington, DC: Gallaudet University Press.

Kisor, H. (1990). *What's that pig outdoors?* New York: Hill and Wang.

Klop, W., Driaire, J., Stiggelbout, A., & Frijns, J. (2007). Cochlear implant outcomes and quality of life in adults with prelingual deafness. *Laryngoscope, 117*(11), 1982–1987.

Kluwin, T. (1999). Coteaching deaf and hearing students: Research on social integration. *American Annals of the Deaf, 144*(4), 339–344.

Kluwin, T., & Gaustad, M. (1991). Predicting family communication choices. *American Annals of the Deaf, 136*(1), 28–34.

Kluwin, T., & Stinson, M. (1993). *Deaf students in local public high schools: Background, experiences, and outcomes.* Springfield, IL: Charles C. Thomas.

Knutson, J., Boyd, R., Reid, J., Mayne, T., & Fetrow, R. (1997). Observational assessments of the interaction of implant recipients with family and peers; Preliminary findings. *Otolaryngology-Head and Neck Surgery, 117*(3), 196–207.

Kochkin, S., Luxford, W., Northern, J., Mason, P., & Tharpe, A. M. (2007, September). Are 1 million dependents with hearing loss in America being left behind? *Hearingreview.com,* 2–12.

Koester, L. S., Papousek, H., & Smith-Gray, S. (2000). Intuitive parenting, communication, and interaction with deaf infants. In P. Spencer, C. Erting, & M. Marschark (Eds.). *The deaf child in the family and at school* (pp. 55–71). Mahwah, NJ: Erlbaum.

Komesaroff, L. (2007). Media representation and cochlear implantation. In L. Komesaroff (Ed.). *Surgical consent: Bioethics and cochlear implantation* (pp. 88–119). Washington, DC: Gallaudet University Press.

Kozol, J. (2005). *The shame of the nation: The restoration of apartheid schooling in America.* New York: Crown.

Krentz, C. (2007). Letters to the editor: Not Deaf enough. *The Chronicle Review.* Retrieved March 8, 2007, from http://chronicle.com/temp/email2.php?id=YS6SVvyz5vSSKT9kJp8FpbpsDGzNH68x.

Ladd, G., Munson, H., & Miller, J. (1984). Social integration of deaf adolescents in secondary-level mainstreamed programs. *Exceptional Children, 50,* 420–428.

Ladd, P. (1994). Deaf culture: Finding it and nurturing it. In C. Erting, R. C. Johnson, D. Smith, & B. Snider (Eds.). *The Deaf way* (pp. 5–15). Washington, DC: Gallaudet University Press.

Ladd, P. (2003). *Understanding Deaf culture.* Clevedon, UK: Multilingual Matters.

Ladd, P. (2007). Cochlear implantation, colonialism, and Deaf rights. In L. Komesaroff (Ed.). *Surgical consent* (pp. 1–29). Washington, DC: Gallaudet University Press.

Ladd, P. (2008). Colonialism and resistance: A brief history of Deafhood. In H-D. Bauman (Ed.), *Open your eyes: Deaf Studies talking* (pp. 42–59). Minneapolis, MN: University of Minnesota Press.

LaFromboise, T., Coleman, H., & Gerton, J. (1993). Psychological impact of biculturalism: Evidence and theory. *Psychological Bulletin, 114,* 395–412.

Landsman, G. (2002). Mothers and models of disability. *Journal of Medical Humanities, 26,* 121–139.

Lane, H. (1992). *The mask of benevolence.* New York: Alfred A. Knopf.

Lane, H. (1997). Constructions of deafness. In L. Davis (Ed.). *The disability studies reader* (pp. 153–171). New York: Routledge.

Lane, H. (2005). Ethnicity, ethics, and the Deaf-World. *Journal of Deaf Studies and Deaf Education, 10*(3), 291–310.

Lane, H., Hoffmeister, R., & Bahan, B. (1996). *A journey into the Deaf-World.* San Diego, CA: DawnSign Press.

Lane, H., Pillard, R., & French, M. (2000). Origins of the American Deaf-World. *Sign Language Studies, 1*(1), 17–44.

Lang, H. (2004). *Edmund Booth: Deaf pioneer.* Washington, DC: Gallaudet University Press.

Lang, H. (2007). Genesis of a community: The American deaf experience in the seventeenth and eighteenth centuries. In J. Van Cleve (Ed.). *The deaf history reader* (pp. 1–23). Washington, DC: Gallaudet University Press.

Lang, H., & Meath-Lang, B. (1995). *Deaf persons in the arts and sciences.* Westport, CT: Greenwood Press.

Langholz, D., & Rendon, M. (1991–1992). The deaf gay/lesbian client: Some perspectives. *Journal of the American Deafness and Rehabilitation Association, 25,* 31–34.

Laroche, C., Garcia, L., & Barrette, J. (2000). Perceptions by persons with hearing impairment, audiologists, and employers of the obstacles to work integration. *Journal of the Academy of Rehabilitative Audiology, 23,* 63–90.

LaSasso, C., & Wilson, A. (2000). Results of two national surveys of leadership personnel needs in deaf education. *American Annals of the Deaf, 145*(5), 429–435.

Laszlo, C. (1994). Is there a hard-of-hearing identity? *Journal of Speech-Language Pathology and Audiology, 18,* 248–252.

Leary, M., & Tangney, J. (Eds.). (2003). *Handbook of self and identity.* New York: Guilford.

Lederberg, A., & Prezbindowski, A. (2000). Impact of child deafness on mother–toddler interaction: Strengths and weaknesses. In P. Spencer, C. Erting, &

M. Marschark (Eds.). *The deaf child in the family and at school* (pp. 73–92). Mahwah, NJ: Erlbaum.

Legge, J. (2004). Bullied no more! *Volta Voices, 11,* 37–38.

Leigh, I. W. (1987). Parenting and the hearing impaired: Attachment and coping. *The Volta Review, 89,* 11–21.

Leigh, I. W. (1990). Impact of communication on depressive vulnerability in deaf individuals. *JADARA, 23,* 68–73.

Leigh, I. W. (1999a). Inclusive education and personal development. *Journal of Deaf Studies and Deaf Education,* 4(3), 236–245.

Leigh, I. W. (Ed.) (1999b). *Psychotherapy with deaf clients from diverse groups.* Washington, DC: Gallaudet University Press.

Leigh, I. W. (2003). Deaf: Moving from hearing loss to diversity. In J. Mio & G. Iwamasa (Eds.). *Culturally diverse mental health* (pp. 323–339). New York: Brunner-Routledge.

Leigh, I. W., & Brice, P. (2003). The visible and the invisible. In J. Robinson & L. James (Eds.). *Diversity in human interactions* (pp. 175–194). New York: Oxford University Press.

Leigh, I. W., Brice, P., & Meadow-Orlans, K. (2004). Attachment in deaf mothers and their children. *Journal of Deaf Studies and Deaf Education, 9,* 176–188.

Leigh, I. W., & Lewis, J. W. (1999). Deaf therapists and the deaf community: How the twain meet. In I. W. Leigh (Ed.). *Psychotherapy with deaf clients from diverse groups* (pp. 45–65). Washington, DC: Gallaudet University Press.

Leigh, I. W., Marcus, A., Dobosh, P., & Allen, T. (1998). Deaf/hearing cultural identity paradigms: Modification of the Deaf Identity Development Scale. *Journal of Deaf Studies and Deaf Education,* 3(4), 329–338.

Leigh, I. W., Maxwell-McCaw, D., Bat-Chava, Y., & Christiansen, J. (2009). Correlates of psychosocial adjustment in deaf adolescents with and without cochlear implants: A preliminary investigation. *Journal of Deaf Studies and Deaf Education,* advance access October 14, 2008, doi:10.1093/deafed/edd038, forthcoming.

Leigh, I. W., & Stinson, M. (1991). Social environments, self perceptions, and identity of hearing impaired adolescents. *Volta Review,* 93(7), 7–22.

Levesque, J. (1992–1993/2001). CBS hurt Deaf children with "Caitlin's Story." In L. Bragg (Ed.). *Deaf world* (pp. 40–42). New York: New York University Press.

Levinson, K. (1990, July). Ken Levinson. *DeafLife,* 19–25.

Levinson, K. (2002). Ken Levinson. In J. Reisler (Ed.). *Voices of the oral deaf* (pp. 81–93). Jefferson, NC: McFarland & Company.

Liebkind, K. (1999). Social psychology. In J. Fishman (Ed.). *Handbook of language and ethnic identity* (pp. 140–151). New York: Oxford University Press.

Liebkind, K. (2006). Ethnic identity and acculturation. In D. Sam & J. Berry (Eds.). *The Cambridge handbook of acculturation psychology* (pp. 78–96). New York: Cambridge University Press.

Lietz, K. (2002). The place of the school for the deaf in the New Reich. In D. Ryan & J. Schuchman (Eds.). *Deaf people in Hitler's Europe* (pp. 114–120). Washington, DC: Gallaudet University Press.

Linton, S. (1998). *Claiming disability: Knowledge and identity.* New York: New York University Press.

Lloyd, K., & Uniacke, M. (2007). Deaf Australians and the cochlear implant: Reporting from ground level. (2007). In L. Komesaroff (Ed.). *Surgical consent: Bioethics and cochlear implantation* (pp. 174–194). Washington, DC: Gallaudet University Press.

Loohauis, J. (1999). Matlin tells of struggle with success. *JSOnline*. Retrieved May 26, 2006, from http://www2.jsonline.com/enter/daily/0330matlin.asp?format=print.

Luckner, J., & Muir, S. (2001). Successful students who are deaf in general education settings. *American Annals of the Deaf, 146,* 435–446.

Luczak, R. (Ed.). (2007). *Eyes of desire 2: a deaf GLBT reader.* Minneapolis, MN: Handtype Press.

Luterman, D. (1987). *Deafness in the family.* Boston: College Hill Press.

Luterman, D. (2004, November 16). Children with hearing loss: Reflections on the past 40 years. *The ASHA Leader, 6–7,* 18–21.

Lyddon, W. (1995). Forms and facets of constructivist psychology. In R. Neimeyer & M. Mahoney (Eds.). *Constructivism in psychotherapy* (pp. 69–92). Washington, DC: American Psychological Association.

Lytle, L. (1987). Identify formation and developmental antecedents in deaf college women (Doctoral dissertation, The Catholic University, 1987). *Dissertation Abstracts International, 48(3-A),* 606–607.

MacDonald, R. (1994). Deaf-blindness: An emerging culture? In C. Erting, R. C. Johnson, D. Smith, & B. Snider (Eds.). *The Deaf way* (pp. 496–503). Washington, DC: Gallaudet University Press.

Mackelprang, R., & Salsgiver, R. (1999). *Disability: A diversity model approach in human service practice.* Pacific Grove, CA: Brooks/Cole.

Marcia, J. (1993). The relational roots of identity. In J. Kroger (Ed.). *Discussions on ego identity* (pp. 101–120). Hillsdale, NJ: Lawrence Erlbaum.

Marschark, M. (2004). Developing deaf children or deaf children developing? In D. Power & G. Leigh (Eds.). *Educating deaf students: Global perspectives* (pp. 13–26). Washington, DC: Gallaudet University Press.

Marschark, M., Lang, H., & Albertini, J. (2002). *Educating deaf students: From research to practice.* New York: Oxford University Press.

Martin, D., & Bat-Chava, Y. (2003). Negotiating deaf–hearing friendships: Coping strategies of deaf boys and girls in mainstream schools. *Child Care, Health, & Development, 29,* 511–521.

Martinez, A., Linden, J., Schimmenti, L., & Palmer, C. (2003). Attitudes of the broader hearing, deaf and hard of hearing community toward genetic testing for deafness. *Genetics in Medicine, 5,* 106–112.

Maxon, A., & Brackett, D. (1992). *The hearing impaired child: Infancy through high-school years.* Boston: Andover Medical Publishers.

Maxwell-McCaw, D. (2001). Acculturation and psychological well-being in deaf and hard-of-hearing people (Doctoral dissertation, The George Washington University, 2001). *Dissertation Abstracts International, 61(11-B),* 6141.

Maxwell-McCaw, D., & Zea, M. C. (submitted). The Deaf Acculturation Scale (DAS): Development and validation of a 58-item measure.

McAdams, D. (1993). *The stories we live by.* New York: Guilford.

McAdams, D. (2001). Psychology of life stories. *Review of General Psychology, 5,* 100–122.

McAdams, D., Josselson, R., & Lieblich, A. (2006). Introduction. In D. McAdams, R. Josselson, & A. Lieblich (Eds.). *Identity and story: Creating self in narrative* (pp. 3–11). Washington, DC: American Psychological Association.

McCrone, W. (2004). School bullying: A problem for deaf and hard of hearing students? *Odyssey, 5*(2), 4–9.

Meadow-Orlans, K. (1985). Social and psychological effects of hearing loss in adulthood: A literature review. In H. Orlans (Ed.). *Adjustment to adult hearing loss* (pp. 35–57). San Diego, CA: College-Hill Press.

Meadow-Orlans, K., Mertens, D., & Sass-Lehrer, M. (2003). *Parents and their deaf children.* Washington, DC: Gallaudet University Press.

Meadow-Orlans, K., & Steinberg, A. (1993). Effects of infant hearing loss and maternal support on mother–infant interactions at eighteen months. *Journal of Applied Developmental Psychology 14,* 407–426.

Merriam, G., & C. Merriam (1980). *Webster's new collegiate dictionary.* Springfield, MA: G. & C. Merriam.

Merriweather, K. (2008). History of NBDA. Retrieved February 17, 2008, from http://www.nbda.org/history_NBDA.html.

Middleton, A. (2004). Deaf and hearing adults' attitudes toward genetic testing for deafness. In J. Van Cleve (Ed.). *Genetics, disability, and deafness* (pp. 127–147). Washington, DC: Gallaudet University Press.

Middleton, A., Hewison, J., & Mueller, R. (1998). Attitudes of deaf adults toward genetic testing for hereditary deafness. *American Journal of Human Genetics, 63,* 1175–1180.

Middleton, A., Hewison, J., & Mueller, R. (2001). Prenatal diagnosis for inherited deafness—What is the potential demand? *Journal of Genetic Counseling, 10*(2), 2001.

Miles, M. (2000). Signing in the seraglio: Mutes, dwarfs, and jestures at the Ottoman Court 1500–1700. *Disability and Society, 15*(1), 115–134.

Miller, M., & Moores, D. F. (2000). Bilingual/bicultural education for deaf students. In M. Winzer & K. Mazurek (Eds.). *Special Education in the 21st Century* (pp. 221–256). Washington, DC: Gallaudet University Press.

Miller, M., Moores, D. F., & Sicoli, D. (1999). Preferences of deaf college students for the hearing status of their children. *JADARA, 32*(3), 1–8.

Miller, R. H. (2004). *Deaf hearing boy.* Washington, DC: Gallaudet University Press.

Miner, I. (1999). Psychotherapy for people with Usher syndrome. In I. W. Leigh (Ed.). *Psychotherapy with deaf clients from diverse groups* (pp. 307–327). Washington, DC: Gallaudet University Press.

Mio, J., Trimble, J., Arredondo, P., Cheatham, H., & Sue, D. (1999). *Key words in multicultural interventions: A dictionary.* Westport, CT: Greenwood Press.

Mischel, W., & Morf, C. (2003). The self as a psycho-social dynamic processing system: A meta-perspective on a century of the self in psychology. In M. Leary & J. Tangney (Eds). *Handbook of self and identity* (pp. 15–43). New York: Guilford.

Mishler, E. (2004). Historians of the self: Restorying lives, revising identities. *Research in Human Development, 1,* 101–121.

Mitchell, D. (2006). Flashcard: Alternating between visible and invisible identities. *Equity and Excellence in Education, 39*(2), 137–145.

Mitchell, R. (2006a). How many deaf people are there in the United States? Estimates from the survey of income and program participation. *Journal of Deaf Studies and Deaf Education, 11*, 112–119.

Mitchell, R. (2006b). Comments on "W(h)ither the Deaf Community." *Sign Language Studies, 6*(2), 210–219.

Mitchell, R., & Karchmer, M. (2004). When parents are deaf versus hard of hearing. *Journal of Deaf Studies and Deaf Education, 9*, 133–152.

Mitchell, R., Young, T., Bachleda, B., & Karchmer, M. (2006). How many people use ASL in the United States? *Sign Language Studies, 6*, 306–335.

Mo, B., Lindbæk, M., & Harris, S. (2005). Cochlear implants and quality of life: A prospective study. *Ear and Hearing, 26*(2), 186–194.

Möller, K., & Danermark, B. (2007). Social recognition, participation, and the dynamic between the environment and personal factors of students with deaf blindness. *American Annals of the Deaf, 152*(1), 42–55.

Monaghan, L., Schmaling, C., Nakamura, K., & Turner, G. (Eds.). (2003). *Many ways to be Deaf; International variation in Deaf communities.* Washington, DC: Gallaudet University Press.

Montgomery, G. (1991). Bionic miracle or megabuck acupuncture? The need for a broader context in the evaluation of cochlear implants. In M. Garretson (Ed.). *Perspectives on deafness* (pp. 97–106). Silver Spring, MD: National Association of the Deaf.

Montoya, L., Camberg, J., & Rall, E. (2005, May). *Counseling hard of hearing children/families.* Paper presented at the meeting of ADARA, Orlando, FL.

Moore, M. (2007). *About the conference.* Retrieved May 15, 2007, from http://www.deafpeopleofcolor.org/about_this_conference/index.html.

Moores, D. F. (2001). *Educating the deaf: Psychology, principles, and practices* (5th ed.). Boston: Houghton Mifflin.

Moores, D. F. (2005/2006). Editorial. *American Annals of the Deaf, 150*(5), 399–400.

Moores, D. F. (2006). Comments on "W(h)ither the Deaf Community." *Sign Language Studies,6*(2), 202–209.

Moores, D. F., Jatho, J., & Dunn, C. (2001). Families with deaf members: American Annals of the Deaf, 1996–2000. *American Annals of the Deaf, 146*(3), 245–250.

Moradi, B., & Rottenstein, A. (2007). Objectification theory and Deaf cultural identity attitudes: Roles in deaf women's eating disorder symtomatology. *Journal of Counseling Psychology, 54*(2), 178–188.

Morton, D. (2000). Beyond parent education: The impact of extended family dynamics in deaf Education. *American Annals of the Deaf, 145*(4), 359–365.

Moskowitz, G. (2005). *Social cognition: Understanding self and others.* New York: Guilford.

Most, T., Wiesel, A., & Blitzer, T. (2007). Identity and attitudes towards cochlear implant among deaf and hard of hearing adolescents. *Deafness and Education International, 9*(2), 68–82.

Mottez, B. (1990). Deaf identity. *Sign Language Studies, 68*, 195–216.

Mottez, B. (1993). The deaf-mute banquets and the birth of the deaf movement. In J. Van Cleve (Ed.). *Deaf history unveiled* (pp. 27–39). Washington, DC: Gallaudet University Press.

Mudgett-DeCaro, P. (1995). On being both hearing and Deaf: My bicultural-bilingual experience. In I. Parasnis (Ed.). *Cultural and language diversity and the Deaf experience* (pp. 272–288). New York: Cambridge University Press.

Mundy, L. (2002). A world of their own. Retrieved January 23, 2003, from http:www.washingtonpost.com/ac2/wp-dyn?pagename=article&node=&contented=A231 . . .

Murray, J. (2006). Genetics: A future peril facing the global deaf community. In H. Goodstein (Ed.). *The Deaf Way II reader* (pp. 351–356). Washington, DC: Gallaudet University Press.

Murray, J. (2008). Coequality and transnational studies: Understanding Deaf lives. In H-D. Bauman (Ed.). *Open your eyes: Deaf Studies talking* (pp. 100–110). Minneapolis, MN: University of Minnesota Press.

Musselman, C., Mootilal, A., & MacKay, S. (1996). The social adjustment of deaf adolescents in segregated, partially integrated, and mainstreamed settings. *Journal of Deaf Studies and Deaf Education, 1*(1), 52–63.

Nakamura, K. (2003). U-turns, Deaf Shock, and the hard of hearing: Japanese deaf identities at the borderlands. In L. Monaghan, C. Schmaling, K. Nakamura, & G. Turner (Eds.). *Many ways to be Deaf; International variation in Deaf communities* (pp. 211–229). Washington, DC: Gallaudet University Press.

Nance, W. (2003). The genetics of deafness. *Mental Retardation and Developmental Disabilities Research Reviews, 9*(2), 109–119.

Nance, W. (2004). The epidemiology of hereditary deafness. In J. Van Cleve (Ed.). *Genetics, disability, and deafness* (pp. 94–105). Washington, DC: Gallaudet University Press.

Nash, J. (2000). Shifting stigma from body to self: Paradoxical consequences of mainstreaming. In P. Spencer, M. Marschark, & C. Erting (Eds.). *The deaf child in the family and at school* (pp. 211–227). Mahwah, NJ: Lawrence Erlbaum.

National Association of the Deaf (1991). Report of the task force on childhood cochlear implants. *The NAD Broadcaster, 13,* 1–2, 6–7.

National Association of the Deaf (2000). *NAD position statement on cochlear implants.* Retrieved June 7, 2007, from http://www.nad.org/ciposition.

National Association of the Deaf (2002). *How deaf and hard of hearing Americans are using instant messaging and e-mail at home and at work.* Retrieved June 8, 2007, from http://www.nad.org/site/pp.asp?c=foINKQMBF&b=186376.

National Association of the Deaf (2005). *What is wrong with the use of these terms: "Deaf-mute," "Deaf and dumb," or "Hearing-impaired"?* Retrieved October 11, 2005, from http://www.nad.org/site/pp.asp?c=foINKQMBF&b=103786.

National Association of the Deaf (2006). *What is the difference between a Deaf and a hard of hearing person?* Retrieved February 15, 2006, from http: www.nad.org/site/pp.asp?c=foINKQMBF&b=180410.

Ng, S. (1996). Power: An essay in honour of Henri Tajfel. In W. P. Robinson (Ed.). *Social groups and identities* (pp. 191–214). Oxford, England: Butterworth Heinemann.

Nielsen, K. (2006). Was Helen Keller deaf? Blindness, deafness, and multiple identities. In B. J. Brueggemann & S. Burch (Eds.). *Women and deafness* (pp. 21–39). Washington, DC: Gallaudet University Press.

Nikolaraizi, M., & Hadjikakou, K. (2006). The role of educational experiences in the development of deaf identity. *Journal of Deaf Studies and Deaf Education*, 11(4), 461–476.

Nover, S. (1995). Language and English in deaf education. In C. Lucas (Ed.), *Sociolinguistics in deaf communities* (pp. 109–163). Washington, DC: Gallaudet University Press.

Nowak, R. (2006, November 23). Ear implant success sparks cultural war. *New Scientist, 2579*, 16–17.

Nunes, T. Pretzlik, U, & Olsson, J. (2001). Deaf children's social relationships in mainstream schools. *Deafness and Education International, 3*, 123–136.

Nybo, W., Scherman, A., & Freeman, P. (1998). Grandparents' role in family systems with a deaf child. *American Annals of the Deaf, 143*(3), 260–267.

Oakes, P. (1996). The categorization process: Cognition and the group in the social psychology of stereotyping. In W. P. Robinson (Ed.). *Social groups and identities: Developing the legacy of Henri Tajfel* (pp. 95–119). Oxford, England: Butterworth-Heinemann.

Oglethorpe, R. (2006). Making ourselves heard: The promise of no-barriers communication. In H. Goodstein (Ed.). *The Deaf Way II reader* (pp. 356–362). Washington, DC: Gallaudet University Press.

Ohna, S. E. (2003). Education of deaf children and the politics of recognition. *Journal of Deaf Studies and Deaf Education, 8*(1), 5–10.

Ohna, S. E. (2004). Deaf in my own way: Identity, learning and narratives. *Deafness and Education International, 6*(1), 20–38.

Oliva, G. (2004). *Alone in the mainstream.* Washington, DC: Gallaudet University Press.

Olkin, R. (1999). *What psychotherapists should know about disability.* New York: Guilford.

Olney, K. (2007). The Chicago Mission for the Deaf. In J. V. Van Cleve (Ed.). *The deaf history reader* (pp. 174–208). Washington, DC: Gallaudet University Press.

Onorato, R., & Turner, J. (2004). Fluidity in the self-concept: The shift from personal to social identity. *European Journal of Social Psychology, 34*(3), 257–278.

Osgood, R. (2005). *The history of inclusion in the United States.* Washington, DC: Gallaudet University Press.

Padden, C. (1980). The deaf community and the culture of deaf people. In C. Baker & R. Battison (Eds.). *Sign language and the deaf community* (pp. 89–103). Silver Spring, MD: National Association of the Deaf.

Padden, C. (1996). From the cultural to the bicultural: The modern deaf community. In I. Parasnis (Ed.). *Cultural and language diversity and the Deaf experience* (pp. 79–98). New York: Cambridge University Press.

Padden, C., & Humphries, T. (1988). *Deaf in America: Voices from a culture.* Cambridge, MA: Harvard University Press.

Padden, C., & Humphries, T. (2005). *Inside Deaf culture.* Cambridge, MA: Harvard University Press.

Page, C. (2006, October 25). Listening to the deaf. *Chicago Tribune*, 21.

Pandya, A., & Arnos, K. (2006). Genetic evaluation and counseling in the context of early hearing detection and intervention. *Seminars in Hearing, 27*(3), 205–212.

Parasnis, I., & Fischer, S. (2005). Perceptions of diverse educators regarding ethnic-minority deaf college students, role models, and diversity. *American Annals of the Deaf, 150*(4), 343–349.

Parasnis, I., Samar, V., & Fischer, S. (2005). Deaf college students' attitudes toward racial/ethnic diversity, campus climate, and role models. *American Annals of the Deaf, 150*(1), 47–58.

Parents and Families of Natural Communication, Inc. (1998). *We CAN hear and speak!* Washington, DC: Alexander Graham Bell Association for the Deaf.

Percy-Smith, L., Jensen, J., Josvassen, J., Jonsson, M., Andersen, J., Samar, C., Thomsen, J., & Pedersen, B. (2006). Parents' perceptions of their deaf children's speech, language, and social outcome after cochlear implantation. *Ugeskr Laeger, 168*(33), 2659–2664.

Peters, E. (2000). Our decision on a cochlear implant. *American Annals of the Deaf, 145*, 263–267.

Peterson, C., & McCabe, A. (2004). Echoing our parents: Parental influences on children's narration. In M. Pratt & B. Fiese (Eds.). *Family stories and the life course* (pp. 27–54). Mahwah, NJ: Lawrence Erlbaum.

Phinney, J. (2002). Ethnic identity and acculturation. In K. Chun, P. B. Organista, & G. Marín (Eds.). *Acculturation* (pp. 63–81). Washington, DC: American Psychological Association.

Phinney, J., & Rosenthal, D. (1992). Ethnic identity in adolescence: Process, context, and outcome. In G. Adams, T. Gullotta, & R. Montemayor (Eds.). *Adolescent identity formation* (pp. 145–172). Newbury Park, CA: Sage.

Pilling, D., & Barrett, P. (2008). Text communication preferences of deaf people in the United Kingdom. *Journal of Deaf Studies and Deaf Education, 13*(1), 92–103.

Pipp-Siegel, S., Sedey, A., & Yoshinaga-Itano, C. (2002). Predictors of parental stress in mothers of young children with hearing loss. *Journal of Deaf Studies and Deaf Education, 7*, 1–17.

Plann, S. (2008). "Bad Things": Child abuse and the nineteenth-century Spanish National School for the Deaf and Blind. *Sign Language Studies, 8*(2), 181–210.

Plies, J., & Coles, R. (2002). Summary health statistics for U.S. adults: National Health Interview Survey, 1998. *Vital Health Statistics Volume 10(209)*. Washington, DC: National Center for Health Statistics.

Pollard, R. Q. (2004). *Psychological diversity in context.* Invited address, National Technical Institute for the Deaf, Rochester, NY.

Power, D. (2005). Models of deafness: Cochlear implants in the Australian Daily Press. *Journal of Deaf Studies and Deaf Education, 10*(4), 451–459.

Power, D., Power, M., & Rehling, B. (2007). German deaf people using text communication: Short message service, TTY, relay services, fax, and e-mail. *American Annals of the Deaf, 152*(3), 291–301.

Power, M., Power, D., & Horstmanshof, L. (2007). Deaf people communicating via SMS, TTY, relay service, fax, and computers in Australia. *Journal of Deaf Studies and Deaf Education, 12*(1), 80–92.

Preisler, G., Tvingstedt, A., & Ahlström, M. (2005). Interviews with deaf children about their experiences using cochlear implants. *American Annals of the Deaf, 150*(3), 260–267.

Preston, P. (1994). *Mother father deaf: Living between sound and silence.* Cambridge, MA: Harvard University Press.

Prilleltensky, I., & Gonick, L. (1994). The discourse of oppression in the social sciences: Past, present, and future. In E. Trickett, R. Watts, & D. Birman (Eds.). *Human diversity* (pp. 145–177). San Francisco: Jossey-Bass.

Punch, R., Creed, P., & Hyde, M. (2006). Career barriers perceived by hard of hearing adolescents: Implications for practice from a mixed methods study. *Journal of Deaf Studies and Deaf Education, 11*(2), 224–237.

Punch, R., Hyde, M., & Creed, P. (2004). Issues in the school-to-work transition of hard of hearing adolescents. *American Annals of the Deaf, 149*(1), 28–38.

Punch, R., Hyde, M., & Power, D. (2007). Career and workplace experiences of Australian university graduates who are Deaf or hard of hearing. *Journal of Deaf Studies and Deaf Education, 12*(4), 504–517.

Putz, K. (2005). 'Sound and Fury' update: A family comes together again. Retrieved October 11, 2005, from http://www.handsandvoices.org/articles/misc/V8-4_soundfury.htm.

Quartararo, A. (2008). *Deaf identity and social images in nineteenth-century France.* Washington, DC: Gallaudet University Press.

Raggatt, P. (2006). Multiplicity and conflict in the dialogical self: A life-narrative approach. In D. McAdams, R. Josselson, & A. Lieblich (Eds.). *Identity and story: Creating self in narrative* (pp.15–35). Washington, DC: American Psychological Association.

Ramsey, C. (1997). *Deaf children in public schools: Placement, context, and consequences.* Washington, DC: Gallaudet University Press.

Ravaud, J., & Stiker, H. (2001). Inclusion/Exclusion. In G. Albrecht, K. Seelman, & M. Bury (Eds.). *Handbook of disability studies* (pp. 490–512). Thousand Oaks, CA: Sage.

Reagan, T. (2002). Toward an "Archeology of Deafness": Etic and emic constructions of identity in conflict. *Journal of Language, Identity, and Education, 1*(1), 41–66.

Redding, R. (2000). Teacher expectations and their implications for ethnically diverse deaf students. In K. Christensen & G. Delgado (Eds.). *Deaf plus* (pp. 254–263). San Diego, CA: DawnSign Press.

Rée, J. (1999). *I see a voice.* New York: Metropolitan Books.

Reinharz, S. (1994). Toward an ethnography of "voice" and "silence." In E. Trickett, R. Watts, & D. Birman (Eds.). *Human diversity* (pp. 178–200). San Francisco: Jossey-Bass.

Reisler, J. (2002). *Voices of the oral deaf.* Jefferson, NC: McFarland & Company.

Rentmeester, L. (2006/2007). *Annual report, Clarke School for the Deaf/Center for Oral Education,* p. 7.

Risdale, J., & Thompson, D. (2002). Perceptions of social adjustment of hearing-impaired pupils in an integrated secondary school unit. *Educational Psychology in Practice, 18,* 21–34.

Robinson, M. (2006, June 1). Signing and dancing to showcase a "different world." *Washington Post, Montgomery Extra,* pp. 5–6.

Robinson, S. (2006). The extended family: Deaf women in organizations. In B. J. Brueggemann & S. Burch (Eds.). *Woman and deafness* (pp. 40–56). Washington, DC: Gallaudet University Press.

Rolland, J., & Williams, J. (2006). Toward a psychosocial model for the new era of genetics. In S. Miller, S. McDaniel, J. Rolland, & S. Feetham (Eds.).

Individuals, families, and the new era of genetics (pp. 36–75). New York: W.W. Norton.

Ross, M. (2001). Definitions and descriptions. In J. Davis (Ed.). *Our forgotten children: Hard of hearing pupils in the schools* (3rd ed.) (pp.11–37). Bethesda, MD: SHHH Publications.

Ross, M. (2005, Fall). Personal and social identity of hard of hearing people. [Electronic version]. *IFHOH Journal,* 6–9.

Rudmin, F. (2003). Critical history of the acculturation psychology of assimilation, separation, integration, and marginalization. *Review of General Psychology, 7,* 3–37.

Rust, P. (1996). Finding a sexual identity and community: Therapeutic implications and cultural assumptions in scientific models of coming out. In E. Rothblum & L. Bond (Eds.). *Preventing heterosexism and homophobia* (pp. 87–123). Thousand Oaks, CA: Sage.

Rutman, D. (1989). The impact and experience of adventitious deafness. *American Annals of the Deaf, 134*(5), 305–311.

Ryan, D., & Schuchman, J. (Eds.). (2002). *Deaf people in Hitler's Europe.* Washington, DC: Gallaudet University Press.

Sacks, O. (1993, March 10). To see and not see: A neurologist's notebook. *The New Yorker,* 59–73.

Sam, D., & Berry, J. (Eds.). (2006). *The Cambridge handbook of acculturation psychology.* New York: Cambridge University Press.

Sandel, M. (2007). *The case against perfection.* Cambridge, MA: Harvard University Press.

Sanders, E. (1986). The establishment of a Deaf Studies major. *Journal of Rehabilitation of the Deaf, 19,* 19–23.

Sandler, W., Meir, I., Padden, C., & Aronoff, M. (2005, February 15). The emergence of grammar: Systematic structure in a new language. *PNAS, 102*(7), 2661–2665.

Sarason, B., Pierce, G., & Sarason, I. (1990). Social support: The sense of acceptance and the role of relationships. In B. Sarason, I. Sarason, & G. Pierce (Eds.). *Social support: An interactional view* (pp. 97–128). New York: Wiley.

Sari, H. (2005). An analysis of the relationship between identity patterns of Turkish deaf adolescents and the communication modes used in special residential schools for the hearing impaired and deaf. *Deafness and Education International, 7*(4), 206–222.

Sass-Lehrer, M., & Bodner-Johnson, B. (2003). Early intervention: Current approaches to family-centered planning. In M. Marschark & P. Spencer (Eds.). *Oxford handbook of deaf studies, language, and* education (pp. 65–81). New York: Oxford University Press.

Scheer, J. (1994). Culture and disability: An anthropological point of view. In E. Trickett, R. Watts, & D. Birman (Eds.). *Human diversity* (pp. 244–260). San Francisco: Jossey Bass.

Schein, J. (1989). *At home among strangers.* Washington, DC: Gallaudet University Press.

Schemo, D. (2006, October 30). At college for deaf, trustees drop new leader. *The New York Times.* Retrieved June 28, 2007, from http://tinyurl.com/yh927c.

Scherich, D., & Mowry, R. (1997). Accommodations in the workplace for people who are hard of hearing: Perceptions of employees. *Journal of the American Deafness and Rehabilitation Association, 31,* 31–43.

Schildroth, A., & Hotto, S. (1995). Deaf students and full inclusion: Who wants to be excluded? In B. Snider (Ed.) *Inclusion? Defining quality education for deaf and hard of hearing students* (pp. 173–194). Washington, DC: College for Continuing Education, Gallaudet University.

Schneider, D. (2004). *The psychology of stereotyping.* New York: Guilford.

Schowe, B. (1979). *Identity crisis in deafness.* Tempe, AZ: The Scholars Press.

Schuchman, J. (1988). *Hollywood speaks.* Urbana, IL: University of Illinois Press.

Schuchman, J. (2002). Misjudged people: The German deaf community in 1932. In D. Ryan & J. Schuchman, J. (Eds.). (2002). *Deaf people in Hitler's Europe* (pp. 98–113). Washington, DC: Gallaudet University Press.

Schuchman, J. (2004). The silent film era: Silent films, NAD films, and the Deaf community's response. *Sign Language Studies, 4*(3), 231–238.

Scott-Hill, M. (2004). Impairment, difference, and "identity." In J. Swain, S. French, C. Barnes, & C. Thomas (Eds.). *Disabling barriers—enabling environments* (2nd ed.) (pp. 87–93). London: Sage.

Searls, S., & Johnston, D. (1996). Growing up Deaf in Deaf families: Two different experiences. In I. Parasnis (Ed.). *Cultural and language diversity and the Deaf experience* (pp. 201–224). New York: Cambridge University Press.

Sedano, R. (1997/2001). Traditions: Hispanic, American, Deaf culture. In L. Bragg (Ed.). *Deaf world* (pp. 124–128). New York: New York University Press.

Seelman, K. (2001). Science and technology policy: Is disability a missing factor? In G. Albrecht, K. Seelman, & M. Bury (Eds.). *Handbook of disability studies* (pp. 663–692). Thousand Oaks, CA: Sage.

Seligman, M., & Csikszentmihalyi, M. (2000). Positive psychology: An introduction. *American Psychologist, 55,* 5–14.

Shapiro, J. (1993). *No pity.* New York: Time Books.

Shavelson, R., Hubner, J., & Stanton, J. (1976). Self-concept: Validation of construct interpretations. *Review of Educational Research, 46,* 407–441.

Sheldon, A. (2004). Changing technology. In J. Swain, S. French, C. Barnes, & C. Thomas (Eds.). *Disabling barriers: Enabling environments* (2nd ed.) (pp. 155–160). London: Sage.

Sheridan, M. (2001). *Inner lives of deaf children.* Washington, DC: Gallaudet University Press.

Sheridan, M. (2008). Deaf adolescents: Inner lives and lifeworld development. Washington, DC: Gallaudet University Press.

Shultz Myers, S., Myers, R., & Marcus, A. (1999). Hearing children of deaf parents: Issues and interventions within a bicultural context. In I. W. Leigh (Ed.). *Psychotherapy with deaf clients from diverse groups* (pp. 121–148). Washington, DC: Gallaudet University Press.

Silver, N. (2003). When one size doesn't fit one! *Odyssey, 4,* 24–27.

Simon, B. (1999). A place in the world: Self and social categorization. In T. Tyler, R. Kramer, & O. John (Eds.). *The psychology of the social self* (pp. 47–69). Mahwah, NJ: Lawrence Erlbaum.

Singleton, J., & Tittle, M. (2000). Deaf parents and their hearing children. *Journal of Deaf Studies and Deaf Education, 5*(3), 221–236.

Skelton, T., & Valentine, G. (2003). "It feels like being Deaf is normal": An exploration into the complexities of defining D/deafness and young D/deaf people's identities. *Canadian Geographer, 47*(4), 451–466.

Sleeter, C., & Grant, C. (2005). Illusions of progress: Business as usual. In H. Shaprio & D. Purpel (Ed.). *Critical social issues in American education: Democracy and meaning in a globalizing world* (3rd ed.) (pp. 89–107). Mahwah, NJ: Lawrence Erlbaum.

Smedley, A., & Smedley, B. (2005). Race as biology is fiction, Racism as a social problem is real. *American Psychologist, 60*(1), 16–26.

Smiler, K., & McKee, R. (2007). Perceptions of *Māori* deaf identity in New Zealand. *Journal of Deaf Studies and Deaf Education, 12*(1), 93–111.

Smith, D. (1998). Families joined or divided by silence; Film shed light on emotional issues of the deaf. *The New York Times.* Retrieved May 26, 2006, from http://query.nytimes.com/gst/fullpage.html?res=9F00E7D7133AF932 A25755C0A96E958.

Smith, P. K., & Sharp, S. (1994). The problem of school bullying. In P. K. Smith & S. Sharp (Eds.). *School bullying: Insights and perspectives* (pp. 1–19). New York: Routledge.

Solomon, A. (1994, August 28). Defiantly Deaf. *The New York Times Magazine,* 38–45, 62, 65–68.

Sorkin, D. (2000). *Developing an identity for people with hearing loss.* Retrieved September 6, 2000, from http://www.ifhoh.org/sorkin.htm.

Sorrells, S. (2006, October 4). Rockville student rails against stereotypes. *The Gazette,* B-21.

Sparrow, R. (2005). Defending Deaf culture: The case of cochlear implants. *The Journal of Political Philosophy, 13*(2), 135–152.

Spencer, P., & Hafer, J. (1998). Play as "window" and room: Assessing and supporting the cognitive and linguistic development of deaf infants and young children. In M. Marschark & M. D. Clark (Eds.). Psychological perspectives on deafness, Volume 2 (pp. 131–152). Hillsdale, NJ: Lawrence Erlbaum.

Spencer, P., & Marschark, M. (2003). Cochlear implants: Issues and implications. In M. Marschark & P. Spencer (Eds.). *Oxford handbook of deaf studies, language, and education* (pp. 434–448). New York: Oxford University Press.

Stainback, M. (2000). The inclusion movement: A goal for restructuring special education. In M. Winzer & K. Mazurek (Eds.). *Special education in the 21st century* (pp. 27–40). Washington, DC: Gallaudet University Press.

Steinberg, A., Davila, J., Collazo, J., Loew, R., & Fischgrund, J. (1997). "A little sign and a lot of love...": Attitudes, perceptions, and beliefs of Hispanic families with deaf children. *Qualitative Health Research, 7*(2), 202–222.

Stern, S., Arnos, K., Murrelle, L., Welch, K., Nance, W., & Pandya, A. (2002). Attitudes of deaf and hard of hearing subjects towards genetic testing and prenatal diagnosis of hearing loss. *Journal of Medical Genetics, 39,* 449–453.

Stern, S. Oelrich, K., Arnos, K., Murrelle, L., Nance, W., & Pandya, A. (2000). The attitudes of deaf and hard of hearing individuals toward genetic testing of hearing loss. *American Journal of Human Genetics, 67*(4), Suppl. 2:32.

Stewart, D. (1991/1993). *Deaf sport.* Washington, DC: Gallaudet University Press.

Stewart, D., & Ellis, K. (2005). Sports and the Deaf child. *American Annals of the Deaf, 150*(1), 59–66.

Stewart, L. (1992). Debunking the bilingual/bicultural snow job in the American deaf community. In M. Garretson (Ed.). *Viewpoints on deafness* (pp. 129–142). Silver Spring, MD: National Association of the Deaf.

Steyger, P. (2004). A researcher looks back. *Odyssey, 5,* 22–23.

Stinson, M., & Antia, S. (1999). Considerations in educating deaf and hard-of-hearing students in inclusive settings. *Journal of Deaf Studies and Deaf Education, 4*(3), 163–175.

Stinson, M., Chase, K., & Bondi-Wolcott, J. (1988). *Use of social activity scale as part of personal/social development activities during "Explore Your Future."* Working paper, National Technical Institute for the Deaf, Rochester, NY.

Stinson, M., & Foster, S. (2000). Socialization of deaf children and youths in school. In P. Spencer, C. Erting, & M. Marschark (Eds.). *The deaf child in the family and at school* (pp. 191–209). Mahwah, NJ: Lawrence Erlbaum.

Stinson, M., & Kluwin, T. (1996). Social orientations toward deaf and hearing peers among deaf adolescents in local public high schools. In P. Higgins & J. Nash (Eds.). *Understanding deafness socially* (pp. 113–134). Springfield, IL: Charles C. Thomas.

Stinson, M., & Kluwin, T. (2003). Educational consequences of alternative placements. In M. Marschark & P. Spencer (Eds.). *Oxford handbook of deaf studies, language, and education* (pp. 52–64). New York: Oxford University Press.

Stinson, M., & Whitmire, K. (1992). Students' views of their social relationships. In T. N. Kluwin, D. F. Moores, & M. G. Gaustad (Eds.). *Toward effective public school programs for deaf students* (pp. 149–174). New York: Teachers College Press.

Stinson, M., & Whitmire, K. (2000). Adolescents who are deaf or hard of hearing: A communication perspective on educational placement. *Topics in Language Disorders, 20,* 58–72.

Stokoe, W. (1960). Sign language structure: An outline of the visual communication system of the American Deaf. *Studies in Linguistics, Occasional paper,* Buffalo, NY.

Stokoe, W. (1989). Dimensions of difference: ASL and English based cultures. In S. Wilcox (Ed.). *American Deaf culture: An anthology* (pp. 49–59). Burtonsville, MD: Linstok Press.

Stokoe, W., Croneberg, C., & Casterline, D. (1965). *A dictionary of American Sign Language on linguistic principles.* Washington, DC: Gallaudet University Press.

Stone, J. (Ed.). (2005). *Culture and disability.* Thousand Oaks, CA: Sage.

Stone, R., & Stirling, L. (1994). Developing and defining an identity: Deaf children of deaf and hearing parents. In C. Erting, R. C. Johnson, D. Smith, & B. Snider (Eds.). *The Deaf way* (pp. 49–54). Washington, DC: Gallaudet University Press.

Storbeck, C., & Magongwa, L. (2006). Teaching about Deaf culture. In D. Martin & D. Moores (Eds.). *Deaf learners* (pp. 113–126). Washington, DC: Gallaudet University Press.

Sue, D. W., & Sue, D. (2008). *Counseling the culturally diverse: Theory and practice* (5th ed.). New York: Wiley.

Suggs, T. (2001). Threat of anthrax real for these postal workers. *Silent News, 33*(12), 1, 18.

Swiller, J. (2007). *The unheard. A memoir of deafness and Africa.* New York: Henry Holt.

Szapocznik, J., & Kurtines, W. (1993). Family psychology and cultural diversity. *American Psychologist, 48,* 400–407.

Tajfel, H. (1981). *Human groups and social categories.* Cambridge, England: Cambridge University Press.

Taneja, P., Pandya, A., Foley, D., Nicely, L., & Arnos, K. (2004). Attitudes of deaf individuals towards genetic testing. *American Journal of Medical Genetics Part A, 130*(1), 17–21.

Tatum, B. (1997). *Why are all the black kids sitting together in the cafeteria?* New York: Basic Books.

Tellings, A. (1996). Cochlear implants and deaf children. The debate in the United States. *Journal of the British Association of Teachers of the Deaf, 20*(1), 24–31.

Thoits, P., & Virshup, L. (1997). Me's and We's: Forms and functions of social identities. In R. Ashmore & L. Jussim (Eds.). *Self and identity* (pp. 106–133). New York: Oxford University Press.

Thumann-Prezioso, C. (2005). Deaf parents' perspectives on deaf education. *Sign Language Studies, 5*(4), 415–440.

Treni, K. (2002). Kathleen Suffridge Treni. In J. Reisler (Ed.). *Voices of the oral deaf* (pp. 133–142). Jefferson, NC: McFarland & Company.

Triandis, H. (1996). The psychological measurement of cultural syndromes. *American Psychologist, 51,* 407–415.

Trimble, J. (2005). Ethnic identity. In C. B. Fisher & R. Lerner (Eds.). *Encyclopedia of applied developmental science, Vol. I* (pp. 415–420). Thousand Oaks, CA: Sage.

Tucker, B. (1995). *The feel of silence.* Philadelphia: Temple University Press.

Tucker, B. (1998a). Deaf culture, cochlear implants, and elective disability. *Hastings Center Report, 28,* 6–14.

Tucker, B. (1998b). *Cochlear implants: A handbook.* Jefferson, NC: McFarland & Company.

Turner, G. (1994). How is Deaf culture? Another perspective on a fundamental concept. *Sign Language Studies, 83,* 103–125.

Turner, J. (1996). Henri Tajfel: An introduction. In W. P. Robinson (Ed.). *Social groups and identities: Developing the legacy of Henri Tajfel* (pp. 1–23). Oxford, England: Butterworth-Heinemann.

Turner, J., & Onorato, R. (1999). Social identity, personality, and the self-concept: A self-categorization perspective. In T. Tyler, R. Kramer, & O. John (Eds.). *The psychology of the social self* (pp. 11–46). Mahwah, NJ: Lawrence Erlbaum.

U.S. Public Health Service. (1990). *Healthy people 2000.* Washington, DC: Government Printing Office.

Valentine, G., & Skelton, T. (2007). Re-defining "norms": D/deaf young people's transitions to independence. *The Sociological Review, 55*(1), 104–123.

Valentine, P. (1993). Thomas Hopkins Gallaudet: Benevolent paternalism and the origins of the American Asylum. In J. Van Cleve (Ed.). *Deaf history unveiled* (pp. 53–73). Washington, DC: Gallaudet University Press.

Van Cleve, J. (1993). *Deaf history unveiled.* Washington, DC: Gallaudet University Press.

Van Cleve, J., & Crouch, B. (1989). *A place of their own: Creating the Deaf community in America.* Washington, DC: Gallaudet University Press.

Vash, C., & Crewe, N. (2004). *Psychology of disability* (2nd ed.). New York: Springer.

Vérte, S., Hebbrecht, L., & Roeyers, H. (2006). Psychological adjustment of siblings of children who are deaf or hard of hearing. *The Volta Review, 106,* 89–110.

Vesey, K., & Wilson, B. (2003). Navigating the hearing classroom with a hearing loss. *Odyssey, 4,* 10–13.

Wald, R., & Knutsen, J. (2000). Deaf cultural identity of adolescents with and without cochlear implants. *Annals of Otology, Rhinology & Laryngology* (Suppl. 185), *12*(2), 87–89.

Wallis, D., Musselman, C., & MacKay, S. (2004). Hearing mothers and their deaf children: The relationship between early, ongoing mode match and subsequent mental health functioning in adolescence. *Journal of Deaf Studies and Deaf Education, 9*(1), 2–14.

Warick, R. (1994). A profile of Canadian hard-of-hearing youth. *Journal of Speech Language Pathology and Audiology, 18,* 253–259.

Warick, R. (2004). Voices unheard: The academic and social experiences of university students who are hard of hearing. (Doctoral dissertation, The University of British Columbia, 2003). *Dissertation Abstracts International, 64*(12), 4390.

Warren, C., & Hasenstab, S. (1986). Self-concept of severely to profoundly hearing—impaired children. *The Volta Review, 88,* 289–295.

Watson, L., Hardie, T., Archbold, S., & Wheeler, A. (2008). Parents' views on changing communication after cochlear implantation. *Journal of Deaf Studies and Deaf Education, 13*(1), 104–116.

Watson, N. (2002), Well, I know this is going to sound very strange to you, but I don't see myself as a disabled person: Identity and disability. *Disability and society, 17,* 509–527.

Wauters, L., & Knoors, H. (2008). Social integration of deaf children in inclusive settings. *Journal of Deaf Studies and Deaf Education, 13*(1), 21–36.

Weinberg, N., & Sterritt, M. (1986). Disability and identity: A study of identity patterns in adolescents with hearing impairments. *Rehabilitation Psychology, 31,* 95–102.

Weiner, M., & Miller, M. (2006). Deaf children and bullying: Directions for future research. *American Annals of the Deaf, 151*(1), 61–70.

Weisel, A., & Kamara, A. (2005). Attachment and individuation of deaf/hard-of-hearing and hearing young adults. *Journal of Deaf Studies and Deaf Education, 10*(1), 51–62.

Wendell, S. (1996). *The rejected body.* New York: Routledge.

Wheeler, A., Archbold, S., Gregory, S., & Skipp, A. (2007). Cochlear implants: The young people's perspective. *Journal of Deaf Studies and Deaf Education, 12*(3), 303–316.

White, B. (2001). This child is mine. In L. Bragg (Ed.). *Deaf world* (pp. 68–80). New York: New York University Press.

Whitestone, H. (2008). Retrieved February 16, 2008, from http://www.heatherwhitestone.com/site/content/bio.shtml.

Williams, C., & Abeles, N. (2004). Issues and implications of Deaf culture in therapy. *Professional Psychology: Research and Practice, 35,* 643–648.

Williams, L. (2007). Black deaf pagan lesbian tomfemme. In R. Luczak, (Ed.). *Eyes of desire 2: A deaf GLBT reader* (pp. 7–14). Minneapolis, MN: Handtype Press.

Williamson, C. (2007). Black Deaf students: A model for educational success. Washington, DC: Gallaudet University Press.

Wilson, E. (2001). Foreword. In J. Davis (Ed.). *Our forgotten children: Hard of hearing pupils in the schools* (3rd ed.) (pp. 7–8). Bethesda, MD: SHHH Publications.

Winefield, R. (1987). *Never the twain shall meet.* Washington, DC: Gallaudet University Press.

Woll, B., & Ladd, P. (2003). Deaf communities. In M. Marschark & P. Spencer (Eds.). *Oxford handbook of deaf studies, language and education* (pp. 151–163). New York: Oxford University Press.

Woodcock, K. (1992/2001). Cochlear implants vs. Deaf culture? In L. Bragg (Ed.). *Deaf world* (pp. 325–332). New York: New York University Press.

Woodward, K. (1997). Concepts of identity and difference. In K. Woodward (Ed.). *Identity and difference* (pp. 7–50). Thousand Oaks, CA: Sage Publications.

Woodward, K. (2002). *Understanding identity.* London: Arnold Publishers.

Wu, C., & Grant, N. (1999). Asian American and Deaf. In I. W. Leigh (Ed.). *Psychotherapy with deaf clients from diverse groups* (pp. 203–226). Washington, DC: Gallaudet University Press.

Yetman, M. (2000). Peer relations and self-esteem among deaf children in a mainstream school environment (Doctoral dissertation, Gallaudet University, 2000). *Dissertation Abstracts International, 63,* AAT3038028.

Zaidman-Zait, A. (2008). Everyday problems and stress faced by parents of children with cochlear implants. *Rehabilitation Psychology, 53*(2), 139–152.

Zazove, P. (1993). *When the phone rings, my bed shakes.* Washington, DC: Gallaudet University Press.

Zazove, P., Meador, H., Derry, H., Gorenflo, D., Burdick, S., & Saunders, E. (2004). Deaf persons and computer use. *American Annals of the Deaf, 148*(5), 376–384.

INDEX